To Restore American Democracy

To Restore American Democracy

Political Education and the Modern University

Edited by
ROBERT E. CALVERT

ROWMAN & LITTLEFIELD PUBLISHERS, INC.
Lanham • Boulder • New York • Toronto • Oxford

ROWMAN & LITTLEFIELD PUBLISHERS, INC.

Published in the United States of America
by Rowman & Littlefield Publishers, Inc.
A wholly owned subsidary of The Rowman & Littlefield Publishing Group, Inc.
4501 Forbes Boulevard, Suite 200, Lanham, Maryland 20706
www.rowmanlittlefield.com

PO Box 317
Oxford
OX2 9RU, UK

British Library Cataloguing in Publication Information Available

Library of Congress Cataloging-in-Publication Data

To restore American democracy : political education and the modern
university / edited By Robert E. Calvert.
    p. cm.
Includes bibliographical references and index.
ISBN 0-7425-3454-5 (cloth : alk. paper) —
ISBN 0-7425-3455-3 (pbk. : alk. paper)
    1. Higher education and state—United States. 2. Education, Higher—
Political aspects—United States. 3. Political socialization—United States.
I. Calvert, Robert E.
LC173.T6 2006
378'.015—dc22   2005022246

Printed in the United States of America

Contents

Foreword

A volume of this kind inevitably moves from idea to reality along an uncertain path, through a process involving much time and the work of a great many people. For me, the origin of this publication was July 1999. At that time, the national leadership of Campus Compact invited several college and university officials to meet in Aspen, Colorado. The purpose of the meeting was to explore our common concern that while voluntary service had increased significantly among college students, there was little evidence that a community service commitment carried over into participation in the democratic process. Volunteer service and political involvement appeared unconnected. Our meeting focused upon what the public purposes of education should be. How, in practice, might colleges and universities not only renew a commitment to service generally but also awaken in their students the very ideals of democracy itself?

It is important to note that the point of the meeting was not to blame students, whose earlier education seems to have failed them, for their lack of political involvement. Rather, we sought to think about ways in which we in higher education could take up that challenge ourselves, the ways in which colleges and universities might teach the knowledge and values necessary to democracy—and more broadly to challenge educational institutions across the country to live up to their obligations to teach and model good citizenship. After some reflection, Thomas Ehrlich, the former president of Indiana University, crafted a statement summarizing our discussion, and the "Presidents' Fourth of July Declaration on the Civic Responsibility of Higher Education" was created. After the initial participants of the conference signed on, Campus Compact circulated the declaration to the higher education community and the presidents of well over five hundred institutions signed the document.

It is fair to say that the Aspen conference, as we know from recent elections, did not reverse the dismaying trend toward youthful political disengagement. What it did do, however, was to help me formulate a proposal I would send to the Mellon Foundation for doing something here at DePauw, however modest, about that trend.

I had several long conversations about this project with Pat McPherson, the vice president of Mellon. After serving over a decade as president of a liberal arts college, I had three interrelated questions about what our kind of education might achieve:

- What could we do to encourage a potentially positive role for religion in the public square?
- What did good citizens have to *know* as well as *do,* and what curricular reforms might help to develop an informed civic responsibility in our students?
- In our efforts to prepare leaders for American society, how might we link "leadership" more closely with the call to service for the common good?

My proposal, which was funded, allowed DePauw to convene faculty discussion groups, which met for a year and a half, concentrating on three discrete but intertwined topics: religion in society, civic responsibility, and leadership. I asked Professor Robert Calvert to lead the group on civic responsibility, and the symposium on Political Education and the Modern University grew out of his work.

The claim that the proper role for a college is teaching civic responsibility, together with cultivating a civically informed religion and leadership, will likely conflict with other values potential students have absorbed from contemporary American society. A number of the essays in this volume speak to these conflicts. Scan most college Web sites and admissions brochures. They boast of the leaders they produce, and properly so. When they hold forth the lure of quality graduate school placement and rewarding careers after college, those promises also are not empty. We in higher education are also committed to an open and discrimination-free society and are proud to say so.

Now all of these roles and ways of being an adult American involve a kind of character development and, yes, a healthy civic order to which properly educated citizens will contribute. But in advertising ourselves we say little or nothing about citizenship or character development, even though most would grant that undergraduate education does shape the character of college students. In fact, outside of our Web sites and recruiting literature, our publicly stated commitments spark only a series of "small conversations" in the life of the college as such. Missing from our common life is that necessary "big conversation" about the conditions of a healthy civic order, calling on the virtues of the democratic citizen, that will provide the context within which our smaller conversations can assume a larger meaning.

I believe colleges and universities have a calling to contribute to their students' understanding of themselves as obligated to be active citizens, and I trust these provocative chapters will contribute to the dialogue about this vitally important issue.

Robert G. Bottoms
President, DePauw University
June 2005

Acknowledgments

I have incurred many debts, and it is a pleasure to acknowledge them, beginning with President Bottoms's entrusting me with this project. I was most grateful early on to the members of the discussion group on civic responsibility, mentioned by President Bottoms, for their faithful attendance and the stimulating discussions we all enjoyed; and to Professors Noah Lemos and Marcia McKelligan, the discussion leaders respectively of the religion and leadership groups, for our many informal conversations about how our topics overlapped. For the huge undertaking that was our symposium, I must thank anonymously the literally hundreds of persons, faculty, students, staff, visitors, and Greencastle residents who made that most memorable event possible. More specifically, I extend my appreciation to our guest lecturers, now contributors to our current volume, for their tireless efforts to connect, with us at DePauw and with each other, throughout that fast-paced week. Those lectures, seminars, and panel discussions established a record for serious intellectual activity not likely soon to be surpassed, I'm bold enough to say, here or elsewhere.

On a more personal note, I want to thank old friends and colleagues Ralph and Sally Gray, Marcia McKelligan, Bill Morrow, Bob Newton, Jim Nyman, and Ralph Raymond for helpful comments and criticisms in the preparation of the prologue and of my own chapter. Our extended conversations, and their written commentaries, were invaluable to me in getting my disjointed thoughts together and for preventing at least some of the errors to which they know I am prone. Other more recent colleagues, David H. Smith and Ted Reuter, and my daughter, Jane Calvert, offered detailed editorial criticisms, which went some way toward eliminating obscurities and making what I've written more "reader friendly."

In the same vein I owe a debt particularly to three former students, Caleb Beasley, Philip Exline, and Cullen Howe, who read either the prologue or the essay, or both, in various stages of their preparation and provided useful written commentaries, and also to their many classmates who heard much from their professor about political education and often responded with their own views. I owe a very special debt of gratitude to Charles Carpenter, who was my very diligent and resourceful assistant during that part of the project in which the heaviest labors of editing were required. His own talents as a writer, his sharp editorial eye, his critical sense of what works and what doesn't in an exposition, and his instincts for support and companionship were valuable to me beyond measure. I also want to say how grateful I am to the other contributors in this volume for the delightfully enriching opportunity to take part with them in this extended endeavor. When I needed it most, my wife, Rita, helped me to think calmly and productively about the myriad details and frustrations associated with the project in its several stages, the lofty as well as the mundane. She helped me to tell the one from the other and to cope with both.

Finally, I was always able to call on the unfailing knowledge of publishing detail and the constant encouragement and much-needed support of Jim Langford and Katie Lane of Rowman & Littlefield.

While all of the above persons deserve to share in whatever praise is accorded this volume, its editorial defects are mine alone.

Political Education and the Modern University
Prologue

ROBERT E. CALVERT

The chapters in this volume for the most part were originally delivered as lectures at a symposium at DePauw University in the spring
of 2003, convened to address the complex question whether colleges and
universities can properly regard themselves as called upon to help make
better citizens of their students—to see to their political education. In
these introductory remarks I can only hint at the richness and subtlety
of what follows, and so readers should take what I say here as but an invitation to ponder these essays for themselves. In what follows I try to convey something of the sense of urgency these committed scholars bring to
bear on what it is no exaggeration to call a crisis confronting us Americans
as a people, if of a kind so quiet and protracted and ever-present that it is
not really "news."

To begin, by a "political" education most of our authors have in
mind something other than what may result from the good "civic" works
or local volunteerism, sometimes called "community service" or "service
learning," that is championed increasingly throughout the American educational system at all levels. It was a premise of our symposium, following the lead of Campus Compact, that

we share a special concern about the disengagement of college students from democratic participation. A chorus of studies reveals that students are not connected to the larger purposes and aspirations of the American democracy. Voter turnout is low. Feelings that political participation will not make any difference are high. Added to this, there is a profound sense of cynicism and lack of trust in the political process.[1]

MEET BRIAN

Consider a concrete example of our problem: Shortly after the 2000 election, a column appeared in the DePauw University student newspaper in which the author vigorously defended his freedom of choice *not* to vote. Denying emphatically that as a U.S. citizen he had an obligation to have or voice a political opinion, he insisted to his readers that "I do not follow politics one bit. I do not watch politics, do not listen to politics, do not talk politics, do not care about politics, and don't vote on politics," and went on to tell the "democracy hounds," as he called those who believed otherwise, that his choice to avoid politics had not in any way "affected" him "personally."

It would be incorrect to say this student—let's call him "Brian"—was altogether typical of his politically disengaged peers in that election year, if only because he went public, vigorously, even militantly, with his contempt for politics. He was quick to distance himself from the mass of his quietly apathetic contemporaries, to say nothing of a growing number of Americans generally, who were simply "too lazy," as he put it, to vote— who "ruin it," he said, for the "rest of us with real reasons" for not voting. And what were those reasons? His real reasons for opting out of politics were a mixture of simple contempt for politicians—they are a "dime a dozen"; disdain for the images they presented—you vote not for a president but for "a poster," for "who kisses his wife the right way" or "who has the better smile"; a sense of utter powerlessness to affect the outcome of an election—he alluded to the electoral college; and a deep cynicism about democracy itself: as he put it, "disenchantment with democracy is common and the golden rule reigns: whoever has the gold makes the rules." For his part, Brian conceived of himself as a free-thinking, autonomous individual coexisting with a mass of conformists. "There is no reason whatsoever why anyone should feel pressured to vote merely to fit in and to avoid ridicule," he lectured his peers. "If you feel that the only reason you voted is because of your parents or your friends, you shouldn't have voted. At least I acted on my own accord." "I have survived thus far without any type of political opinion," he concluded, "and will continue to make my free choice in the future."[2]

But I think we can say that Brian *is* quite typical of his apathetic peers in at least one critically important respect. Brian's confidence in his own independence of mind is a conceit engendered by a number of social and economic forces that combine to provide otherwise "diverse" young Americans today with a very common sense of self, an identity of a kind. They constitute an evolving generational culture, importantly nourished and shaped by modern media in its many manifestations, as Benjamin R. Barber, Todd Gitlin, and Cass R. Sunstein will attest in their chapters. Social theorists of the mid-twentieth century speculated presciently about the "mass" society already foreshadowed by Tocqueville; Brian and his cohort turn out to be what they were talking about.

Brian's militant individualism—his belief in his "moral freedom," as Alan Wolfe will describe it—can quite comfortably shelter a multitude of "culturally" nuanced ideological rationales for being a political dropout. In fact, all we know about Brian is that he is male. Yet had his newspaper column been unsigned, one could easily imagine its author to be female; or for that matter black, or Hispanic, or gay, from no particular part of the country, and either religious or not, and so on across a range of differences among our students. Brian's antipolitical views make him almost the archetypal young American individual.

The burden of the chapters in this volume is that Brian is wrong and mistaken—morally wrong in believing that as an American citizen he has no obligation to concern himself with our politics, and factually mistaken in thinking that national politics do not affect him personally.[3] He is even mistaken in believing he doesn't "think about" politics or have a political opinion. His denial of his "public self," widely shared as it is, affects profoundly our polity and how as a nation we do politics—indeed, it casts grave doubt on the very possibility of democracy itself. And if in his later life he continues to be rightly disgusted with much of the contemporary political scene, he will need only to consult the closest mirror to see who is partly responsible for it.

A University for Brian?

Should we in American higher education try to help Brian understand his political responsibilities—and to act on them? There are formidable obstacles to assigning such a task to colleges and universities. For American institutions of higher learning to flourish, or even to survive, they must be generally in accord with the expectations of prospective students and their parents who seek them out. They must share, first, a common conception of the *purpose* in our society of a higher education—both must, at least broadly, agree on what a college education is *for*. William A. Galston states our problem bluntly: "Few [Americans], I submit, support higher education in the hope that it will make their children better citizens."

Second, besides sharing a sense of the purpose of a university education, both students (and parents) and universities must share a common understanding of the grounds that universities claim for the *authority* they will exercise over students, chiefly, of course, academic or intellectual authority, but other kinds as well. Faculties must be able to give reasons that students (and their parents) can accept, if they don't always or at first fully understand them, for offering as "worth knowing about" this or that subject in the curriculum. This is of course all the more important if such subjects or courses are to be *required* of students. Only if both parties understand in broadly the same terms the authority as well as the purpose of such an education can they agree on its basic legitimacy, for both students and the society at large. But such shared conceptions of authority and purpose, to the extent that they center on what we are calling a political education, may be impossible to achieve.

Third, as anyone at all familiar with the higher education scene today will immediately grant, an added difficulty is that *internally* the members of universities, faculty, administrators, and trustees (as well as students) must also agree with each other on these fundamental questions of purpose and authority—on what is worth knowing and why it should be required of students. But with faculties increasingly "professionalized" and fragmented along disciplinary lines, and rewarded less and less for devotion to teaching than for research and publication, such agreement is not easily reached. This means that if our project is a vitally important one, as the contributors here all agree, it is also, to say no more, an exceedingly challenging one. Prospective students know what they want, or think they do; universities are pretty good at satisfying those expectations and have opinions of their own about what students need. This convergence of interests induces a community of sorts on the campus largely sheltered from the unseemly world of politics. Generally missing from these complementary impulses, however, is any serious concern for citizenship.

Our authors approach these broad issues from a number of different angles of vision, each bringing to light a significant feature of the problem of how to conceive of a political education for those young persons who inevitably will constitute in later life a privileged and powerful elite, but who come to us already conditioned against active citizenship. That our universities do in fact produce such an elite, and that few individuals in American life rise to prominence in any field without such an education, are surely reasons enough take seriously our task in this book. The point is made over and over here that *some* sort of orientation toward the political and social world is somehow acquired during the four years of college, even if this means that what students bring with them to college is simply reinforced. Leroy Rouner puts it this way:

> When we are asked whether universities can properly engage in a kind of character education, the answer is that character education is inevitable. We don't have any choice. What's happening in college is that you feed an adolescent in one end and four years later you get a young adult out the other. The kid has matured, developed new interests, new ideas, new values, and his or her teachers have been instrumental in shaping this emerging character.

Whether we intend it or not, and whether our students (and their parents) expect it or not, the education we provide will *somehow*, for good or ill, shape their characters as citizens. So, will the upper classes we inevitably help produce be a politically and socially responsible elite—or merely a rich and powerful one?

More specifically, our authors examine the assumptions that lead students like Brian to imagine they have already achieved their personhood, are complete individuals, at the age of nineteen or so, with little more to learn about who and what they are as members of this society and polity, and to believe they have no duties corresponding to the rights they indubitably enjoy. Our contributors have much to say about why it is that today's universities not only do not see the Brians among their students as any sort of "problem," but in a number of ways are even contributing to their political alienation. Notwithstanding the often powerful and deeply rooted antipolitical tendencies of modern universities, the authors turn their attention concretely to what universities might reasonably be expected to do in the matter of making better citizens of their students.

ANTIGOVERNMENTALISM AND THE TYRANNY OF THE MARKET

Brian comes honestly by his opinions. In the opening essay, "Between Resignation and Utopia: Political Education in the Modern University," William Galston begins his lucid treatment of our broad and urgently important topic with these words: "Citizenship in America is always an endangered species. Judged against other developed democracies, we are a remarkably antistatist and antipolitical people." Before going on to analyze in detail the "embeddedness" of modern universities in both the economy and the culture, he offers a convincing account of the sources of Brian's antipolitical individualism, pointing to the tendency of wealthy societies like our own—because of their very affluence—to encourage in young people an indifference toward obligations beyond their self-defined interests and, as does Brian, to distrust all authority and to embrace only their own self-defined purposes. And all of this Brian brings with him to the university.

Over the last half century the market economy has displaced much of the trust in government that had been generated by the Progressive Era, the New Deal, and the Great Society. During those three moments in recent American history there was at least a temporary relaxation of the antigovernmentalism as old as the Revolution and reinforced by the U.S. Constitution itself.[4] It's not that Americans "trust" the market economy exactly, but when it is performing at least reasonably well, they are inclined to give it the benefit of the doubt. On the embeddedness of today's universities in that economy and its popularly supported assumptions, Michael Sandel offers in graphic and disturbing (if sometimes humorous) detail an analysis of just how deeply committed we academics collectively are to offering to prospective students (and their parents) a scheme of education that promises nothing so much as an intensive preparation for a life of economic success and high social status, along with, of course, a vibrant "social" life (which students may relish more than do their parents). Hence the elaborate emphasis on ever more sophisticated marketing strategies in how universities present themselves to potential consumers of their advertised wares.

With such an education embracing the "market conception" of freedom, one finds little room in curricula predicated on the inviolability of individual choice for the teaching and learning about the *civic conception of freedom* necessary to American citizenship. The "liberal" education once so closely identified with such a conception of freedom and citizenship continues, of course, to be usefully exploited for its prestige value. It is used as part of a marketing strategy for selling to prospective consumers of higher education what in practice is basically vocational preparation. There is much emphasis on "critical thinking" and "thinking for yourself" in such a faux liberal education, as our Brian would be quick to point out, but it is largely silent on thinking *with others* about pursuing common ends.

So if modern capitalism has created a world after its own image, as Marx predicted, modern universities are quite at home in that world, are indeed among its most courted and useful handmaidens—hence also Benjamin Barber's discussion of the "commercialized" or "branded" university. But at home as well in such a society are the mass media, another powerful force making the modern university what it is for its students. In any event, if Brian seeks out a college education because it will help him climb the ladder of success, thinking critically for himself as he climbs, he will obviously be joined by a host of fellow climbers, also thinking critically for themselves, whose aspirations are essentially indistinguishable from his own. Together they will have been prepared, en masse, by the mass media and popular culture, before they even set foot on campus, to be the kind of individuals they imagine themselves to be, and in some respects actually are.

A MEDIA-ENHANCED PRIVATIZATION

To say that such students are bearers of an economically oriented culture reinforced by the media, hostile or indifferent to politics, and distrustful of government, means a lot more than that the news media over the last four decades or so have bombarded the American populace with a relentless and monotonous tale of political and governmental scandal, corruption, dishonesty, and incompetence, or even that the media have all but usurped the role of such political institutions as political parties— important as all this is. This might in itself be enough to persuade Brian that he wanted nothing whatever to do with the institutions, and those who act within them, by which we are governed. But no, the alienating effect of modern media extends much beyond such a simple (political) immorality tale, influential as that has been.

This is to say, media-encouraged cynicism about government and politics aside, that many of our incoming students may well be impervious to any part of their college education that substantially contradicts their already deeply ingrained expectations about what life in our society ought to be for them. This is the important and dismaying argument that Barber makes about "America's invisible tutors." Taking the long view, he argues that educational institutions, public schools as well as colleges and universities, no longer serve to educate citizens, as the American Founders hoped they would, that role having been usurped by the mass media and entertainment industry, as well as the commercial economy. When it comes to even the most basic political information, for example, we professors will compete with—and lose to—the television news of the day. More than this, the impact of the "media, the mall, and the multiplex," according to Barber, is not so much ideologically neutral as civically and politically irrelevant. "Radical or conservative, the academy is no longer the paramount institution for the socialization and education of the young. It doesn't really matter what or how we teach, as long as content on the Web, the tube, and the silver screen are controlled by the nation's power elites." In any event, bringing Jefferson up to date, Barber considers an education for American national citizenship at the university level as less important for the average American than local civic activity or membership in the world being produced by globalization.

Todd Gitlin does not share Barber's reservations about American national citizenship. Yet in making his case for that dimension of our individual identities, centering on the principles we share as members of this polity, not on the ethnicities or religions that may divide us from each other or from others in the world, Gitlin focuses even more heavily than does Barber on the tendency of modern media to separate, isolate, individualize, even in a sense to deracinate American youth, and above all to make it hard for them to attend to or to participate in reasoned deliberation on complex issues of public import. It is not possible to do justice here to Gitlin's rich analysis of the proliferation of media in which we are immersed today. He argues convincingly that "this condition of half-attention" it produces in our students is not "the focus that is required for intellectual mastery—learning a language, performing a complex computation, grasping the contours of history, assessing rival explanations of a given phenomenon, assessing the moral implications of complex realities. It is not a mood conducive to education—or citizenship."

Calling on a theme dealt with in different ways by our previous contributors, Cass R. Sunstein brings out starkly the negative implications—for active American citizenship—of a higher education permeated by Gitlin's "values of media" driven by a market conception of life. Is a college education, along with other kinds of culture, a commodity like any other, simply a good that can be bought and sold? One of our symposium questions put it this way: "In the end, isn't liberal education, as a practical matter, defined by what students and parents are willing to spend their money for?" Sunstein argues that liberal education is not that at all, and therefore that to tailor it simply to meet the expectations of its "customers" is to negate it.

This conclusion raises three further questions at the heart of our problem. First, since untrammeled choice is at the center of what Sandel calls the "market conception of freedom," does conceiving of higher education as something other than just another commodity mean that freedom of choice is somehow limited in a properly constructed curriculum? Sunstein's answer is an emphatic yes. Drawing an ingenious parallel between the public forum doctrine concerning freedom of speech and what ought to be offered to students in a well-designed curriculum, Sunstein argues that central to both is the benefit of unchosen or unexpected experiences—whether in the former being exposed to ideas you might have wanted to avoid, or in the latter being required to study a subject you might think doesn't interest you.

Second, though, curtailing our natural right as consumers to choose is to invoke a conception of authority that is very tenuous indeed in the case of universities. Where do universities come by the authority to tell students what they "must" study—if they or their parents are paying to attend? One source of this may be the epistemic authority of hard science as applied in certain professional programs, and by extension in any course of a specifically vocational sort. "This is what you must know if you want to be a _____; we professors have that sort of knowledge and you as students don't, so you must trust us." But, and here is where it gets sticky, it isn't obvious that there is in today's university a kind and degree of authority, epistemic or simply institutional, to which our (self-styled) freely and critically thinking students of today will readily defer when it comes to an education called "political."

Finally, guaranteeing that students as future citizens will confront and have to contend intellectually with unchosen and unexpected ideas and other experiences means that they will be to that extent drawn out of their media-induced isolation, or what may be even more pernicious, the tendency of their "own" ideas to become ossified as they are reinforced by the associations they freely choose. "Forced" in the ordinary course of a rightly conceived college education to think about ideas and ways of life different from their own, Sunstein suggests, they will tend to adopt a broader, more comprehensive view of the life they inescapably share with others. It is the move from what the ancient Greeks called the "idiocy" of the merely private or apolitical life to something approaching a citizen's grasp of a political or common life. It may sound harsh to put it this way, but, left to his own devices, our Brian, as he thinks critically for himself, may well end up an ancient Greek kind of idiot—and a dogmatic one at that.

Whatever his claims to independence of mind, we may doubt that young Brian is quite the "master of his fate" and the "captain of his soul" he may believe he is. We are inclined to doubt this all the more when we reflect on Tocqueville's observations about the "philosophical method of the Americans," their penchant for consulting only their own experience, where "Each therefore withdraws narrowly into himself and claims to judge the world from there."[5] Indeed, the more thoroughly and radically American individualists reject the influence on themselves of all "external" institutions, the more alike they become, which poses, in such an egalitarian society that never had a democratic revolution, the ever-present threat of majority tyranny at worst and a troubling social conformity at best.

LIBERAL EDUCATION AND THE HERO: A CIVIC INDIVIDUALISM?

Well, if Brian and his contemporaries are a youthful herd of independent minds,[6] listening to the echoes from their peers of their own uncertain and hesitant internal moral voices, we can doubt that they are on their way to becoming citizens suitable to a viable liberal-democratic republic. What if, as the early American republicans believed, such a citizen must be prepared to sacrifice in ways great and small, even if necessary his life, for a good beyond himself? No one believes—certainly that generation of Americans did not—that we are born with such "republican virtue," that we are just "naturally" self-sacrificing, let alone heroic. Though, as Jefferson and the Scottish Enlightenment had it, we are born with a "moral sense," it is precisely education that strengthens and refines such a sense. So, can a properly conceived liberal education in any way foster such *political* virtues in students, and thus help to promote the right sort of citizenship for our kind of "constitution," broadly speaking? These questions are brought forcefully to our attention by James B. Stewart's dramatic account of the life, and death, of Rick Rescorla. Where did Rick come by his strong sense of personal responsibility, his selfless commitment to standards of conduct that led him knowingly, we must suppose, to give his life to save his coworkers in the World Trade Center on September 11, 2001?

We know from Stewart's stirring narrative that Rick Rescorla lacked the benefit of a formal college education. We also learn, however, that he had, quite on his own, steeped himself in a wide range of the classics of the Great Books tradition in liberal education, and that he often drew pointed inspiration from them as he coped with the vicissitudes of a very active, often a very perilous, and ultimately a fatally dangerous life. By contrast, as Stewart pointedly reminds us, his other works have been a series of books about Wall Street felons, many of whom were products precisely of a liberal education at some of the nation's most prestigious institutions, where evidently they "learned" how to be not civic heroes, but selfish villains. The best we can conclude, perhaps, is that even a liberal *self*-education *can* shape a good kind of character and that a formal education at the "best" schools can result in the opposite. We should wonder what might happen if we stopped giving students what they've been conditioned to want and instead aimed deliberately at shaping the right kind of character necessary not only to autonomous individuals but also to a self-governing polity.

RELIGION, MORALITY, AND POLITICAL EDUCATION

Some of these contributions explore the proper place of religion in American public life, a perennial issue in American politics and hence in an education for citizenship. Our authors were invited to respond to this much contested issue by the question, "With blood being shed all over the world in the name of religion, can there be—should there be—any place for religion in the education of *American* citizens? Is ours not a secular republic?" Now the spheres of religion, morality, and public life are surely different. But do they at all overlap? George Washington thought they did: "Of all the dispositions and habits, which lead to political prosperity," he said in his Farewell Address, "Religion and Morality are indispensable supports. In vain would that man claim the tribute of Patriotism, who should labor to subvert these great pillars of human happiness, these firmest props of the duties of Men and Citizens. The mere Politician, equally with the pious man, ought to respect and to cherish them." But he also said to his countrymen that "With slight shades of difference, you have the same religion, manners, habits, and political principles." Washington and the other Founders in fact made no *institutional* provision for ensuring the continuance in generations to come of this fortuitous homogeneity. The First Amendment to the Constitution in its entirety, but especially the first two clauses, saw to that. What persisted instead was a political "creed," rooted in both Athens and Rome as well as Jerusalem, which eventually ended slavery and opened up this "first new nation" to wave upon wave of newcomers. So what are we to think, now, with a nation of great religious and cultural diversity, of the alleged overlapping of religion and morality, and of the link between both and political life? And this especially when American institutions of all kinds are said to be growing weaker?

As Michael Walzer points out, an education for democratic citizenship that is also a *moral* education will be viewed differently by different religious groups, for whom religion, morality, and civic identity are intertwined, some with acceptance, but some with distrust or opposition: Orthodox Catholics, Jews, and Muslims worrying that their children will be "Protestantized"; or fundamentalist Christians, who fear their children will be "secularized." Alan Wolfe tells a revealing story about how American Catholicism is gradually adapting to its American cultural environment, an important element of which is the drive for what he calls "moral freedom." Specifically, this means an assertion on the part of lay Catholics of that characteristic American suspicion of institutional constraints in favor of the freedom of individual choice in matters of morality and beyond. On Wolfe's account it seems exactly that American Catholics are indeed becoming not only Protestantized but also Americanized. Much more recent to these shores, and lacking the indigenous political resources of the Judeo-Christian heritage, some Muslims find themselves in an even more stressful plight as they try to raise their children to be both good Muslims and good (secular?) Americans. We should note that what makes these groups anxious is exactly the very modern and very American culture of individual liberation from traditional constraints.

Though Wolfe is skeptical that universities can be institutions strong enough in an age of moral freedom to shape the character of their students, Leroy Rouner's claim, cited above, that universities inevitably do shape character is enough by itself to make students like our Brian a bit uncertain about their own individuality, just as it should cause the rest of us to think about the possibilities higher education offers. Even a secular political order, it can be argued, requires citizens of a certain character, a certain convergence of private with public morality. But when Rouner also says that "my thesis is that the health of American democracy is dependent on people of a certain character; that that character has a religious dimension; and that it is one of the 'secular' university's responsibilities to produce such people," he makes in the current atmosphere, especially in academia, a very controversial statement indeed. Hence also this symposium question: "Can universities as such properly engage in what amounts to a kind of character education without abandoning the principle of value neutrality central to the disinterested search for truth? Can universities be that kind of advocate?"

The interest in lucrative careers most of our students bring with them, their media conditioning, their sense of absolute moral freedom— all support what we can call demand-side liberal education. This popular conception of what a college education is good for, pragmatically embraced by universities themselves, returns us directly to the question of the purpose of universities and the nature and extent of academic authority. By what authority, by what right, do professors—or does the university as a whole—advocate *any* conception of the good life?

According to William Galston, neither of the dominant conceptions of pedagogical authority in our universities is consistent with an education for American citizenship—all the more so, surely, if that is held to include either a moral or a religious dimension.

On the one hand, our students and their parents overwhelmingly expect what Galston calls the "vocational" conception, aimed, as Sandel argues at length, at equipping them for jobs. This is a conception of knowledge, always congenial to us practical-minded Americans, that in its embrace of technology and its manifold applications has earned the respect of the world. But except as persons so trained would be contributing to the general social and economic well-being, it is not a conception of knowledge that informs the active citizen. And "vocational" has long since lost its religious connotations.

POLITICAL KNOWLEDGE: PLATO OR ARISTOTLE?

When we turn to the other traditional conception of knowledge, which Galston calls "philosophical"(the pursuit of knowledge "for its own sake"), we see that it offers even less support for an education for democratic citizenship, even as it is also in some of its expressions inhospitable to a religiously defined conception of human life. And it is important to understand why this is so. Persons imbued with this philosophical view of educational purpose and authority, as old as Plato and as recent as modern positivist social science, may be deeply if differently engaged with the moral and political dimensions of life, but each will eschew mere practicality. Whether out of philosophic detachment or scientific objectivity, they will address, not the character of the *citizen*, but respectively in different ways the rationality of the *thinker* or the behavior of the *individual*. Between them, we may say, they contemplate both the sublime and the ridiculous, without intruding overmuch, except imaginatively as observers, into either. As philosophers our faculty don't aspire to be kings and queens (or even to advise them), and as social scientists they are always mindful of the distinction between fact and value, of the is and the ought, and struggle to adhere to the former and to avoid the latter.[7] Neither overtly prescribes the good life—or tries to save souls, just as neither lends itself to a self-conscious education for membership in the American polity.

We must recognize a certain irony in seeing positivist social science as part of the philosophical conception of knowledge, consistent though it may be with a Neoplatonic elitism and detachment from the "real" world, as critics of Plato (as well as of mainstream political science) would have it. A look at the history of American political science, at least since the "behavioral revolution," for example, will reveal that its scorn for ideas is second, if at all, only to its indifference to history—which together make it very American as well as antipolitical. When William Galston says we Americans "are a remarkably antistatist and antipolitical people," it may be said indeed that he is also describing some of the most prominent tendencies in the American discipline of political science as well. [8] Benjamin Barber is right that American political science virtually stopped being interested in citizenship after the 1920s and 1930s. Michael Walzer observes that as recently as the 1950s the "dissociation of ethics from the rest of academic work"

> . . . derived in part from a one-sided conception of social science. On this view, statements of value, because they cannot be proven true or false, cannot be studied at all. Values can't be analyzed, we were told in those days, they can only be chosen, and the choice is irrational, ungovernable, without objective criteria. Hence teaching [morality] is impossible, the presumptuous invasion of a mysterious (religious?) realm where professors, with their secular and scientific training, have nothing to say and should therefore say nothing. "Whereof one cannot speak, thereof one must be silent."

The dominant behaviorialism of the 1950s and early 1960s was in fact so adamant about avoiding the "value judgments" that talking seriously about citizenship surely entails that the reaction against such methodological rigidity setting in shortly thereafter never replaced the entrenched creed, despite premature talk about the "post-behavioral era" in the discipline. [9] As for academic philosophy itself, the pursuit of truth for its own sake presupposes a conception of (academic) authority that, unlike the bases of political authority students must be led to understand, is absolute and indisputable. Or so Plato believed.

Nor, as Walzer also suggests, did the "return of grand theory in the human sciences" heralded as early as 1985, though it may have helped to drive value-free behavioralism further underground, do anything to rescue from its near oblivion the idea of citizenship and its attendant concepts. [10] On the contrary, the postmodernism the new grand theory often (but not always) represented became itself ensconced in academe, where it gave rise not so much to a new conception of purpose and authority in the university as to a multifaceted deconstruction of the very ideas of purpose and authority themselves. This in turn provided a grounding, so to speak, for what has been dubbed "advocacy pedagogy," a kind of teaching that by no means shies away from "values" or arguing for this or that cause. [11] Including representatives of all of the social sciences as well as the humanities, this advocacy pedagogy sometimes is described openly as "political" and will even talk the talk of revolution and "subversion" in the name of justice for the oppressed. But for all that, it is firmly and comfortably a part of the academic establishment and rarely concerns itself, except rhetorically, with "politics" in the world outside. (I say more about this in my own chapter.)

Still, this open advocacy would seem to be even more offensive to the philosophical mode of knowledge—without, however, qualifying as any sort of "civic" education, certainly not the political education urged in this volume. On the contrary, it sometimes transforms positivist behavioralism's indifference to a citizenship of the common good into a strident rejection, or ironic dismissal, not only of a politically defined common life and a democratic politics, but also of the very idea of a shared national identity. [12]

In sum it must be said that most of the contributors to this volume reject this legacy, a combination of Thrasymachus and of Plato himself, whether expressed in formal academic philosophy, in what Walzer calls "one-sided social science," or the new "grand theory." Instead they affirm, if only implicitly, that what Aristotle called "the science of politics" is less about *knowing* (for its own sake) than about *acting*, with others, in pursuit of a contested common good, less about demonstrating the validity of an argument than about carrying on a conversation, and is in any case not an "exact" science. But Aristotle's claim that "political science" in his sense was not properly a study for the young and inexperienced? This, of course, they reject! [13]

THE AMERICAN "REGIME": ARISTOTLE PLUS LOCKE

Along with Leroy Rouner, who has much to say about the idea of America's "civil religion," Jean Bethke Elshtain argues that Americans are still a people who understand themselves in religious (and moral) terms, though representing a pluralism of religious traditions. The question she so forcefully raises is whether religious Americans, that is, the bulk of the population, can literally be themselves in politics, whether our reigning "liberal monism," as she describes the impact on our culture of John Rawls's injunction to purge our vocabularies of religious meanings as a precondition of achieving a public consensus, will permit the religious to draw on their religious convictions as they engage in political discourse. Although the U.S. Constitution separates church from state, it does not, she insists, require us to separate our religion from our politics. Indeed, our constitution as a people, in Aristotle's sense, may in some measure preclude such a separation.

There are reasons besides the reigning secularism in the modern academy (tolerating "all" religions is compatible with marginalizing religion as such) that Elshtain's claim about the inseparability of American religion from American politics is likely to cause controversy. For one thing, it evokes exactly the Aristotelian conception of a "constitution" or "regime," a particular "way of life" of a people, suggesting criteria for justice, both distributive and retributive, conceptions of who should rule, and for what ends, even specifying who are citizens, and so on. The fusion of Protestant Christianity with classical republicanism at the time of the American founding, for example, even contained within it seeds of all of the key elements of contemporary American political culture: republicanism itself, of course, but also democracy, liberalism, the rule of law, a rich sense of community, and so on. We might easily imagine a conversation between Locke and Aristotle about how Americans ought to be governed, and we can be certain that neither of them would leave American religiosity out of his calculations. [14]

Yet William Galston is surely correct in saying there is a conception of Aristotelian civic education that is quite incompatible with what he calls the "philosophical" tradition in American education, especially as that was so heavily influenced by the emergence of the modern research university after the German model. Surely, from that point of view, the "inculcation" of the norms of "reasonable patriotism" or "informed loyalty," rather than an investigation into the fundamental aspects of the regime of a sort that doesn't beg the question of its own goodness, would strike the modern philosophical professor, whether actually a philosopher or only a positivist political scientist, as a form of "indoctrination." And any number of "advocacy pedagogues" might be even more deeply offended.

But what if Locke's arguments, plus Aristotle's own investigations into the character of the people for whom he was recommending a constitution, convinced Aristotle that the Americans simply could not accept a "regime" the fundamental "tenets of which" they do "not question"? That is, what if the American regime just *is* a regime built upon questioning, if not indeed on revolution itself? Between them, what Locke and Aristotle might agree upon, then, could be a "constitution" (regime) in Aristotle's sense of the term that was both permeated throughout by liberalism and importantly informed by religion. Democratic? Surely not at first—but then Locke was no more a radical democrat than was Aristotle. Even today, many will argue, the American "constitution's" oligarchic features largely eclipse its democratic ones. Or perhaps it would be a modern sort of Lockean polity in which the too-sharp but ambiguous distinctions between the state of nature, civil society, and government itself are softened and "clarified." "I've got it," one of our two experts might say, "a 'mixed constitution' with a middle-class base, in which governing power is nowhere concentrated, authority is nebulous and its locus uncertain, and in which individual rights are respected. We can decide later about what 'happiness' ought to mean for them." As it happened (to conclude our fantasy), they never got around to finishing their project, and we Americans, left to work that out for ourselves, are still wondering what true happiness, individual and collective, really is. Neither of our constitutional consultants would be altogether satisfied with their joint handiwork, we may suppose, but both would see themselves in the result. We might call it an incipient liberal-democratic republic—a "constitution" that both is but is not yet, both is and is coming to be at the same time, inaugurated but still being consummated, ever a work in the making.

AMERICA AND THE WORLD

Before going further it must be said that one of our contributors, Stephen Holmes, takes sharp issue with the argument about the capture of universities by market forces and that we ought to champion citizen participation. He characterizes that critique as proceeding from a misplaced leftism or communitarianism, faulting it for focusing on a republic and participatory democracy lost beyond recall and for failing to meet the challenges of today and the future. "The problem is not loss of the past and overadaptation to the present, but the contrary. Far from overadapting, universities have underadapted and seem unable to teach a highly diverse group of young people what they need to know in order to live responsibly and fruitfully in a world without walls." Holmes doesn't mount a defense of the market conception of life, nor would he endorse our Brian's modish individualism. But he does understand Brian's cynicism about democracy in noting that "citizens in democracies and semi-democracies around the world are increasingly alienated from civic engagement because civic engagement is often a sham." Yet he would insist that insofar as Brian is a typical student, indeed a typical American, he is scandalously ignorant precisely of the world he inhabits. Citing also the gullibility of the American people in the run-up to the invasion of Iraq, Holmes argues, "Not extreme commercialization, therefore, but extreme public ignorance—which entails extreme vulnerability to being politically manipulated—is the most urgent problem to which universities can contribute an answer."

Though one of those insisting on the negative effects of commercialization, Benjamin Barber agrees with Holmes that we must transcend our "nostalgia" for the old republican kind of polity projected by Jefferson's Declaration of Independence and Washington's Farewell Address, and the American democracy celebrated by Tocqueville, which in any case harbored slavery and the oppression of women. Taking issue implicitly also with the Campus Compact's call to reconnect our students with the national institutions of American democracy, Barber argues that "the very notion of citizenship has a different meaning in a world with vanishing borders whose primary players are not necessarily states. *Citizenship is both transnational and local—rather than strictly national.*" [Emphasis in the original.]

Barber and Holmes are responding in different ways to this symposium question: "If democratic citizenship is problematic in a polity the size of the American republic, is it even conceivable in 'the world' that is not a polity at all?" Critical here is whether there can be institutions on a global scale that link ordinary citizens to centers of governmental power. What will tie "global citizens" to the institutions, when they are developed, *if* they are developed, that connect them to the centers of world power—when *they* are developed? Barber speaks to this challenge when he says, "When power and participation are severed, democracy is imperiled. For power without participation is tyranny while participation without power is a fraud and a provocation to cynicism. . . . Rejoining power and participation is the core task of twenty-first-century democracy. The project entails a redefinition of global civic infrastructure to sustain citizenship in more global terms and the development of that citizenship."

WHAT ARE WE TO THINK ABOUT PATRIOTISM?

Whatever in the future might bind Americans (or members of any other nation today) to others into a cosmopolitan world community, we have to doubt that it will be anything approaching patriotism as that sentiment is commonly understood. The circles of our operative affections are probably not that all-encompassing. Certainly it can't be what is called an "ethnic" nationalism, or indeed (obviously) any kind of *nationalism* at all. Just as certainly, for most of us, such potentially destructive sentiments in our students ought to be discouraged. Consider Stephen Holmes's title. For Holmes the practical meaning of such emotional allegiance is not the "informed loyalty" or "reasonable patriotism" Galston associates with an Aristotelian sort of civic education but is gleaned from Plato's characterization of the good guard dog's disposition—an "instinctive fondness for fellow citizens and xenophobic aversion to foreigners." This, Holmes argues, is what has been encouraged in Americans, especially after 9/11. "The real threat to the university lies here [i.e., "in Plato's conception of patriotism and its relation to the life of the mind"], not in commercialism but in the vulgar jingoism of a few anti-intellectual conservatives who have shown what fatal influence they can wield over an uneducated public in an age of panic induced by terror." Holmes warns against the well-funded right-wing ideologues who are pressuring the academy to be more patriotic, or at least less disloyal. "Campaigning to use the classroom to instill patriotic emotions," he says, "they seem to want to remake our students in the image of Plato's dogs."

It is indeed hard for many of us in the academy, even before the present nationalistic enthusiasm, to have good thoughts about patriotism, especially for those upon whom the 1960s left an indelible mark. [15] But there is a different and arguably a noble kind of patriotism that not only "permits" but *requires* vigorous if politically responsible dissent from the doings or misdoings of national leaders. One can even argue that such a patriotism is indispensable to our Lockean but also Aristotelian "constitution."

A moving discussion of the meaning of this sort of patriotism is announced in the opening paragraphs of Roger Wilkins's very personal story, "The Civic Education of a Black American in a Great Big World." Beyond Wilkins's dissent from the Iraq war, it is the story of a lifelong struggle against racial injustice, indeed demonstrating against it from the "outside" when necessary, but also working hard "within" the American governmental and political system when possible. The latter is made possible, Wilkins insists, precisely by the institutional, political-cultural, and legal legacies we twenty-first-century Americans have inherited from those racist (and sexist, and no doubt homophobic) white Anglo-Saxon Protestant males we call the Founding Fathers—persons, one might add, it is almost taboo in some quarters to mention, let alone praise, even critically. Flawed human beings though they were, Wilkins maintains, they gave black people, and the rest of us, too, the institutional means to protect our rights, to get them expanded, and to do so in the name of American justice. And when all this in fact works, never entirely or immediately but measurably over time, it attaches you to the country you and your ancestors helped to build. No jingoistic nationalism here.

Obviously, none of this makes Roger Wilkins's sort of patriotic American a parochial xenophobe, but such a citizen *is* deeply mindful of the indispensability of the institutional structure of American democracy— and, we must add, of its global responsibilities. Consider Stephen Holmes's suggestion as to how American citizens ought to regard their responsibilities given this country's place in the world and the conduct of the present administration. "As the only electorate in the world with a chance to hold the U.S. government accountable, we may conceivably have an extra moral duty to act as 'virtual representatives' of the rest of mankind." Well said. But before we can begin to rise to this responsibility for holding our government accountable for its actions abroad, we must, in addition to having an "accurate and nuanced" grasp of international affairs, *also* know how to make our electoral institutions (e.g., political parties) work *and* possess the political will to do so. We must hope, that is, that students like Brian can be brought to care about their country and to be willing to work in effective ways to make it better at home and otherwise genuinely to earn the decent respect *of* the opinion of mankind. This would seem to require a certain kind of patriotism. As Wilkins puts it, alluding to the story he tells his students about Ben Franklin,

> At times of crisis our leaders—this is a bipartisan observation—are
> not always strict in their observation of the limits the Constitution
> erects around their power. It is then when the nation needs citizens
> who are *alert to the need to keep their republic.* . . . People in power
> will always find a reason to try to quiet voices that they find incon-
> venient. But it is when the government finds discussion and protest

and organizing most "inconvenient" that such discussion and action are most needed. That is when the requirement to "keep it" is most urgent. . . . Somebody has to teach young Americans those things and if it is not us, then, what's a faculty for?

WHAT A FACULTY IS FOR

Finally, we must note that our authors offer a variety of curricular suggestions, which together should provide much substance for faculties and administrations willing to consider undertaking what we hope they will consider their *political*, as well as their "civic," responsibilities.

The stories Professor Wilkins tells his students—the Ben Franklin Story, The "Real" American Revolution Story, the Weeping Professor Story (a defense of political commitment in professors), the Demonstration Story, all pointing to Blacks and the Vindication of the Founding Ideals—seem to me to constitute a defensible response to those subscribing to what William Galston describes as the philosophical tradition in universities—who worry about "inculcation" and "indoctrination," and who deny that professors may teach from a position that "privileges" one regime, say our own, over another. The same would seem to apply to the pedagogical treatment of religion, especially, of course, as religion has worked for good as well as ill in the development of our institutions. If Roger Wilkins can tell a story whose central theme is that the "black" story and the "white" story are inextricably interrelated, so must students understand that the story of religion in America, as presented by scholars such as Jean Elshtain and Alan Wolfe, is also on some level each of their stories as well—that a properly intensive and critical study of that part of the American past can provide the substance for that feat of human rationality that Leroy Rouner identifies as "synoptic intuition," an insight into the larger culture in which they each live, and move, and have their being.

In a different mode, Galston's own "investigative" model of instruction, designed to overcome objections about indoctrination and enculturation, would likely have just that effect, while also being in accord with Todd Gitlin's claim that "for citizenly as well as strictly educational purposes, then, higher education ought to cultivate a disciplined curiosity about the world and an enthusiasm for careful disputation"—which I would hope would be the effect of the debate-structured courses in my own proposal. "In sum," Gitlin says, "higher education has the burden of advancing the intellectual side of citizenship. . . . It enrolls higher education in the defense of the society's highest values. It is not a mission that can be offloaded onto any other institution." Moreover, the second half of Galston's yearlong course, the United States in the World, would seem to coincide nicely with Barber's and Holmes's prescriptions for overcoming our woeful national ignorance about cultures, societies, religions, and governing systems besides our own. And all by itself Cass Sunstein's inspired analysis brings up short those who would abdicate their professional (as well as "political") responsibilities by succumbing to the temptation to open up the curriculum to untrammeled freedom of student choice.

And we might also consider in a new light James Stewart's revealing tale of Rick Rescorla's life and death, and countless other stories like it in the history and literature of our broader culture. Properly and critically pondered by students, might they not contribute to the sort of reflection that, like Rick's own, can constitute a "self-forming" of one's own individual character of the kind that meshes with Michael Sandel's project in the formation of the republican citizen? Moreover, in these essays, but also in our many related sessions at our symposium, we heard countless calls for open, rigorous, and robust debate, with no cows too sacred to avoid critical scrutiny, with no intellectual holds barred, and all in the spirit of sparking curiosity and subsequent reflection, in line with Galston's and Gitlin's suggestions above. And the constant subtext of these many calls was that all this heated yet carefully focused and structured debate was importantly at least part of the education necessary to citizens of a political order such as our own. Indeed, provided students are deeply enough engaged in such an investigative yet argumentative examination of the fundamental principles of our political and social order, they will in fact be *doing,* as well as merely thinking about, what citizens in our "constitution" do, and so will in some measure become such citizens. Such debate over the meaning of the common life would be an existential lesson about the *purpose* of democratic citizenship under the auspices of the kind of (challengeable) *authority* that makes it possible. Through such a "participatory political education" students might come to understand that there can be no enduring individual freedom, negative or positive, without politics; that there can be no equality, economic or political, unless there is a *democratic* politics; and that there can be no politics of any kind unless there is a common life, which some want to preserve, some to change, or others only to make more extensively or deeply shared. We might even surmise that Aristotle would regard this as a civic education for our time and place he would support.

I'll close by recommending to the reader's careful attention Michael Walzer's complex and uncompromising argument in support of his claim about the three-way connection between liberal education, morality, and democratic citizenship, and specifically his description of the sort of course devoted to moral reasoning about politics that, in his view, undergraduate students should be required to take. *Required?* This returns us to our beginning claim about purpose and authority in the modern university, and how the tensions between the two, and between them and the social context within which out institutions exist, should be resolved in favor of a certain kind of political education. So if democratic citizenship is the purpose of the university, or one of them, what does Walzer have to say to our Brian (and his parents)—*and* our morally timorous modern faculty—about why student Brian *ought* to be conversant with and act on his responsibilities as a citizen in this democracy?

Because of the First Amendment to the Constitution, we don't have an established church, Walzer says, but the Constitution does establish politics and a certain kind of state, complete with a multiplicity of "offices."

Think of citizenship as a political office: surely future officeholders should learn something about the responsibilities the office entails. Or better, the current officeholders should teach the next generation what they think they have learned about those responsibilities. For the reproduction of democratic politics is never a sure thing. We have to prove to our children that we really believe in the values that make democracy possible. That means, first of all, that we have to live by those values; it also means that we should not be afraid to insist on their study. For very good reasons, citizenship, unlike medicine or law, doesn't require a license; students don't need a passing grade in democratic politics. But they should definitely take the course.

NOTES

1. Campus Compact, "Presidents' Fourth of July Declaration on the Civic Responsibility of Higher Education," July 1999. Most of our contributors also reject a specific source of much of the cynicism and disengagement of today's

youth, fashionable in some quarters—I refer to the "realist"-cum-postmodern claim, articulated in part by "Brian" below, that "political" is simply a synonym for the ideological interests of this or that group or segment of the whole, indeed that "the whole" has no meaning other than what is somehow imposed by the powerful on the weak. This is the argument of Thrasymachus, early in the *Republic,* brought up to date. In either case, a political education thus cynically regarded would be a study in how to serve some particular interest, whether of the traditionally powerful or the historically oppressed.

2. It is true that student voices like Brian's were at least muted in the campaign of 2004. Despite the initial optimism about the surge in the youth vote, however, there are reasons to be skeptical that the turnout for the 2004 national election signifies a reversal of our thirty-year trend toward nonvoting. Again, it is true that the turnout of younger eligible voters in 2004 markedly exceeded that of 2000, but it is also true that this increase in the youth vote, according to what experts are now saying, only equaled the increase in the vote of the general population. And it is also true, we must note, that enormous efforts to mobilize the youth vote in 2004 were not directed at any other segment of the electorate. Then, too, if we keep in mind that special circumstances in 2004 may uniquely have boosted turnout across the board, we may have to conclude that younger citizens are not quite yet on their way to becoming better ones. Thomas Patterson puts it succinctly: "It cannot be assumed that a healthy increase in turnout in a single election marks a turnaround in the longer-term pattern. Turnout jumped 5 percentage points in 1992 among younger and older voters alike, only to fall by an even larger amount four years later" (www.vanishingvoter.org/Releases/Vanishing_Voter_Final_Report_2004_Election.pdf). Whatever the fluctuations in voter turnout in the immediate future, we can be assured that the fundamental conditions that have produced such political disengagement on the part of the American electorate, and especially of those of college age, will not appreciably have changed. Such long-term trends of political withdrawal, like the decline of Rome, were not the work of a day and are not likely to be quickly overcome.

3. As Bernard Crick has observed, "The person who wishes not to be troubled by politics and to be left alone finds himself the unwitting ally of those to whom politics is a troublesome obstacle to their well-meant intentions to leave nothing alone." *In Defence of Politics* (Chicago: University of Chicago Press, 1962), 12. Crick's is the point that "you can ignore politics, but politics won't ignore you," as one of my professors at Berkeley, Peter H. Odegaard, told our class. This bit of common sense (to many of us), which at the least posits a private realm that must at times be protected "from" politics (even if the means of that protection is also *through* politics), is rejected by certain voices in both American behavioral political science and the postmodern or cultural left. In the first case, see Robert A. Dahl and Bruce Stinebrickner, *Modern Political*

Analysis, 6th ed. (New York: Prentice-Hall, 2003), on the "ubiquity" of politics, 24–28. That orientation in political science has been with us for a very long time, as noted below. For a more recent expression of a "boundaryless" politics, see the debate over whether universities can be "depoliticized" in Robert L. Simon, *Neutrality and the Academic Ethic* (Lanham, Md.: Rowman & Littlefield, 1994), especially the selections by Henry David Aiken and Sidney Hook.

4. It was Herbert Croly's view that the American people distrust their government in part because their government distrusts them. "The founders of the Constitution did succeed in giving some effect to their distrust of the democratic principle . . . ; and this was at once a grave error on their part and a grave misfortune for the American state. Founded as the national government is, partly on a distrust of the American democracy, it has always tended to make the democracy somewhat suspicious of the national government." *The Promise of American Life* [1909] (Boston: Northeastern University Press, 1989), 33.

5. Alexis de Tocqueville, *Democracy in America* , ed. Harvey C. Mansfield and Delba Winthrop (Chicago: University of Chicago Press, 2000), 404.

6. Harold Rosenberg's characterization of New York intellectuals.

7. On the former, see Mark Lilla, "The Lure of Syracuse," *New York Review of Books*, September 20, 2001. It's quite possible to find would-be philo-tyrants in academia, as Lilla points out. As for a modern value-free social science, Max Weber's *Science as a Vocation* is the classic statement. Though it's possible to argue that American social scientists have misread Weber, he leaves no doubt that "science," and certainly science in the classroom, cannot answer for us the important questions we've since called "normative." Bernard Crick quotes Dwight Waldo, a political scientist at Berkeley, as saying that according to the norm of scientific objectivity, a "new amorality became almost a requisite for professional respect." *The American Science of Politics* (Berkeley and Los Angeles: University of California Press, 1959), 73–74. Today's students in effect attempt to hold their professors to this norm when they accuse them of being "biased," even if much of the reigning academic culture holds that objectivity or neutrality is impossible and that bias is all there is.

8. See generally Crick, *The American Science of Politics*. On the long-range effect of the search for a genuine science of politics, see Robert A. Dahl, "The Behavioral Approach in Political Science: Epitaph for a Monument to a Successful Protest," *American Political Science Review* 55, no. 4 (December 1961): 763–72. Though mostly sympathetic to the behavioral movement, Dahl did note and criticize its neglect of history and its aversion to "bold theory" and "speculation"— which Tocqueville had noted as traits in us Americans a long time before. Ironically, despite its scientific detachment, or perhaps because of it, this mainstream political science may itself be so "close" to American political culture, indeed so much its expression, that it is unable to understand it.

9. See George J. Graham Jr. and George W. Carey, *The Post-Behavioral Era: Perspectives on Political Science* (New York: David McKay, 1972). Dahl got it right, I think, when he said, writing in 1961 ("The Behavioral Approach in Political Science," cited above), that the behavioral movement will "gradually disappear. By this I mean only that it will slowly decay as a distinctive mood and outlook. For it will become, and in fact already is becoming, incorporated into the main body of the discipline." Still, in 1984 the question of citizenship resurfaced in *P.S.* (vol. 17, no. 2 [Spring 1984]), with thoughtful articles by some prominent political scientists. Yet I think we can be confident that our essayists here are right that, as between the lingering behavioralism and the newer postmodernism, citizenship is a subject from which the discipline today by and large distances itself, except, perhaps, among those who link citizenship simply with local community service.

10. See Quentin Skinner, ed., *The Return of Grand Theory in the Human Sciences* (Cambridge: Cambridge University Press, 1985), with essays on Althusser, the *Annales* historians, Derrida, Foucault, Gadamer, Habermas, Kuhn, Levi-Strauss, and Rawls. Skinner's own work has helped keep alive what he variously calls the "classical republican" or "neo-Roman" view of political life. See the review of Skinner's works by Keith Thomas, "Looking for Liberty," in the *New York Review of Books*, May 26, 2005.

11. These issues (and many related ones) are discussed in Patricia Meyer Spacks, ed., *Advocacy in the Classroom: Problems and Possibilities* (New York: St. Martin's Press, 1996); and Darryl J. Gless and Barbara Herrnstein Smith, eds., *The Politics of Liberal Education* (Durham, N.C.: Duke University Press, 1992).

12. See Alan Wolfe, "Anti-American Studies," *New Republic*, February 10, 2003. The huge gulf that would seem to exist between the rigorously value-free social science of the 1950s and today's postmodern advocacy pedagogy may not be as wide as it first appears. True enough, that earlier generation of scholars produced a "science" criticized at the time as a conservative defense of the status quo, as serving a "system maintenance function," where some of today's scholars talk of radically transforming the existing order, or at least of "subverting" it. But recall the enormous influence in the field (of political science) of A. F. Bentley, Charles Merriam, Harold Lasswell, David B. Truman, David Easton, and Robert A. Dahl, to cite only some of the most prominent. With varying degrees of emphasis, these writers tended to slight or disparage the historical and philosophical (the "normative") dimensions of political life and the polity, especially as those have helped shape such concepts as the common good or the public interest, not to mention the idea of the "state" (or centralized government), and active citizenship itself—each of which concepts had in any case a shaky status at best in American political culture. While they were at it, they systematically exposed as "myths" those norms and values essential to a liberal-democratic republic that their methods wouldn't allow them to take seriously. We must note with a sense of irony that Charles A. Beard's

"economic interpretation" of the Constitution has come back into favor with those who want "realistically" to highlight the base motives of the Framers. But my favorite dismissal of the "central referent of the political," as Sheldon Wolin called it, was this almost casual remark of David Truman's, explaining why certain objections to his "group interpretation of politics" could be ignored:

> Assertion of an inclusive "national" or "public" interest is an effective device in many . . . situations. . . . In themselves, these claims are part of the data of politics. However, they do not describe any actual or possible political situation within a complex modern nation. In developing a group interpretation of politics, therefore, we do not need to account for a totally inclusive interest, because one does not exist. *The Governmental Process* (New York: Alfred A. Knopf, 1951, 1971), 50–51.

No postmodern critical theorist could have put it any better—or as clearly.

13. *Nichomachean Ethics*, Book 1, Chapters 2–3, 1094b–1095a, in Richard McKeon, ed., The *Basic Works of Aristotle* (New York: Random House, 1941), 935–37. We should add that the boundaries between the political and the nonpolitical for us being less precise than they were for Aristotle, our young will already have "experienced" enough of their "constitution" to make a formal study of it not something altogether new to them.

14. There is hardly a more vigorously contested issue than the significance, past and present, of the religious component of American culture. In addition to the seminal works of such scholars as Perry Miller, Edmund Morgan, Donald Lutz, Barry Alan Shain, Sacvan Bercovitch, Martin Marty, and Gordon Wood, who insist on the salience of that component, see Alan Wolfe, "What God Owes Jefferson," in *New Republic,* May 23, 2005, a review of Jim Wallis's *God's Politics: Why the Right Gets It Wrong and the Left Doesn't Get It,* and *Taking Faith Seriously,* ed. Mary Jo Bane, Brent Coffin, and Richard Higgins.

15. There are powerful voices in today's left that are not repeating the mistake of the 1960s, which was, in effect, to surrender the flag to the militant jingoistic right. Even at the time John H. Schaar, a man of the left, spoke against that proclivity of the New Left. As he put it, "The radicals of the 1960s did not persuade their fellow-Americans, high or low, that they genuinely cared for and shared a country with them. And no one who has contempt for others can hope to teach those others. A revived radicalism must be a patriotic radicalism. It must share and care for the common things, even while it has a 'lovers' quarrel' with fellow-citizens." "A Case for Patriotism" (1973), *Legitimacy in the Modern State* (New Brunswick, N.J.: Transaction Publishers, 1989), 287. More recently, see Todd Gitlin, *Letters to a Young Activist* (New York: Basic Books, 2003), chap. 11; Michael Kazin, "A Patriotic Left," *Dissent,* Fall 2002; Richard Rorty, *Achieving Our Country* (Cambridge, Mass.: Harvard University Press, 1998); and Michael Walzer, "Can There Be a Decent Left?" *Dissent,* Spring 2002.

TWO

Between Resignation and Utopia
Political Education in the Modern American University

WILLIAM A. GALSTON

THE PROBLEM

Citizenship in America is always an endangered species. Judged against other developed democracies, we are a remarkably antistatist and antipolitical people. Some recent studies suggest that substantial percentages of Americans are not particularly interested in enhanced political participation and would be happy if more public decisions were left up to nonelected, nonpartisan experts or successful businesspeople. Other studies indicate that many Americans actively flee the conflict they see as endemic to politics. As American history is written from the perspective of the twenty-first century, it would not be surprising if scholars converged on the view that the period of relative national unity and civic activism from the Great Depression through the 1960s constituted an aberration without either predictive or normative force for the future.

Whatever the merits of these views, they encourage premature acquiescence in a disturbing state of affairs. I share the sense, which many individuals and groups have forcefully articulated, that civic life in America is weaker than it has been, and should be. It is not unequivocally bad for democracy if citizens mistrust government, as a substantial majority of Americans now do. [1] But it is troubling when virtually every quantitative index charts a steady decline in the percentage of Americans who are interested in politics, take the time to inform themselves, and feel sufficiently motivated to participate, even to the modest extent of voting for president.[2]

The trend toward disengagement is particularly pronounced among young adults. A research center I direct has documented disturbing developments, such as a one-third decline over the past three decades in youth voter turnout and a decline of more than one-half in the percentage of young adults who report reading a newspaper regularly. (Their use of new sources of political information, such as cable television and the Internet, does not come close to plugging the gap that the collapse in newspaper reading has opened.)[3] These trends help explain what would otherwise be a paradox: although the median level of formal education has soared during the past half century, the level of political knowledge hasn't budged.[4] There may be many more highly trained professionals than there were in our grandparents' time, but the percentage of informed citizens is no higher.

Scholarly and popular publications alike are crammed with competing explanations for the weakening of citizenship. Some analysts, such as Michael Schudsen,[5] argue that the decline is more apparent than real: traditional political participation has waned, he claims, because newer and more relevant rights-based civic practices have emerged to replace it. Among scholars who are willing to concede the reality of the decline, the list of possible culprits is dizzying: public perception of government as unresponsive, ineffective, and corrupt; the withering of political parties; the weakening of national civic organizations; rising economic inequality; and the pervasive influence of the mass media, to name but a few.

There is some truth to each of these explanations, to which I would add an argument based on broad cultural change. Daniel Yankelovich has documented what he calls the "affluence effect."[6] As societies become wealthier, individualism tends to become more pronounced, and unfettered individual choice becomes an ever more important value. Generations who grow up taking affluence for granted are likely to focus less on traditional social bonds and more on undertakings they freely assume. In this context, it is hardly surprising that according to a recent survey, most young Americans see voting as a right or choice rather than as a responsibility or duty. Nor is it surprising that these trends are hardly confined to the United States. A recent survey of advanced industrial societies shows that in most countries the younger generation is uninterested in politics, cynical about public affairs, and less inclined than were their parents and grandparents to participate in enduring civic organizations.

There is a connection, I believe, between the rise of choice and the decline of citizenship. The reason is this: in large societies, a calculus guided by narrow self-interest will typically conclude that it is more rational to be a free rider on, than a participant in, collective ventures. Voting is the most familiar example of this logic: because the chance that any one vote will prove decisive is vanishingly small, it makes no sense to expend more than a minimal effort to cast one's ballot. Unless one somehow comes to believe that voting is a responsibility not appropriately subjected to the calculus of self-interest, the logic of abstention will predominate. And as I have already observed, fewer and fewer young people find the language of duty at all persuasive.

Most (not all) religious and philosophical traditions agree that a sense of duty is not innate and that unless societies decide they can get along without it, they must somehow arrange their formative institutions so as to promote it. But few of the forces that shape today's young Americans do this, and many do the opposite. The choice-centered structure of economic markets has colonized social life, and the media strongly reinforce this outlook. For its part, government expects little of young people; the shift away from the military draft to an all-volunteer armed force wiped out the most concrete example of civic responsibility and promoted instead an understanding of citizenship as optional and spectatorial. Most remarkably we have reshaped family life, the traditional symbol of bonds among its members "until death do us part," into an institution guided as much by individual choice as by moral responsibility. Whatever the merits of no-fault divorce, it sends many children the message that adults have the right to choose (and often have chosen) to put their personal well-being first. This is not to say that all or even most parents fail to convey some understanding of responsibility to their children, but it is to say that the legal structure of the family no longer works to reinforce that teaching.

We are left, then, with three kinds of social forces that might shape young people's moral and political sensibilities: faith-based groups, the professions, and educational institutions. The first of these opens up questions too vast to address in this chapter; suffice it to say that much depends on how connected young people are to the norms and practices of their faith, and also on the content of that faith. More observers have noted a shift away from an understanding of God as stern and demanding and toward the idea of God as companion and source of happiness, and also away from denominational identities based on clear theological conviction and toward a more diffuse "spirituality" that sees religious identification as a matter of personal inclination. To the extent that these trends predominate, they are bound to diminish the effectiveness of faith as a counterweight to a choice-centered culture.

The professions, too, present a mixed picture. On the one hand, we find occupations—such as public safety, firefighting, and military service—that make a point of training their members for responsibility toward one another and to the larger society. The performance of these occupations in the aftermath of September 11 is testimony to the effectiveness (and crucial importance) of this formative process. On the other hand, professions such as medicine and law, which once prided themselves on an ethic of service, have increasingly absorbed the logic of the market, with negative consequences for broader conceptions of responsibility. And one need not be an enemy of corporations to believe that developments during the past generation have widened the gap between executives and lower-level employees and weakened ties between businesses and local communities, or that these developments have eroded many executives' sense of responsibility as a check on naked self-interest.[7]

That leaves educational institutions, on which I will focus for the remainder of this chapter; not all of them, but rather on institutions of higher education and learning. Not many observers believe that these institutions have addressed themselves seriously to issues of citizenship and civic responsibility in recent decades. The real question is the extent to which they can do so, and how effectively, given the constraints under which they must operate.

The body of this chapter addresses this question, in three steps. First, I will review, in an optimistic but firmly antiutopian spirit, the social context that both empowers and constrains the modern university. Second, I will examine the considerations that might shape forms of civic education that universities may appropriately conduct. Finally, I will sketch the basic elements of the civic education to which my analysis points.

Beginning from Where We Are:
The Modern University

I begin with the most obvious of all points: there is no such thing as "the" modern university. The diversity of institutions of higher education and learning in the United States is astonishing. Some are huge, others compact. Some are public, others private. Some ("colleges") are more focused on teaching; others ("universities," properly speaking) tilt toward research. Some have a meaningful link to a religious denomination, while others (the majority) have no such ties.

These are distinctions that make a difference for the topic at hand. It is easier for a private institution to adopt a specific stance toward political life than it is for a public institution. It is easier still for a private institution with a serious religious affiliation to draw on that tradition in shaping its program of political education. It is easier for a college than for a university to focus on the goal of political education, which by its nature is more closely connected to teaching than to research. And all other things being equal, it is easier for smaller institutions than for larger ones to achieve some unity of pedagogical purpose across their departments and divisions.

We may reasonably conclude that large public universities present the most difficult case for political education, with large private universities not far behind. Such universities are internally heterogeneous, with multiple functions and constituencies. Conversely, if a small private college truly wants to make political education central to its mission, it can probably do so, in the same way that St. John's has been able to place and keep the Great Books at the core of its pedagogy.

Higher education in America is not only diverse but also voluntary. It is structurally different from elementary and secondary education, where diversity is limited and attendance is mandatory. Higher education, then, is more marketlike than elementary and secondary schooling. Students choose not only whether to attend colleges and universities but also where, and what kind. That means that each institution must pass a market test: its program must be attractive to a steady stream of students who have the option of going elsewhere. In deciding whether to institute new curricular requirements, such a core curriculum with a significant component of political education, institutions must consider their potential impact on student recruitment. It is somewhat easier for public institutions, which enjoy some ongoing support from governments, to pass a market test than it is for private institutions, which depend almost exclusively on student tuition and alumni contributions. Nonetheless, as state governments cut back on appropriations for higher education in response to hard times and mounting pressures to fund health care and public safety, the fiscal gap between public and private institutions is narrowing. (Some states have gone so far as to propose cutting their public universities loose altogether from the public purse.)

It is in this context that universities have turned increasingly to the private sector, not only to fund research, but also to sustain ongoing operations, a trend that has sparked serious anxiety about market colonization of higher education. While such concern is not misplaced, it is important to realize that the current debate concerning the impact of the market on higher education is but the latest iteration of a long-standing worry. Indeed, the relationship between the life of the mind and its material conditions has never been simple. Socrates criticized the Sophists for accepting fees for teaching, and many rabbis of the Talmudic period raised questions about the practice as well. It was vital, they argued, to maintain the dignity and independence of the quest for truth, which the demands of the market threatened to distort. The scholar-patron relationship that dominated the intellectual life of early modern Europe raised similar issues (and fears).

The migration of American scholarship into the German-style research university changed the scope and venue of this tension, but not its essential character. A century ago, Thorstein Veblen charged that business principles were rendering higher education a "merchantable commodity."[8] A half century later, in the early 1950s, Richard Hofstadter lamented that "It has been the fate of American higher education to develop in a pre-eminently businesslike culture."[9] The pragmatic, instrumental understanding of teaching and research, he feared, would inevitably devalue education understood as a means in itself, that is, as advancing knowledge and cultivating worthier human beings.

I offer this brief history, not to dismiss or trivialize contemporary anxieties, but to place them in the context of an enduring structural tension that we can manage but cannot hope to abolish. To some extent, the piper-payers will always call the tune. The challenge for contemporary higher education is not to become too dependent on any single patron and to distinguish between patrons' demands that threaten the essence of the life of the mind and those that do not.

This line of argument, however, raises the question of whether any "patron," public or private, is willing to pay for an increased emphasis on political education. It is easy to see why pharmaceutical and biotechnology firms are willing to support university-based research, but how many businesses and corporations are interested in funding political education? (For reasons of their own, some may decide to subsidize programs of business ethics, typically within business schools.) Equally concrete considerations move citizens to pay taxes for the support of public higher education: the expectation of concrete benefits, such as job preparation for their children, local economic development, and contributions to public issues such as health care, transportation, and public safety. Beyond specifics, some citizens embrace a diffuse Enlightenment faith that the life of the mind conduces to the improvement of "man's estate," often in unanticipated ways. Few, I submit, support higher education in the hope that it will make their children better citizens. Fewer still support higher education as an end in itself. While citizens may regard it as a "light" (that is, an informed guide to important public questions), they are far less inclined to think of it as an "ornament" that ennobles civic life through its intrinsic worth. In this respect, among many others, what Alexis de Tocqueville observed in the 1830s remains largely true today: higher education in America "aims only at some specialized and profitable objective; . . . and only matters of immediate and recognized practical application receive attention." The explanation has deep roots in our democracy: "there is no class in America in which a taste for intellectual pleasures is transmitted with hereditary wealth and leisure and which holds the labors of the mind in esteem."[10]

These reflections lead me to a gloomy hypothesis, which I will phrase in the language of economics: like citizenship itself, civic education may be a "public good" that self-interested individuals, groups, and institutions are not adequately motivated to supply. The result is likely to be a chronic shortage of civic-mindedness, relieved only occasionally and temporarily when events conspire to heighten national unity and reinforce the efforts of the beleaguered band of civic educators.

Universities are embedded, not only in the economy, but also in the culture. Regrettably, contemporary American culture creates additional obstacles for the partisans of civic education. The heightened importance of individual choice, to which I have already adverted, weakens all authority, including academic authority. Diversity, understood not only as fact but also as norm, throws supporters of uniform curricular requirements on the defensive, all the more when requirements are defended as promoting a shared or common citizenship. And features of our everyday culture too numerous to list combine to thin out knowledge of, and serious regard for, intellectual, religious, and historical traditions. Every teacher I know has had the experience of mentioning central figures from the Bible, Greek mythology, European culture, or even American civilization, only to be greeted with students' blank stares. To the extent that civic education draws from such traditions, it is forced to begin almost from scratch.

Although institutions of higher education and learning are embedded in American society, it would be a mistake to regard them purely as a product of external social forces. These institutions are designed, after all, to be partially insulated from these forces, in the hope that they can serve to some extent as a counterweight to a society dominated by the pursuit of power, profit, and pleasure.

When we inspect the inner life of these institutions, we see three different kinds of education at work. The first may be called in the broad sense "vocational"—directed toward preparing students for a dizzying variety of gainful occupations. It is the hope of occupational qualification and advancement that draws most students to higher education (and does the most to make parents and citizens willing to subsidize it). The professoriat tends to look down on vocational education, but we must acknowledge that for the most part that is the function we are serving in our classes.

At the other end of the continuum is the form of education I will call "philosophical"—not the narrow discipline, but in the broader sense of an endeavor guided by the pursuit of truth for its own sake. This quest motivates some professors some of the time, and it attracts the small minority of students who share this passion. The development of the research university constitutes an amendment to Tocqueville's characterization of the intellectual life in America: while we do not have an hereditary aristocracy, we do now have a substantial academic meritocracy, a portion of which spends its time in activities that Tocqueville's landed nobility would recognize and applaud.

This brings me to the third kind of education we find in American colleges and universities—civic or political education, preparation for citizenship. While these institutions have always served multiple purposes, it seems fair to say that explicit civic education was more central to their endeavors in the nineteenth century, prior to the rise of the research university, than it is today. In fact, one can number on the fingers of two hands the contemporary American colleges and universities that devote even one-tenth of their efforts and resources to civic education.

It is not hard to see why civic education is neglected. Unlike vocational education, it is not gainful and does not always serve students' self-interest. Any fair account of citizenship must acknowledge that it involves giving as well as getting, and sometimes uncompensated sacrifice. Absent a live moral vocabulary of responsibility and duty, citizenship is bound to be a hard sell. And as we have already seen, in today's culture this vocabulary is anything but robust.

The tension between civic and philosophic education is subtler, but just as real and no less important. A genuinely truth-seeking inquiry into political life cannot begin with the presumption that any particular regime form is preferable to others. The normative comparison of regimes is at the heart of traditional political philosophy, and it has not always led to a full-throated endorsement of democracy as the best mode of political organization. Since Aristotle, by contrast, civic education is seen as relative to, and supportive of, a specific regime whose tenets it does not question. The ultimate aim of civic education, so understood, might be described as informed loyalty or reasonable patriotism, but certainly not the pursuit of the whole truth about the regime of which one is a member. It is not hard to depict this form of civic education as inculcation or indoctrination, a process that many professors regard as antithetical to the core mission of higher education.

In short, civic education lacks a strong constituency within academia because it stands in tension with both vocational and philosophical education, both of which do enjoy vigorous support. This does not mean that strengthening civic education in higher education is a lost cause, however. For better or worse, colleges and universities constitute the pool from which the vast majority of our country's leaders are and will be drawn. Whether professors and academic administrators like it or not, the decisions they make today help shape the men and women who will direct the affairs of the Republic for much of this century. Academia must accept a share of responsibility if university-educated leaders know little about their own country and even less about the rest of the world, or if they care mainly about personal advancement and little about the public interest.

Perhaps university teachers and administrators are absorbed with professional and institutional advancement at the expense of civic responsibility. Still, self-interest rightly understood should lead the leaders of the academy to give civic education a higher priority than they now do.

CIVIC EDUCATION: CONTEXT AND PRINCIPLES

Having reached this point of equipoise between pessimism and optimism, we must take a closer look at civic education itself. I take as my point of departure the tension between philosophic education and the Aristotelian conception of civic education. One possibility is simply to accept the tension, with the result that a part of university-based pedagogy would pursue truth while another part promoted patriotism. I doubt that this "inculcative" model of civic education would prove politically viable, however; many professors would go into open revolt, as would many students and outside groups.

The alternative is to adopt what I will call the investigative model. This strategy of civic pedagogy would adopt the American regime as its point of departure while problematizing it as an object of inquiry. So, for example, students would be asked to reflect on the fact that each of the principal structural features of American democracy—liberalism, constitutionalism, and representation—represents a contestable choice within the broader democratic tradition. They would be exposed to key arguments for and against democracy, contrasted with historical and contemporary alternatives. They would consider the relation between democracy and meritocracy, which some leading American democrats (Thomas Jefferson among them) have seen as mutually consistent while others have regarded them as opposed in principle and practice. And they would ponder alternative objects of loyalty: to one's country; to intimate attachments such as family, friends, and tribe; to institutions and aggregations of individuals beyond national boundaries; or to an ultimate source of meaning that transcends humanity itself.[11]

Civic education is intimately connected with citizenship, but the investigative strategy would refrain from giving students a single canonical conception of citizenship. Instead, they would be exposed to a wide range of different, and to some extent competing, models. Supportive citizens obey the law and do their part to maintain the regime, more or less as it is. Active citizens adopt engagement as their central norm; they take care to inform themselves, vote, communicate with their representatives, and faithfully fulfill civic duties such as serving on juries. Critical citizens measure their country's practices by its principles and work for the reform of practices inconsistent with those principles. Radical citizens criticize, not only practices, but also the principles of their country; they are citizens rather than revolutionaries because they use persuasion, law, and nonviolence rather than force to effect fundamental regime change. Students would look at examples of these models, drawn from American history and the experience of other nations, and they would explore the strengths and weaknesses of each.

The investigative model of civic education would also ask students to consider the reasons and motivations for being a citizen. They would explore, for example, the ideas (some mutually exclusive) that citizenship arises through choice or contract; that it is a requirement of reciprocity (the kind of claim Socrates sketches in the Crito); that it is a duty (as Immanuel Kant argues); that it is an essential element of human development and flourishing; and that it is one of the ties of sentiment that inescapably define our identity.

At this juncture one might object, reasonably enough, that teaching about citizenship and patriotism in the investigative mode is not the same as fostering them. (Indeed, the relation between knowledge and virtue is one of the oldest philosophical perplexities.) My response is twofold. First, in a complex modern society, a measure of civic knowledge is a necessary condition for effective citizenship. For example, unless citizens have some understanding of public budgets, they will be unable to judge whether candidates' proposals are feasible or pie-in-the-sky. Second, a large and growing body of research suggests that knowledge contributes to active citizenship.[12] Citizens equipped with basic civic knowledge are better able than others to understand their interests, as individuals and as members of groups; to achieve consistency among their views on different topics; and to acquire additional knowledge of public affairs. In addition, civic knowledge reduces generalized mistrust, builds tolerance, and increases support for democratic values. And finally, it promotes political engagement: all other things being equal, the more knowledge citizens have, the more likely they are to participate in politics and civic life.

I do not want to overstate the connection between knowledge and decent politics, however, because freedom of the mind does not invariably strengthen democracy. During the Weimar period, for example, the most profound philosophic inquiry led professors and students toward the antidemocratic extremes of left and right. Even in the far more settled republican circumstances of the United States, it would be unwise to rule out the possibility that investigative civic education could incline some students toward less than fully democratic regimes.

Nor, conversely, is it the case that democracy always provides the most supportive environment for freedom of inquiry. We have already encountered Tocqueville's argument that the life of the mind finds its most natural home among hereditary aristocrats, even when (or perhaps because) strong monarchs restrict their political activities. The life of the mind, which is inherently meritocratic, is bound to abrade certain understandings of democratic equality. American history is replete with populist attacks on academic intellectuals, who were regarded as elitist and even subversive. The question whether academics are loyal and useful democratic citizens will, I suspect, always remain open, a reality that is bound to make the conduct of university-based civic education politically delicate as well as pedagogically complex.

THE PRACTICE OF CIVIC EDUCATION IN AMERICAN UNIVERSITIES

We reach, finally, the specifics of a political education program that may prove feasible, even in the less than welcoming environment of the modern American university. The first component of this program is curricular, beginning with a two-semester course required of all students. The first semester would focus on American history and civic institutions as well as key concepts and debates. The second semester might be called "The United States in the World." It would examine war, diplomacy, international economics, and international law and organizations and would as well offer a broad introduction to comparative culture and religion. As much as possible, this course would feature case studies that exemplify key issues and invite discussion and disagreement. In addition to this requirement, each of what I have called the vocational tracks would be asked to craft a course that examines ethical issues specific to its profession in the context of broader civic concerns.

The second component of university-based political education would address internal institutional life. University leaders would conduct their affairs with maximum feasible transparency to facilitate treating their institution as a subject for civic inquiry. They would encourage robust political debate by subsidizing the distribution of major national and regional newspapers, supporting a range of student-run newspapers and journals, minimizing restraints on speech, and encouraging political debates. And rather than imposing top-down regulations about membership and internal governance, they would allow the widest possible range of campus groups and associations, and they would treat inevitable controversies about exclusionary practices as opportunities for public dialogue rather than as occasions for legal or administrative discipline.

Finally, university officials would foster a range of links between the university and its civic and political environment. For example, rather than diverting federal work-study funds for student jobs in campus libraries and dining halls, they would use a substantial percentage of those funds for their original intended purpose—namely, fostering community service. Officials would encourage students (and faculty and staff as well) to participate in organized engagement with surrounding communities. (Potential areas of engagement include public schools, social services, economic development, and the environment.) And they would maximize incentives and opportunities for student voter registration.

While this three-pronged program of political education is ambitious, it is far from utopian. During the past decade a major national organization, Campus Compact, has emerged to encourage campus-based civic and political activities; its membership now numbers nearly one thousand college and university presidents. Five years ago, numerous college and university presidents drafted and endorsed a declaration on the civic responsibility of higher education and developed a template that universities can use to assess the status of their civic responsibility activities. Individual universities have come forward as leaders. To mention but a few: Tufts has probably gone the farthest in suffusing its entire curriculum with a sense of civic mission. The University of Pennsylvania has developed a multifaceted engagement with West Philadelphia, as has Indiana University–Purdue University, Indianapolis with its surrounding neighborhoods. The University of Minnesota and the University of Maryland have worked effectively to organize internal constituencies in support of an expansive civic mission.

We do not yet know how much these kinds of institutional strategies will do to kindle a rebirth of citizenship among students. (Institutions of higher education and learning are notoriously lax about, even resis-. tant to, evaluating any aspect of their activities.) But we do already know that with leadership and patience, even large diverse public institutions, which I have argued present the great challenge for would-be political educators, can overcome opposition and inertia to put in place wide-ranging programs of political education, backed by significant resources and buy-in from faculty and students. Rather than endlessly bemoaning the obstacles posed by the U.S. economy and culture, faculty members and university administrators committed to serious political education should roll up their sleeves and get to work.

NOTES

1. For some basic statistics, citations, and analysis of our current situation, see *A Nation of Spectators?* (Final Report of the National Commission on Civic Renewal, College Park, Md., 1998).

2. On the tradition of American antigovernmentalism, see Garry Wills, *A Necessary Evil: A History of American Distrust of Government* (New York: Simon & Schuster, 1999). Again, liberal democracy is predicated on a certain distrust of government. But for those of us who think both that a strong but limited state with an active government is necessary to American liberty and justice *and* that such a government must be democratically grounded and ought to be democratically driven, the antigovernmentalism Wills describes is a serious problem.

3. My statistics are drawn from Michael Olander, *Media Use among Young People* (College Park, Md.: Circle: Center for Information and Research on Civic Learning and Engagement, 2003).

4. The formidable barriers to civic consciousness and active engagement posed by a media culture are explored at length by Benjamin R. Barber, Todd Gitlin, and Cass R. Sunstein in their contributions to this volume. See also Gitlin's *Media Unlimited: How the Torrent of Images and Sounds Overwhelms Our Lives* (New York: Henry Holt, 2002) and Sunstein's *Republic.com* (Princeton, N.J.: Princeton University Press, 2001).

5. Michael Schudsen, *The Good Citizen: A History of American Civic Life* (New York: Free Press, 1998).

6. Daniel Yankelovich, "How Changes in the Economy Are Reshaping American Values," in *Values and Public Policy,* ed. Henry J. Aaron, Thomas E. Mann, and Timothy Taylor (Washington, D.C.: Brookings, 1994).

7. The Wall Street criminals so tellingly portrayed by James Stewart in his chapter here and in his other work are only the most flagrant examples of this tendency. See also his *Den of Thieves* (New York: Simon & Schuster, 1992).

8. Quoted and discussed in Eyal Press and Jennifer Washburn, "The Kept University," *Atlantic Monthly,* March 2000, 45–46.

9. Press and Washburn, "The Kept University," 54.

10. Alexis de Tocqueville, *Democracy in America.* For the overall argument, see vol. 2, part 1, chap. 10; for the quotation, see the version translated by George Lawrence and J. P. Mayer (Garden City, N.Y.: Doubleday, 1969), 460.

11. See the exchange on exactly this issue, among others, between Martha Nussbaum and her respondents in *For Love of Country* (Boston: Beacon Press, 2002) and the chapter in this volume by Benjamin R. Barber.

12. For the best single roundup of the evidence on this question, see Michael X. Delli Carpini and Scott Keeter, *What Americans Know about Politics and Why It Matters* (New Haven, Conn.: Yale University Press, 1996).

THREE

Liberal Education
and the Civic Project

MICHAEL J. SANDEL

O ur subject is political education and the modern university. But this raises an immediate question. What does a university education have to do with politics? Universities exist for at least two obvious reasons: to pursue and transmit the truth, and to prepare students for successful, productive careers. Why should colleges and universities take on the further project of shaping the moral and civic character of their students? In fact, doesn't the whole idea of political education and character formation smack of partisanship and indoctrination, antithetical to the ideals of the university? Shouldn't a college education free students to choose their values for themselves?

Yes and no. A college education should be a liberal education, that is, one that equips young men and women for freedom, to be free citizens. But freedom does not simply consist in the pursuit of wants and desires unimpeded. A college education that merely equipped students to get good jobs and to pursue their wants and desires effectively would not be a liberal education. In order to see why, we need to distinguish two conceptions of freedom.

The first might be called the market conception of freedom. On this conception, to be free is to pursue my own interests and ends without interference. It is a market conception because it imagines the setting of freedom to be something like a shopping mall, in which the extent of my liberty depends on the range of goods available and the money I have at my disposal. But there are two problems with the market conception of freedom. The first is that it takes people's wants, desires, and preferences as given, as wholly unexamined. It does not ask where those wants and desires come from, or whether they are worthy or unworthy. Nor does it ask whether I have correctly identified my interests and ends, whether I am clearheaded or deluded in seeking after them. Acting simply to ful-fill the interests and desires I happen to have, without subjecting them to critical examination, makes me a slave to my appetites, not the mas-ter of my fate. This line of reasoning led Immanuel Kant to conclude that freedom, properly understood, cannot consist in answering to the promptings of our inclinations.

The second difficulty with the market conception of freedom is that it takes as given the structure of choices. When I walk into a shopping mall, I may find the range of choices so dazzling that it distracts me from asking why these choices, rather than some others, are on offer in the first place. A preoccupation with satisfying my preferences and desires by choosing among the products arrayed before me may distract me (and my fellow shoppers) from wondering how the structure of choices was designed, how it was given its shape, character, and content.

These two problems with the market conception of freedom have led some thinkers in the history of political philosophy to a different, more demanding understanding of freedom, one that might be called the civic conception. According to the civic conception of freedom, to be free is not to pursue my wants and desires unimpeded but to share in self-rule, to have a meaningful say in shaping the destiny of the political community as a whole. To be a free citizen, according to the civic tradi-tion, is to participate in self-government.

But why does participating in self-government require character for-mation? Why can't people participate in self-government by going to the ballot box and casting their vote for whatever party or candidate seems most likely to advance their interests? According to the civic conception of freedom, sharing in self-rule requires more than the ability to identify my own interests. It also requires the capacity to deliberate well about the common good, which requires in turn that citizens possess certain qualities of character, or civic virtues.

To deliberate well about the common good requires knowledge of public affairs, good judgment, and the capacity to weigh competing alternatives from the standpoint of the public good. Beyond these deliberative capacities, good citizenship also requires a certain moral disposition—an orientation to common purposes and ends, rather than simply to my own individual interests. It requires that citizens possess or come to acquire a sense of identity with the good of the whole, a sense of obligation to one's fellow citizens. The civic conception of freedom requires a formative project so that citizens will acquire the habits and dispositions, the qualities of character, that will equip them for self-rule.[1]

It is this second conception of freedom, the civic conception, that points to the civic purpose of the university. But it is important to notice that the civic purpose of the university is always in possible tension with the practical, vocational, preprofessional aspects of education, for the following reason: Insofar as universities aim at preparing students for good jobs and successful careers, they do so by fitting students to the world, or, more precisely, by fitting students to social and economic roles that confer certain rewards. But the civic mission of the university pulls in another direction. For the civic mission to succeed, it is important that the university not fit students to society too well, or too completely. In fact, a liberal education does not produce a perfect fit between students and the social roles and conventions the world has to offer at any given moment. It produces misfits. By misfits I mean students who do not take their society's established roles and practices as given but who regard these practices as open to criticism, contest, argument, dispute, and revision. In this sense, at least, the civic mission of the university counsels the cultivation of misfits, students who will be sufficiently uneasy with established social and economic arrangements that they will become questioning, critically minded citizens.

Given this understanding of the civic mission of the university, political education can take many forms. There is no single recipe. It might include travel abroad, community service, student government, journalism, debate. Activities such as these can lift students from their parochialism, provide an occasion for engagement with public questions, and provoke or inspire students to reflect critically on the moral and political arrangements they find around them. And somewhere in the course of their undergraduate career, students should be exposed to the systematic reflection on moral and political arrangements to be found in the history of political thought—in the work of thinkers such as Plato, Aristotle, Machiavelli, Hobbes, Locke, Rousseau, Kant, Hegel, Marx, Mill, Nietzsche.

One could add to the list, ideally to include lines of political and moral reflection to be found in various religious traditions. The particular list of thinkers and texts is less important than the way they are studied and taught. What matters is that these thinkers and texts not be studied simply as artifacts in the history of ideas—as serene but distant museum pieces—but as episodes in arguments in which we are still engaged.

In his chapter in this volume, Michael Walzer defends the idea that "students should study moral and political philosophy, and that their attention should be focused on the problems of moral choice in political and professional life." I agree. I share Walzer's view that exposure to moral and political philosophy is an essential part of a liberal education, and that such a course should be taught in a spirit of democratic argument, as an occasion for students to reflect critically on their moral and political convictions. While a course in moral and political philosophy should include some of the great works of moral and political thought, it need not necessarily approach these works historically. While some understanding of historical context sheds light on the meaning of Aristotle's *Politics* or Locke's *Second Treatise of Government* or Kant's *Groundwork of the Metaphysics of Morals*, students should be invited to approach these texts as interlocutors—to critically assess the claims they make about the purpose of government, the obligations of citizens, the nature of rights, the role of consent, the status of democracy, the meaning of freedom, and so on.

One way of making these texts come alive is to juxtapose readings from, say, Aristotle, Locke, and Kant with discussion of contemporary legal and political controversies that raise philosophical questions—debates about distributive justice, for example, or freedom of speech, or just and unjust wars, or the role of religion in public life. If those discussions go well, students are likely to find that, in order to defend their views, they need to appeal to moral and political principles of the kind elaborated by the philosophers. This discovery, in turn, gives students a sense that something important is at stake for them in philosophical texts that might otherwise seem abstract, distant, and daunting. They might even find that their encounter with the philosophers leads them to revise or rethink (or otherwise deepen) the opinions and convictions with which they began. The primary purpose is not to teach students about ancient Athens or seventeenth-century England (though they will learn something about these times and places along the way) or to ask, anachronistically, what Kant would think about affirmative action. The point is to equip students to engage in reasoned moral and political argument, and to provide them an occasion to sort out their own moral and political convictions in the company of thinkers worthy of their attention.

In his chapter, Walzer explores the possible tension between an education that cultivates students' capacity for moral and political argument and religious communities that might view such an education as threatening and unwelcome. The tension that concerns Walzer runs deep in the history of political thought. Political education has often been defined in opposition to religious teachings and assumptions. For example, Hobbes and Locke rejected the divine right of kings and offered accounts of political authority that sought to refute faith-based claims to sovereign power. Today, however, political education faces a different challenge. The primary rival to the civic mission of the university is not religion but economics and the utilitarian cast of mind that prevails in market-driven societies. If the purpose of a liberal education is to free students from the grip of unexamined assumptions, universities today should worry less about religious dogmas than about market values and their deepening hold on social institutions once insulated from commercial pressures.

The challenge of political education in a consumer-oriented, commercial society is complicated by the fact that higher education is itself increasingly defined by market values. In order to clarify what it means to produce students equipped to reflect critically on the social and economic roles that await them, consider a university whose sole purpose is to produce students who will fit, not question, those roles. The university I have in mind is a place of learning set on an eighty-acre campus in the Midwest. As David Kirp describes it, the campus is a "verdant landscape ... dotted with ponds and meandering trails, a setting that invites conversation among students and teachers. . . . The classrooms, many of them seminar-sized, are wired for the electronic age. This is a highly selective school, which draws its students and its faculty from around the globe."[2] In fact, the student body is drawn from 119 countries, and the university provides simultaneous translation in twenty-eight foreign languages. Some 5,800 students attend this cosmopolitan place each year. The school: McDonald's Hamburger University, which confers degrees in "Hamburgerology." According to Diane Thomas, the dean of Hamburger University, the school's mission is to teach McDonald's employees "about quality, service, cleanliness and value, the core principles of McDonald's."[3]

My point in mentioning Hamburger University is not to criticize it but to show how its mission can help clarify by contrast the mission of the traditional university and the project of civic education. It cannot quite be said that Hamburger U. undertakes no formative project. According to Eric Schlosser, the courses teach "lessons in teamwork and employee motivation, promoting 'a common McDonald's language' and 'a common McDonald's culture.'"[4] Even a wholly instrumental, vocational training in the fast-food business finds it useful, apparently, to forge a shared corporate language and culture. Unlike an education for citizenship, however, the formative project of Hamburger U. aims at perfecting, not complicating, the fit between its students and the roles they will occupy in the world of work.

Corporate universities like Hamburger University are a growing presence on the educational landscape, up from about fifteen in the 1980s to over two thousand today.[5] Some observers wonder whether corporate universities will begin to challenge traditional ones, especially in vocational fields. The rise of corporate universities is not troubling as such, but as a harbinger of changes taking place within traditional universities. Increasingly, traditional universities are governed by the commercial norms that Hamburger University makes explicit. As traditional universities take on more of the characteristics of corporate universities, the civic project becomes difficult to sustain. This is especially true when universities operate, as they do today, in a society where market pressures are crowding out civic purposes in many spheres of public life.

I would like to offer a few examples of creeping commercialism in higher education. But first, consider this thought experiment: Imagine a university governed wholly by the logic of market values. What would such a university look like? How would it allocate students to classes, for example? Typically, some classes are crowded while others are underenrolled. Why not charge students more for popular classes and offer a discount for classes taught by unpopular professors? And why not pay professors according to the enrollment their courses attract? This is not as far-fetched a proposal as you might think. No less an authority on political economy than Adam Smith recommended this system of compensation for university professors. He argued that paying professors according to the number of students they taught was the best way of rewarding diligence and averting professorial sloth.[6]

While few if any universities have adopted Smith's solution outright, many are adopting revenue-management techniques that give departments an incentive to maximize their enrollments. David Kirp observed a brazen instance of this practice at the University of Southern California. As students lined up to register for courses, "campus units paraded their wares with the fervor of discount merchandisers. Full-page ads in the *Daily Trojan* touted courses such as the drama class that required no reading. ('Tired of reading Shakespeare? Kill off your [general education] requirement, sit back and eat popcorn, and watch it being performed.')"[7]

Market practices are also making inroads in the area of college admissions and financial aid. Prompted in part by a desire to move up in annual rankings, colleges compete fiercely to attract the most desirable students. The competition is heightened by the fact that a college education is an unusual kind of good; the customers, so to speak, are themselves part of the product being sold. When students choose a college, they don't consider only the libraries, sports facilities, and quality of the faculty. They also consider the kind of students who attend. It is not that way with most goods and services. When you buy an airline ticket to St. Louis, you don't normally care who the other passengers are. In this respect, college enrollment is more like the market for hip restaurants and clubs; the desirability of the place depends in part on who else shows up.

Given the unusual character of the good, the competition for students takes on a special intensity.[8] Unlike ordinary businesses, colleges and universities do not seek to maximize profits. But they do seek to maximize qualities such as academic selectivity, excellence, and prestige, all of which cost money. The drive to compete has led many colleges to adopt market-like policies in admissions and financial aid. The most significant is the growing use of "merit aid." For a time, college financial aid policies were aimed primarily at meeting the needs of less affluent students. Increasingly, however, financial aid is being allocated less on the basis of need and more on the basis of "merit." The trend toward merit scholarships is a boon for families who don't qualify for need-based aid and a valuable recruiting tool for colleges eager to compete for the best students. But from the standpoint of the ideal of equal opportunity, merit scholarships are a mixed blessing. More money for students who can afford to pay their way may mean less money for the needy. And the growing use of merit aid represents the intrusion of market values into higher education.

Colleges and universities increasingly treat merit aid as a discount on a product designed to enroll the students they want. In doing so, they are not simply honoring high academic achievement but buying better students than would attend their institution if financial aid were tied to need alone. Like the airlines, many colleges now employ computer-driven "enrollment management" policies that predict the "willingness to pay" of customers in various categories. These days, the cost of attending may vary not only according to the financial circumstances and academic standing of the applicant but also according to race, gender, geography, or proposed field of study. Some schools have found that those who come for a campus interview are more eager to attend and therefore more willing to accept a leaner financial package.

That merit aid is a step in the direction of marketizing college admissions and financial aid can be seen by extending its logic. If the principle is sound, why stop with tuition discounts? If certain students are in great demand—star quarterbacks, for example—why not allow universities to pay salaries to attract them? If market principles argue for discounted tuition, room, and board for desirable students, regardless of financial need, don't the same principles argue for allowing colleges to pay salaries and bounties to enroll the students they want? This scenario is not merely hypothetical. Recently, the City University of New York, in a bid to improve its student body, set up an honors program that offers not only free tuition but also a laptop computer, tickets to theaters and museums, special seminars, personal academic advising, and a $7,500 academic expense account—only a small step short of paying students to enroll.[9]

Buying top students is one side of the marketizing of college admissions; selling admission to the highest bidder is the other. Universities are expensive to run, and the more money they can raise, the more they can spend on worthy things like laboratories and libraries, faculty salaries, and financial aid. According to the market model of the university, what would be wrong with auctioning off a few seats in the freshman class to wealthy parents willing to pay large sums to enroll a son or daughter who would not otherwise be admitted? While no selective college or university holds a public auction for admission, some come surprisingly close to doing so. Many give an edge in admissions to children of alumni, so-called legacies, hoping to build a sense of school spirit that reaches across the generations and leads alumni to contribute more generously to their alma mater. But some schools dispense with the indirection involved in legacy admits and give an edge to children of potential donors who are not alumni, in hopes of a major contribution. During its last capital campaign, Duke University relaxed its admission standards to admit 100–125 wealthy, nonalumni students a year. The parents of students admitted in this category were then recruited to serve on a fund-raising committee. Although the policy did not involve the outright sale of admission, it apparently served its purpose. Duke led all universities in unrestricted gifts to its annual fund from nonalumni parents and successfully completed a $2 billion capital campaign.[10]

Some universities have found more novel ways of raising revenue, such as selling alumni burial plots on campus. The practice gives new meaning to the college reunion. The University of Richmond recently opened "a million-dollar 'columbarium,' a vault with individual niches for cremated remains," available for $3,000 per niche. Graduates of some fifty schools, including the University of Alabama and the University of Virginia, can now go to their final resting place in caskets bearing the insignia of their alma mater, secure in the knowledge that the school will reap a licensing fee from the casket company.[11] The University of New Hampshire found a less ghoulish but more controversial way to raise funds, by allowing alumni to buy their way out of a ban on alcohol at tailgating parties. To cut down on rowdy, drunken behavior, the university had prohibited alcohol at tailgating parties for the homecoming game. But it made an exception for donors to the athletic department. Opponents of drunk driving objected, but a university spokesperson replied that the exception was a good way to raise money for athletic scholarships.[12]

These examples of the marketization of higher education range from the troubling to the merely tawdry. Universities need money to carry out their missions, and not every brush with lucre corrupts. Most worrisome are those forms of commercialization that reach the heart of the academic enterprise, such as corporate-sponsored research agreements that impose secrecy requirements on scientific findings, and the steady erosion of the humanities on many campuses in favor of disciplines more closely aligned with the world of work.[13]

Taken as a whole, the developments I have described illustrate the drift of higher education toward a market mentality that also exerts a growing influence in the wider society. This tendency complicates the task of civic education and also heightens its importance. Some defend liberal education today on the grounds that professions and careers have become so changeable that a college education should be an education in adaptability—learning how to learn, rather than learning anything in particular. But this defense is partial at best. It assumes that education is about fitting students to the world rather than equipping them to argue with the world, and possibly change it. A liberal education that is also a civic education aims at something higher than basic training for a commercial society. It aims at cultivating men and women with the intellectual strength and moral poise to negotiate a world less hospitable than it should be to the life of the mind and the project of self-government.

NOTES

1. I develop the idea of the formative project more fully in Michael J. Sandel, *Democracy's Discontent: America in Search of a Public Philosophy* (Cambridge, Mass.: Harvard University Press, 1996).

2. David L. Kirp, *Shakespeare, Einstein, and the Bottom Line* (Cambridge, Mass.: Harvard University Press, 2003), 1.

3. McDonald's media Web site, at www.media.mcdonalds.com/secured/company/training/ (6/8/05).

4. Eric Schlosser, *Fast Food Nation* (Boston: Houghton Mifflin, 2001), 31.

5. Des Dearlove, "Training Room? No, University," *Times* (London), September 19, 2002, 13 (citing a report by Rob Paton and Scott Taylor).

6. Adam Smith, *The Wealth of Nations*, book 5, chap. 1, part 3.

7. Kirp, *Shakespeare, Einstein, and the Bottom Line,* 116.

8. In this and the following paragraph, I draw from my chapter "The Market for Merit," in Michael J. Sandel, *Public Philosophy: Essays on Morality in Politics* (Cambridge, Mass.: Harvard University Press, 2005), 89–92; the essay originally appeared in the *New Republic*, May 26, 1997, 29.

9. Karen W. Arenson, "To Raise Its Image, CUNY Pays for Top Students and Throws in a Laptop," *New York Times*, May 11, 2002.

10. Daniel Golden, "Many Colleges Bend Rules to Admit Rich Applicants," *Wall Street Journal*, February 23, 2003, 1.

11. Anne Marie Chaker, "The New School Spirit: Burial Plots for Alums," *Wall Street Journal,* July 10, 2002, D1.

12. Alice Giordano, "Here's to You, UNH Donors," *Boston Globe,* October 10, 1998, 1.

13. These trends are well described in Eyal Press and Jennifer Washburn, "The Kept University," *Atlantic Monthly* 285, no. 3 March 2000, 39–54; James Engell and Anthony Dangerfield, "The Market-Model University: Humanities in the Age of Money," *Harvard Magazine,* May–June 1998, 48–111; and Derek Bok, *Universities in the Marketplace: The Commercialization of Higher Education* (Princeton: Princeton University Press, 2003).

FOUR

The Media, the Mall, and the Multiplex
America's Invisible Tutors and the End of Citizenship

Benjamin R. Barber

My title is "The Media, the Mall, and the Multiplex," and my subject is education and citizenship in an era of interdependence, but I'm going to try to raise some questions that go well beyond the confines of that title, for my concerns are a good deal broader. Because everything we do pedagogically, as well as politically, economically, and culturally, is conditioned by globalization and interdependence, I want to use my concern with education and the media to help illuminate the nature of globalization.

Globalization issues out of and helps define *inter*dependence—a new reality that can be measured against the long-standing American story of independence. At the very start of the American story, we are confronted with a memorable Declaration of Independence. Independence was the context for the original conception of public and civic education in America. How far we've come from that conception and with what consequences for citizenship and democracy are my concern in this presentation.

I propose to look at where we're heading in a world of interdependence from the perspective of the history of independence. I will describe the adjustments and accommodations that will have to be made if anything like the Founders' vision of public education and civic pedagogy is to survive into the twenty-first century. Although I must cover a lot of ground, much of that ground has happily already been surveyed by others in this volume, so I hope I can do this with some economy.

Let me begin by recalling that the Founders were deeply persuaded that democracy was an impossibility in the absence of a robust citizenry and that they also believed that while we may be born free, citizens are made rather than born. Jefferson understood rights to be natural inasmuch as they represented God-sanctioned claims, but he regarded citizenship and the responsibilities with which rights were executed as things to be acquired through positive political and educational institutions. Jefferson, John Adams, and many other Founders believed with Madison that the Bill of Rights would always be a parchment parapet from which the defense of rights could never in practice be undertaken—in the absence of citizenship. They argued that unless there were civic and educational institutions capable of forging citizens, the great new American experiment in democracy (narrow as its parameters first were, being limited to propertied white males) would fail. Even among a narrowly defined elite constituency, in the absence of public education it could not possibly succeed.

Jefferson lived these beliefs, making the founding of a great university the paramount achievement of his life. He memorialized his contributions to the establishment of the University of Virginia on his own tombstone—linking it to the Declaration of Independence and the Virginia Bill of Religious Freedom—and clearly thinks it more significant than his presidency, the Louisiana Purchase, and his founding of the Democratic Party, all of which go unmentioned in his epitaph. The implicit link he makes between rights, religious freedom, and independence on the one hand and the public education of citizens on the other speaks eloquently to his deeper convictions.[1]

Well into the nineteenth century, the notion that educational institutions had to have among their aims a concern with—nearly an obsession with—forging citizenship was apparent in the mission statements of nearly all schools and universities both private and public, secular and religious. Schooling in citizenship as a first principle of education was simply an article of faith. Following the Emancipation Proclamation, for example, it was widely agreed that unless the freed slaves received an education, the Thirteenth, Fourteenth, and Fifteenth Amendments would be meaningless, because without schooling manumitted slaves would never become real citizens.[2] For the same reasons, the suffrage movement that eventually delivered the franchise to women was accompanied by a powerful movement for women's education.[3] This widely acknowledged correlation between education, citizenship, and democracy eventually ran afoul of the idea of the research university and a more vocational understanding of education. If we had the time, we might stop here and digress on the baleful impact of the model of the German research university that arrived in America during the Gilded Age and secured immediate attention with the success of the new Johns Hopkins University.[4] In time this model, so bracing for science and research, began to corrupt the meaning of the liberal arts, what had since the Middle Ages been quite literally the arts of liberty by which free men dissociated themselves from the "servile arts" and through the arts of freemen learned to live in liberty. Those manacled to the lower orders of the great chain of being could learn only the servile arts of forging armor or cobbling shoes or cultivating the earth. Those fortunate few born to the status of freemen understood the university as a vital knowledge center for the arts of liberty.[5]

Yet in the last century, liberal arts increasingly became seen as synonyms for scholarly and scientific research around narrowly defined sectors of knowledge of more theoretical than practical interest. Nowadays, academics aiming to restore the liberal arts to their civic mission by trying to establish a community service program or introduce civic education into political science are likely to find themselves confronting a professor who exclaims, "Excuse me, but my field is liberal arts, you can't expect me to concern myself with the citizenship of my students. That may be a worthy goal, but it's not part of our academic mission, and it's certainly not what I'm here to teach." Thus does amnesia allow the liberal arts to be redefined as liberty rather than commitment to civic education.[6]

Following the research university's inroads into the civic mission of liberal education has come an expansive vocationalism that masquerades as "service" by providing trainees for the professions and hence serving not public citizenship but the private economy. Internships, yes, but in the name of professional training. A commitment to serve society, to be sure, but conceived as career preparation, which Robert Calvert argues is a central feature of America's civically indifferent "meritocracy."

Exaggerating only a little, we can say that by the 1950s, in place of the vision of colleges as forges of democracy and training grounds for citizenship, we had a civically sterile notion of a professionalized, self-absorbed, scholastic research university involved in its own research; and of schools as preparatory institutions geared to funnel students to the colleges and universities and the professions. To the degree the liberal arts college can be said to have survived these changes with something of its civic mission still intact, it has surrounded itself with ivy-covered walls inside of which an ivory tower has been constructed that insulates it from vocationalism and service to the economy (a good thing) but at the price of separating itself from its civic mission as well. Imagination still can flourish, but cut off from the world of civic practice and democratic imagination. The "community" is no longer the college or the college in its neighborhood but an entity "out there" to which the college must establish an anxious and ambivalent relationship based on distrust (in both directions).

In short, the ideal and idea of an educational institution as a forge of citizenship necessary to the appropriate and proper functioning of a democracy had been largely lost, relegated to the occasional civics course in high school. Even in political science departments, most scholars regard civics as beside the point—radically disconnected from their activities as political scientists. In the 1920s and 1930s, words like *citizenship* and *civic relations* appeared regularly in professional journals like the *American Political Science Review*. But by the 1950s and 1960s terms such as *citizen* and *civics* had largely vanished from the reviews.

Now it's against this background of what happened to the civic university that the democratic challenge we face today must be measured. Some hope that we might return to the classical American model of the university, but nostalgia for the republican era cannot respond adequately to the changed environment to which education must now respond. The new challenges include commercialization and marketization as part of a core ideology that impacts pedagogy and has helped marginalize educational institutions altogether with respect to the training and intellectual and emotional development of young people. I want to suggest that if we are really serious about education in America, we may be focusing on the wrong institutions if we look at formal schooling only; for that is not where the young are in fact schooled—that has become the role of the media (television, film, advertising, and the

Internet), a theme also explored by Todd Gitlin. Finally I want to look at globalization and the impact that globalization—in combination with commercialization and privatization—has had on education as well.

Before proceeding to an analysis of these issues, I need to detour briefly to address what we may call the nostalgic perspective on them. As I have suggested, my approach to redressing the problems of commercialization and globalization is not that of a nostalgic republican philosopher looking back at the agora or the American Founding as inalterable normative paradigms. The lesson of the new circumstances is precisely that there is no going back, no restoration of lost canons. I am not a cultural conservative and suspect to the degree the traditional canon has come under attack, there are good reasons for it. In part, the canon institutionalized, and legitimized as universal, power relations that in fact were inegalitarian—however well disguised they were by normative language. But more importantly—and here there is a certain confusion about what the canon really is—the "canon" is something less than canonical. It is often misconstrued by those who are its strongest defenders as a museum or mausoleum of ideas, ideals, and values to be conserved and then transmitted to the young with a kind of mechanical rigor. Yet when examined, it turns out to embody a self-critical and subversive methodology that destroys even as it conserves, that swallows up what it memorializes and kills off and then rebirths itself, generation to generation. The figures who have found their way into the canon were themselves subversive critics of those—the canon of that time—who came before them. Had they been in the university today, they presumably would be crying "Down with the canon," for the canon is in effect anticanonical. Machiavelli's role was subversive to the canon to which we attribute his ideas. Same for Rousseau. Or Nietzsche or Freud or Foucault. Recent critics of the canon like Foucault, or contemporary subversives such as Judith Butler and Carole Pateman and Stanley Fish, are likely to be tomorrow's canon.[7] Their ticket that gives them entry to the canon is a systematic challenge to the paradigmatic status of the canon. And it's because those who defend it, defend it with such gradual, rigid, and at times even dogmatic fervor that I think it has been as difficult as it has even to maintain some of it. But I want to come back to that.

Let me turn now to the principal challenges to the model of the civic university as the forge of democracy that I have been praising. Although we cannot preserve it in its original form, the Founders were right about the central principle that citizens are made not born and require civic schooling if democracy is to function. Indeed, there has never been a the-. orist, whether friendly to or critical of democracy, who did not argue that kingship and citizenship alike, if they are to be effective, must be founded on enlightenment. From Plato through Rousseau to Jefferson and Dewey, theorists have insisted that democracy's strengths (as well as its weaknesses) turn on the quality of citizenship and civic knowledge. The difference between the citizen and the private person is the difference that education makes, and without education democracy becomes little more than plebiscitary polling, mass society, and the tyranny of the majority. Certainly those who defend democracy's good name have never defended it by equating it with mob rule or the absence of deliberation. So there is no reason to yield to the simplistic critic's notion that democracy is merely government by the foolish, ignorant masses rather than government by competent citizens.

At the same time, we need to contextualize the discussion sufficiently to recall that in the "great days" of the agora or the early American Republic when the civil society we so miss today was flourishing, republicanism sat comfortably with a slave society. Alexis de Tocqueville, cited by progressives and conservatives alike as an ardent advocate of civil society and citizen education, celebrated municipal liberty and America's robust civil society in the 1830s when African Americans remained in bondage and women were still seventy-five years away from suffrage. Hannah Arendt makes only the briefest of comments on American slavery as she idealizes its republican foundations and makes ancient Athens a powerful venue of a robust civic vigor.[8] Yet Athens too was a slave-based society in which only a limited number of citizens participated. Observers of the decline of social capital like Robert Putnam[9] portrayed the 1940s and 1950s as more civic than today, but in truth the decline of social capital has tracked a growth in the compass of rights, the reach of tolerance and diversity, and a far more inclusive (if far less animated) citizenry. Women today on the whole feel freer and more powerful than they once were, and yet their new empowerment does not seem to figure in the story of social capital's decline. How many men and women of color would choose to live in Tocqueville's America? Or in the heroic age of the 1950s when social capital was high and the great generation that saved the world in World War II was still running the world? Consequently, in seeking historical models for the renewal of civic democracy, care needs to be taken to avoid idealizing earlier eras that were shining examples of civic engagement for those who were actually citizens but in which few were citizens. Another pitfall of nostalgia.

With this caveat in mind, we nonetheless must face the reality that even as society has become more inclusive, more tolerant, and more diversified (perhaps for these very reasons?), civic engagement and social capital have eroded significantly. The story of the growth of rights is also a story of the decline of engagement—which may point to the disjunction that has emerged between rights and responsibilities, what we expect from democracy and what we give to it. This is a paradox I explore in *Strong Democracy*.[10] The challenge is of course how to provide a citizenry whose connections are less communitarian and solidaristic than they once were, whose associations are far thinner than they once were, with something like the fraternity and associative intimacy we attribute to traditional democracy when participation was vigorous but limited and that is indispensable to a well-functioning democracy.

Here we come face to face with the challenges sketched at the outset of my presentation. While money and commerce have always played a role in democracy's rise (a point Stephen Holmes prudently acknowledges), the markers of today's privatization and commercialization point to a far more invasive and corrupting presence. Cass Sunstein in one of our symposium sessions warned us about being too anecdotal in critiquing data (we may miss the real trends underneath by focusing on exceptional anecdotes that point in a different direction). I will argue here, however, that both anecdotes and empirical trends point in the same direction. Starting close to home, for example, we can describe the modern university as a particular victim of the new corporate ideology that insists on the privatization of public goods and the commercialization of the private. The growing dependence of colleges and universities on the capacity to be financially self-sustaining, to turn a profit, is at war with their public responsibility to liberal and civic education (where's the profit, short term, in these ideals?).

To the degree that education today is interested in citizenship, the ideology of privatization has permeated its pedagogy. The state is often defined as a corporate server and the citizen as a client consumer. Perhaps students here today will have some sense of this trivialization of democratic politics. To what extent are students seen as customers of universities? Many student guides to teachers and courses treat professors as vendors or entertainers to be graded on their capacity to "hold" an audience. The course notices tend to look more and more like movie reviews. How did the prof perform? Good jokes? Riveting story line? Why not in a commercialized academy where students are merely consumers trying to get good product for their tuitions? The topography of the college (or university) has also evolved under the last forty years. When I was in college, most schools fed students in a common cafeteria or common eating rooms where students from every part of the college dined together in a dining community. In major universities and colleges today, dining areas are in effect mini–food courts of the kind found in malls. Starbucks and Pizza Hut and McDonald's take the place of a generic cafeteria, and dining itself becomes an exercise in consumerism and brand loyalty. The same developments can be found in high schools, where cola companies are creating beverage monopolies in the name of scholastic sponsorship. Some will say school administrators are merely giving kids what they want and raising revenues at the same time. No point in hiring a nutritionist when all the children want are the brands they are familiar with from television.

The segmenting of America's schools and universities into Pepsi and Coke syndicates is one of the worst effects of the commercialization of education. When I taught at Rutgers, I found myself in a Coca-Cola university where only Coke products could be sold in vending machines and the school's eating facilities. When I moved to the University of Maryland, I was thrust into a Pepsi school and was compelled to readjust my drinking and snacking habits accordingly. Education is about judgment, learning to choose. Some even argue that capitalism is choice understood as competition.[11] Not when it comes to what you drink or buy or consume. A poor lesson in capitalism and a disastrous one in democracy. At one level this may seem trivial, even comical, and so it is. But at the same time it contradicts everything the university is supposed to stand for: critical judgment, the right to choose, open competition among ideas. Students find themselves fussing about limited choices in taking courses (about which they may not have sufficient information to make a meaningful choice in any case), yet glossing over barriers that prevent them from choosing commercial products they can judge very well.

The result is the travesty of the branded university. It's a good deal for the cola companies since they pay only $10 million to $20 million for a ten-year-plus contract that gives them monopoly control over sales, logos, sports advertising, and related rights in an environment of student consumers uniquely vulnerable to advertising and branding—because of the learning environment in which they find themselves. Sports apparel and sneaker companies make similar deals with university sports teams, providing "free" equipment in return for priceless placement and advertising. There are even reports of young people selling their foreheads or haircuts (with logos shaved in) as human billboard advertising for voracious product vendors yearning for access to youth markets.

The deleterious impact on student dignity and identity is obvious, but the more pertinent issue is the compatibility of such corporate advertising and branding strategies with the putative goals and objectives of the university—even in the corrupted version that is the vocationalized university. The extent of commercialization is evident in the Manhattan Hebrew School pupils who sought and received permission to wear yarmulkes with the Nike swoosh stitched into their crowns. How religious Jews can square this with religion I leave it to others to figure out. How anyone can square it with education remains a mystery to me.

The corporatization and commercialization of the university are, then, about much more than corporate research contracts and privatized patents for profit. They infiltrate and corrupt pedagogy at every level. They corrupt identity and undermine citizenship as a form of public identity. To be a citizen in a democracy is to acquire a public identity that—when in conflict with private identities—is intended to trump them. Democratic sovereignty implies that civic identity regulates other identities. It is not more important but plays a regulatory role in making space for identity. In the current climate of privatization, cultural and commercial identities often trump civic identity, inverting the ideal relationship. Our exposure to commercial branding can itself corrupt identity and lead people to believe that the commodities they consume define who they are. We are what we wear—or eat or listen to. Advertisers are blatant in insisting that purchase choices determine character, while lifestyle takes the place of what Habermas calls life plans. Wearing Nikes is not just a matter of putting on a useful pair of shoes or even of being hip; it entails an identity, assuming a Michael Jordan persona, sports oriented, ghetto cool, a Nike kind of person. More than 70 percent of the world's shoes that are sold today are athletic shoes, though no one thinks 70 percent of the world's population are athletes. Why? Because lounging in front of the TV sporting your Air Jordans is a way of telling yourself who you are. These branding effects suggest why the commercialization of the university is so corrupting. Catalyzing rather than resisting and subverting branding, the modern liberal arts college or research university necessarily subverts the civic mission of schooling.

Privatization of schooling also undermines citizenship by assailing the very idea of public goods, of the res publica that are the common ground (literally the common things) of a democratic community. In the controversy over whether required curricula are pedagogically desirable, the fetish of private choice (make your own curriculum) undermines not only canonical teaching but common teaching—the "commonwealth" of the liberal arts college. In abandoning common readings and common courses, whether traditional or postmodern, the modern university abandons common ground and a sense of being part of a civic public. No required curriculum means no common curriculum, which means no public curriculum. Instead private identity, often acquired through commercial branding, creates a world of private identities—of segmentation and fractiousness, of narcissism and solipsism. The liberty that comes with a belief that identity can be chosen is won, but any sense of common responsibilities and common work is lost. Ideally, a curriculum is how we create common ground in educational institutions. If each individual contrives her own, the construction of a public identity becomes highly problematic, and the possibilities of citizenship become correspondingly constrained. Ultimately privatization entails the eclipse of public space not only within the university but also in the world beyond. Rather than challenge the privatizing conventions of the world outside the walls of academe, the university reflects and enhances them.

As a cafeteria of private identities, the university is associated with private choices about whether to join a fraternity or a touch football team or a chess club or the Young Republicans. Morning chapel, common reading assignments, field requirements, common cafeterias give way to private choice and segmented venues. The college experience turns into a succession of private happenings, and common identity, if it exists at all, consists of aggregated private identities. Like students, faculty identify themselves less by the membership in the local college community than in the "field" nationally to which they belong. An assistant professor of history at State U. is only accidentally living in College Park and working on the State U. campus. Her primary identity is as a member of the American Historical Association, and she sees herself first of all as a scholar of Italian Renaissance studies. The absence of a common curriculum allows her to teach her specialty even to undergrads, without being diverted by common courses or field requirements that might take her out of her area. Sold as effective pedagogy that enhances student choice, curricular decentralization and the abolition of requirements are actually the equivalent of professorial paradise: you can go on elaborating your PhD thesis for the rest of your life. Teach a different chapter of your latest book each semester, without the slightest obligation to public responsibility or the slightest need to serve some higher civic mission of a putative public academic community. How very convenient!

The argument between postmodernists and canonical neoconservatives is fascinating and worthy of common debate. But you need a common curricular space where debate is possible. Privatized curricula serve pluralism (you do your canon and I will do my postmodernism), but they allow the shirking of all responsibility. Absent a common place to argue about our differences, they are entrenched as fractious and incommensurable prejudices that can be taught without being justified and that break up a community of learning into opinionated fractions who need not talk to one another. In a world of diversity (desirable in a democracy), we need commonality (necessary in a democracy), and if not in our schools and colleges, where are we likely to find it? College is where we learn to choose and criticize and individuate, but it is also where we learn the meaning of community and the arts of liberty that make community life possible. Defined exclusively by our differences, we become them. Farewell, citizenship. Goodbye, democracy.

Of course keen observers of modern culture will notice that the arguments about the virtues and vices of privatized schools are largely beside the point nowadays because in truth schools and universities are no longer the primary venues for education or character formation in modern society. Do the math: I am a university teacher, supposedly a major influence on my students for good or ill. But I have students in my class three hours a week in the classroom. A primary school teacher does better than that, but he is unlikely to see his pupils more than twenty-five hours a week for thirty weeks a year. How then can we compete with the real educators of our students, the ubiquitous media? Those omnipresent screens are the true modern tutors—the silver screen at the multiplex, the glowing tube of the television, the dancing pixels on the computer screen. There, the young may spend sixty or more hours a week, fifty-two weeks a year. Who then is really educating the young? Commercial education begins with the Teletubbies at the age of one and continues into the old age home. College "common rooms" are privatized virtually by TV sets looming from their high perches, drawing students away from conversation and community building into passive spectatorship and private reveries. What we think and who we are clearly are more influenced by what we watch on the screens than what we experience at DePauw or Maryland or Harvard. The invisible tutors made omnipresent by a cunning commercial society overwhelm formal schooling.

And when it worries that formal schooling may interfere with branding, the commercial society is canny enough to develop product for the classroom. If students cannot be drawn to the mall, put the mall in their schools. If the classroom critiques TV, get TVs into the classroom. That is what Channel One (originally the brainchild of the Whittle Corporation, which had the good sense to hire Yale's ex-president to legitimize its encroachment on schools) has been doing. In twelve thousand high schools and forty-nine states across the nation, Channel One brings nine or so minutes of television news lite laced with three minutes of advertising. Sponsors pay nearly as much for time on Channel One as on the Superbowl, so enticing is the prospect of selling to children in the legitimizing atmosphere of a classroom. In schools all over America, then, high school students watch advertising as part of their education. Even as schools yield their tutorial role to commercial society, commerce comes to the classroom to secure its dominion over young minds. Poor schools unable to afford their own equipment are pushed by this devil's bargain to expose children already least advantaged by life's lottery to the additional burden of advertising in the classroom, enhancing the effects of what is already the marginalization of formal educational institutions like schools and universities and colleges by the informal education that goes on outside the classroom.

These developments in commercialization and privatization suggest that this debate about appropriate curricula and the civic deficiencies of higher education really matters less than we would like it to. Cultural conservatives may think the issue is feminist studies or too much radical postmodernism in freshman courses while progressives worry about conservative curricula and too little choice for students. But both might find common ground by asking whether Disney, Paramount, NBC, Cable

News Network, the Shopping Network, and eBay are not the more intimidating threat to modern education. Neither the canon nor gender studies but *Sex and the City* and Nintendo Kung Fu. Maybe it's a good thing—popular education. Put the future of America in the hands of some Hollywood hack or Internet popup ad writer out to make a buck by trivializing the big issues in a popular show. Whatever we teach our political science majors about the Middle East or Al Qaeda, the greater portion of what they learn about the world will come from their local television news. Which means they are likely to learn nothing at all or, worse, learn nonsense. Universities may be biased, but their biases are overt and subject to critical assessment, unlike those that accompany the unexamined perspective of television.

Perhaps I am being too hard on the Internet, you may think. Television and film are obviously and overtly antieducational, but the World Wide Web is a pure medium of knowledge. Google is its paradigm, a permanent search engine that can access every knowledge archive known to man. To be sure, the Internet has potential as a democratic medium that can offer everyone access to endless information. For those who know how to use it, it is a tool by which almost every fact, every book, every artwork, every idea ever conceived by the human race can be found. An amazing engine, if you know what you're doing. Yet alongside all the mountains of data and systems of knowledge are mountains of garbage and systems of malice. Every conspiracy theory, every scrap of malicious gossip, every racial lie and social prejudice and religious bigotry ever conceived by the endlessly perverse human imagination is also to be found online. In equal portions with the "truth." There is no way the uninformed user can tell the difference between the truth and the lies, between the verified facts and the mad hypotheses, between honest stories and the manipulative gossips. No wonder 55 percent of Americans believe that extraterrestrials from time to time kidnap *Homo sapiens*, plug electrodes (or their extraterrestrial equivalents) into their brains, and release them again—spies in our midst, or God knows what. No wonder such remarkable numbers will attest to the materiality of witches and warlocks and to the theory that Jewish CIA agents bred HIV agents in the laboratory to keep American blacks under control. On the Internet there is both "evidence" for and "evidence" against almost anything you might want to believe, but nothing to help determine what constitutes evidence.

CNN is little more respectable. Larry King offers a diet of serious politicians, scandal-sheet actors, failed preachers, and helpful spiritualists who channel the dead for call-in listeners, with King ooh-ing and ah-ing at the interviewees' adeptness. "Can you get my husband? He died three years ago," whispers the caller. The spiritualist starts talking with the husband, passing on messages, while King looks on admiringly. When he's done, he moves on to his Colin Powell interview. Then to a K Street actor interacting with James Carville, who is a real political consultant—or is he an actor now?—is this the now defunct HBO "reality" show "K Street" or an interview on the real presidential race (and is there any difference anymore?)? Are television viewers really stupid or at fault when they fail to recognize the difference between fact and fiction, when they abandon the criteria of critical judgment they learned in school? I've seen interviews with Kermit the Frog. Serious interviews. It's the "Other Tutor" at work.

Yes, it's funny, but then again it's not so funny. What is happening to our capacity to understand and discern and make distinctions? Here we come to one of the real issues facing the university. Teaching is not just about conveying or transmitting knowledge or information. It's also about critical judgment and the capacity to think and judge. It teaches the faculties needed to make sense out of the Internet, to distinguish fact from fiction and truth from gossip. These faculties by which we learn to judge the Internet can hardly be learned from merely using the Net. The Internet is an extraordinary instrument for people who are already educated and have acquired editorial judgment. It's deeply dangerous for those who don't because it unleashes floods of undigested, unreflected information. It does to adult sense what light and action does to the infant's senses. Lights and sounds, but not the shapes and meanings that intelligence in time gives to them.

The task of the university is not to replicate the Internet as an information archive—which is what remote education has increasingly tried to do: eliminate teachers and put every student at the end of a camera somewhere with a screen in front of him. It is rather to help students understand how to use the Internet and other information sources, to turn information into knowledge and knowledge into wisdom. A cafeteria of information is not a good definition of higher education. To reproduce on the Web the endless overload of information that characterizes society at large isn't an improvement. To teach students how to make discriminating judgments about what they find online, on the other hand, is to teach the kinds of critical judgment in which the liberal arts excel (and which predate electronic data).

We spend too much time on internal academic arguments that are marginal with respect to the learning (a kind of studied socialization by popular culture) young people are exposed to in the world beyond the academy—perhaps because it flatters our view of ourselves as critical players in the education of the young. And so cultural conservatives focus on the radical professoriat in the humanities (although the majority of academics are actually conservative if engineering and science and law and business are taken into account), while cultural radicals focus on the overall institutional conservatism of the corporatized academy. But the decisions that determine how the young think are being made by forces in the marketplace that academic radicals and academic conservatives cannot affect. Radical or conservative, the academy is no longer the paramount institution for the socialization and education of the young. It doesn't really matter what or how we teach, as long as content on the Web, the tube, and the silver screen are controlled by the nation's power elites. With privatization, control shifts from public education to private entertainment, and what is taught in the public sector simply matters much less.

Academic teachers may in fact have to become remedial instructors trying to undo the impact of commercial socialization. Every picture imprinted on a young mind by television becomes a challenge to the educator. Do we have enough years with students to meet the challenge? It seems unlikely. A single picture of the corpse of a young soldier being dragged naked through a square in Mogadishu forced the Clinton administration to abandon its campaign in Somalia. Arnold Schwarzenegger's films bought him the governor's mansion in California.

These rather numbing considerations suggest that the world in which Jefferson and Madison lived is no longer our world, and the civic shibboleths that worked in the eighteenth and nineteenth century may no longer be relevant to our own realities. For our world *is* privatized, *is* commercialized, and *is* globalized in ways Jefferson could not possibly have foreseen. If civic education and training for democracy are to become possible again today, they will have to respond to new conditions and not simply try to resurrect a world that has vanished. (This is the sin of most traditional civics curricula.) The very notion of citizenship has a different meaning in a world with vanishing borders whose primary players are not necessarily states. *Citizenship is both transnational and local, rather than strictly national.* For Tocqueville, of course, the neighborhood was the locus of both citizenship and liberty. One might speak of Indiana citizenship or even Greencastle citizenship. To a degree that remains true today, since our first civic loyalties still play out locally in our schools, our neighborhood councils, about getting the roads plowed, the mail delivered, about the local traffic cops, about safety, health, the clinic down the street. That's where citizenship starts and always has.

But it no longer ends there. Because each of the forces that affect transportation, safety, health, environment are no longer within the purview of the neighborhood. The state capital is no longer sovereign, the national government no longer paramount. Globalization is no longer a soft aspiration of dewy-eyed idealists. It's a hard fact, a description of the reality that is offered us by environmentalism and ecology, by trade, telecommunications, and public health. The latest epidemic, SARS, does it scare you? Why should it, it's Guangdong Province. No it's not, it's Toronto. Which means Chicago and probably by now Greencastle. But you can't just call out the doctors and address Greencastle SARS. It is not an Indiana problem, or an American issue. It must be dealt with globally or not at all. There's no Indianapolis virus, only a West Nile virus, which means Africa is a problem for Indiana. HIV doesn't carry a passport. Nor do terrorists (a different kind of global health problem) stop for customs inspections.

The terrorists who perpetrated the horrors of 9/11 did not come from the outside at all but had been living in the United States for years. When the president said after 9/11 that he would hold responsible and go after states that harbored terrorists, I wondered for a moment whether he meant Florida and New Jersey (where I was living at the time). The president continues to go after states as supporters of terrorism, but terrorists are not states but quite precisely agents of a malevolent interdependence who deny the relevance and sovereignty of states. Al Qaeda looks more like a malevolent NGO than a state. Such groups are part of a new interdependent networking world in which our nonstate adversaries are both inside and outside, here and not here, part of our national fabric and not part of our national fabric. Policies rooted in old nineteenth-century conceptions of the sovereign nation-state and its powerful national armies are unlikely to be effective in the war against terrorism. Not because America's sovereign military forces are not omnipotent, but because they are incommensurable with our adversaries. There is a deep asymmetry of forces that allows a handful of guerrillas and terrorists to defeat a standing army that, though it can vanquish any other standing army (and did in Iraq), cannot defeat a handful of dedicated terrorists. Tank against tank, plane against plane, America wins. Asymmetrical guerrilla war, who knows? What can well-trained, heavily armed tech-nofighters do against angry men who are supposed to behave toward this superior force as if they have been liberated by it but instead launch rocket-propelled grenades at it?

In the war on terrorism, America ended up picking the enemy it could find, recognize, and defeat rather than the one it couldn't see and didn't know how to overcome—even though it was the latter adversary who was our enemy. But, for all we knew, he was down the road having a drink at the local bar, getting ready to annihilate Chicago.

The president continues to insist on American sovereignty and the nation's sovereign right to combat terrorism however it sees fit. But the American sovereign could not protect its headquarters at the Pentagon and has seen its sovereignty over the economy, the environment, and public health vanish in the last thirty years. The sovereignty claim is all posturing, no substance. No wonder it doesn't impress our adversaries— or even our friends and allies. America will not permit its soldiers to serve under foreign commanders, even if they are from NATO, Canada, or the UK. But it cannot prevent a single job from hemorrhaging abroad, can-not stop corporations from picking up their capital, their plants, and their jobs and walking away to any country they want. Yet America continues to worry about how to hold on to the forms of a nineteenth-century sov-ereignty whose substance has largely vanished in the last thirty or forty or fifty years.

What are the entailments of this dour perspective on globalization for education, for the colleges and universities for which we work? For starters, it means we cannot today be thinking about citizenship and democracy the way Jefferson thought about it. The Founders focused on local liberty: for Jefferson, the ward was the appropriate venue for lib-erty. Yet in a globalized world of interdependence, democratic power has become paradoxical. For while participation and citizenship remain local, power has become ever more central and hierarchical. The real levers of power are no longer to be grasped by fingers reaching out in the neighborhood. When power and participation are severed, democracy is imperiled. For power without participation is tyranny, while participation without power is a fraud and a provocation to cynicism.

Rejoining power and participation is the core task of twenty-first-century democracy. The project entails a redefinition of global civic infrastructure to sustain citizenship in more global terms and the development of that citizenship. How to make citizenship in some meaningful sense transnational or global without making it so thin that it loses the capacity to bind us together—that is the challenge. Too many of the levers of power lie beyond our shores: not just terrorists, but corporations, financial capital, job markets. It is not only the terrorists we can't find; the corporations that control our economic destiny are often equally invisible. (Half the time it seems like we can't find Dick Cheney.) Power, whether legitimate or illegitimate, disappears into a larger interstitial world defined less by sovereign territorial national states with boundaries and customs barriers and frontier patrols than by virtual telecommunication linkages that are everywhere but nowhere in particular. In this world (the president is right when he says this) the old doctrines of self-defense cannot work. Once upon a time nations could live within their little garrisons, fence in the boundaries, and wall out the world. Cross our frontier and you are at war with us. That was self-defense. But in this interstitial networked world this kind of traditional defense doesn't make much sense. Our "foreign" adversaries come from the inside as well as the outside. From below as well as above. We can't wait, the president said, for "proof of intentions" to manifest itself in the form of a mushroom cloud, which complicates America's defense predicament. But preventive war has failed to preempt terrorism, and destroying tyranny has turned out to be a recipe for anarchy rather than democracy.

Perhaps the university should be playing a more crucial role. We ought to be able to think our way into this new world, because we have the luxury of reflection. Yet we seem even more caught up in the old paradigms than our colleagues charged with responsibility for action in the real world. Professor Holmes said wisely during the symposium that so many of the old arguments between ideologists, between left and right, arguments about the canon and postmodernism, are no longer relevant. By the same token, one may say that the Bush administration is searching for new doctrines—preventive war is one of them. The president has recognized that deterrence and containment may not be appropriate strategies for the new era. That interdependence makes new demands on American strategic policy. Even the terrorists get it; they understand interdependence and use its anarchy brilliantly to forward their destructive ends. They use technology, the new telecommunications as well as international finance, against us. The terrorists exploit the harsh realities of a novel interdependence while we continue to argue the cultural wars.

Finally, I need to say a word about the kinds of curricular and pedagogical adjustments the challenges I have depicted here appear to mandate. How might we adapt our approach in the academy to interdependence? Professor Holmes mentioned geography: surely the study of place, topography, and geography belongs in every high school and college in America. In the period of its empire, geography was part of the British core curriculum. Yet in this era of a global America, few Americans are acquainted with the world they aspire to democratize (or dominate). No student would survive long at DePauw without knowledge of the location of the library and the student union, the climate of the campus, the connecting roads into town. Today, the world is our campus, but we have no idea where the connecting roads are. Geography belongs in the curriculum. Professor Holmes joked in conspiratorial tones about how maybe somebody took geography off the curriculum so that Americans wouldn't be able to navigate the modern world. It might as well be true.

The tools needed to navigate the modern interdependent world are obvious enough: geography, of course, but also government, anthropology, history, and religion. With an accent on comparative: comparative government, comparative anthropology, comparative history, comparative religion. The need to compare, to see the other, to understand the different, is absolutely crucial. At a time when our multiculturalism and diversity ought to allow us to understand and be part of a plural, differentiated world far better than when we were a nation of white Protestants, we see as through a glass darkly.

Languages are so obviously of importance that it should be unnecessary to mention them at all. Except that language study is in steep decline, and PhD programs that once required two foreign languages now require one—and the requirement for one may often be met by statistics. The absence of Arabic speakers is a factor in the failure of American armies to do as well in the peace as they have in the war.

Todd Gitlin's chapter should remind us that media studies is also a curricular necessity in a global world dominated by telecommunications conglomerates. Naturally. To understand the media in a world where media rule is a way of understanding power.

If the media are where all the action is, there should also be an academy of the Internet—an ivory radio tower where students learn the McWorld curriculum from which broadcasters and Web users operate. Too many young people still believe in the new electronic frontier as a gate to postmodern democracy and fail to see the degree to which its early democratic promise has been overtaken by virtual commerce. Many of the Web's basic characteristics gainsay the conditions of democracy. Its vaunted speed, for example, is in tension with democratic deliberation, which calls for slow, even ponderous, reflection and debate. The Net's virtue is a vice for democracy, and the challenge is how to slow it down, how to put deliberative speed bumps on the electronic highway. Assessing the democratic (or antidemocratic) proclivities of electronic technology requires scholarship that crosses boundaries. Universities teem with computer experts who, however, know little about democracy; there are legions of social scientists and theorists of democracy, on the other hand, who know little about computers or software. Figuring out both is challenging—a few, like Andrew Shapiro or our colleague Cass Sunstein, have managed to think about both.[12] Exploring the intersection of technology and democracy needs to become a common feature of a liberal arts curriculum. If we don't get our "republic.com" straight, we may lose our republic.

It is of course not just about what we study, it's about how we study. Interdependence challenges our traditional curricula. It points to the need for interdisciplinary work across boundaries. The professionalization and vocationalization of the curriculum tend to chop it up and fragment scholarship, when interdependence ought to be yielding more integrative and dialectical ways of understanding the world. Breaking down the boundaries and borders that have accrued in the academy since the model of the German research university was imported into John Hopkins University is a paramount task. We have been raising walls when we should have been razing them. Of all the walls we have raised, none is more devastating than the one between the university and the community, the university and the world. When academics speak of the community they generally mean "it"—that community, the community outside and beyond the university's walls. "Them" not "us." That the university is both itself a community and part of a community is scarcely recognized. Break down the walls, that remains the challenge.

Programs of education-based community service that combine critical reflection in the classroom with experience of service outside the classroom can punch holes in the walls that keep the university from the community of which it is a part. Experiential education, Dewey's ideal, was never more relevant than today when schools seem to be both too isolated from the world of democracy and too embedded in the world of commerce. In the absence of a linkage between the classroom and the street, knowledge can become abstract and ethics theoretical. Race relations are understood in the library, forgotten in the bar. I have taught for many decades and have marveled that in all these years and in all the classrooms in which I've taught I have never met a bigot. Not once. I have listened to admirable discussions of prejudice and heard admirable condemnations of prejudice. Never a bigot. Occasionally, just to put the reality to the test, I have asked bigots to identify themselves; "Raise your hand if you're a bigot," I will say; and nobody has ever raised a hand, not even a finger. Tolerance, respect, and equality rule . . . in the classroom. Then on my way from the classroom to my office, I stop in the men's room and there, to my amazement, I see these extraordinary things written on the wall above the urinal. Slanders and slurs. And I tell myself, well, it could not have possibly been *my* students who wrote these terrible things because there are no bigots among them. And when frat boys yell themselves hoarse demeaning the girls passing by in the street in front of their frat houses, they must be visitors, because none of my frat-boy students are sexist pigs. The problems of discrimination and bigotry that afflict the real world are not the doing of my students (or anyone else's), it must be dropouts or immigrants. Or is it rather a matter of a convenient wall separating the classroom podium from the frat-house porch? The wall separating the part of a young man's head labeled "student" from the part called "consumer" or "just plain guy" or even "citizen"? Only experiential education and curricula that challenge the walls are likely to remedy the deep hypocrisies that modern insular education makes possible.

I mean to suggest then in these remarks that although the model of citizenship forged by the educational institutions that helped make our incomplete democracy first work two hundred years ago is still in principle relevant, it needs to be adapted to the challenges of our era. Retrieval and restoration will not do the job. We may be able to go home but we can't go backward. To go forward is to stretch the university, to innovate, to unwed ourselves from our paradigms and our comfortable professional niche. Whether that niche is to be found in some neoconservative Platonic canon or in postmodernist subversive attacks on that canon, it cannot save the university. Nostalgia is no remedy. Imagination is demanded. Yet I remain optimistic. The university retains its potential as a community of learning in a world beset by ignorance. It remains a potential transgressor of boundaries, the only venue left in our society in which seeking, learning, subverting, and innovating are still defining characteristics, the only alternative to the pedagogical power of the media monopolies and the marketplace. In the liberal arts college we have the possibility of not only being educators but also of being the makers of citizens—citizens of Greencastle, of Indiana, of the United States, but also citizens of the world.

NOTES

1. See my "Education and Democracy: Summary and Comment," in *Thomas Jefferson and the Education of a Citizen*, ed. James Gilreath (Washington, D.C.: Library of Congress, 1999), 134–52.

2. For the complex story of education and the freed slaves, see Eric Foner, *Reconstruction: America's Unfinished Revolution* (New York: Harper & Row, 1988).

3. The famous Seneca Falls Declaration (1848) asserted that "Man" has never permitted "woman" to "exercise her inalienable right to the elective franchise." "He has made her, if married, in the eye of the law, civilly dead." And "he has denied her the facilities for obtaining a thorough education, all colleges being closed against her." This constituted an important part the agenda of the women's suffrage movement at the end of the nineteenth century and beginning of the twentieth leading to the Nineteenth Amendment granting women the right to vote.

4. Charles W. Anderson presents an incisive analysis of this legacy in *Prescribing the Life of the Mind: An Essay on the Purpose of the University, the Aims of Liberal Education, the Competence of Citizens, and the Cultivation of Practical Reason* (Madison: University of Wisconsin Press, 1993).

5. John Dewey speaks to this point in *Democracy and Education* (New York: Macmillan, 1916), 160.

6. On the civic mission of the university, see Benjamin R. Barber, *An Aristocracy of Everyone: The Politics of Education and the Future of America* (New York: Ballantine Books, 1992), chap. 6.

THE MEDIA, THE MALL, AND THE MULTIPLEX | 77

7. Representative of their works are Judith Butler, *Excitable Speech: A Politics of the Performative* (New York: Routledge, 1997); Stanley Fish, *There's No Such Thing as Free Speech: And It's a Good Thing, Too* (New York: Oxford University Press, 1994); Michel Foucault, *The Foucault Reader* (New York: Pantheon Books, 1984); Carole Pateman, *The Disorder of Women: Democracy, Feminism, and Political Theory* (Palo Alto, Calif.: Stanford University Press, 1990).

8. See Hannah Arendt, *On Revolution* (New York: Viking, 1963), 57, 65–66, 110.

9. Robert D. Putnam, *Bowling Alone: The Collapse and Revival of American Community* (New York: Simon & Schuster, 2000).

10. The twentieth anniversary edition of which has just been published. Benjamin R. Barber, *Strong Democracy* (Berkeley and Los Angeles: University of California Press, 2004).

11. See, e.g., Milton and Rose Friedman, *Free to Choose* (New York: Harcourt, 1980); and *Capitalism and Freedom,* fortieth anniversary edition (Chicago: University of Chicago Press, 2002).

12. Cass Sunstein offered in one of our symposium panel discussions his favorable opinion about the television series *Six Feet Under.* I'm glad he likes HBO, because that's where his students are getting their education about homosexuality, business, capitalism, and the mortuary business. Not law school or macroeconomics courses or gender studies.

The Values of Media, the Values of Citizenship, and the Values of Higher Education

Todd Gitlin

What Media Cultivate

Talk about values is in the American grain, and so it has gone since 1776, when America was deliberately imagined as a nation distinguished by its ideals rather than by the nationality of its inhabitants. In principle, Americanness is a matter of principle. There is, of course, a recurrent nativist streak, which looks to ethnic or racial origin as a stand-in for qualification, but nevertheless, no other nation speaks so incessantly about values as the foundation of its existence.[1]

To an extraordinary degree, the way this civilization spends its time is as spectators, listeners, recipients, and donors of communication. We spend our time in the presence of media. The nonstop arrival and flow of story and sound and image is a huge, unacknowledged fact of our collective life. We prefer to think of ourselves as an information society, but this label simplifies the experience that takes place in human experience as the stories, songs, and images never cease to arrive. Sometimes we pay more attention and sometimes less, but all in all, we live among media to such a degree that time with media is the bulk of the time that people have at their disposal when they're not asleep or at work—and in fact since much of the time when they're at work or on their way to or from work is with media, the point is underscored.

In the course of some twenty-five years of writing about media, among other things, it often felt to me that the deepest truth about media was slipping through my fingers, something for which I didn't have an analytical category. While working on other projects, I sometimes collected note cards under the gaudy rubric "ontology," notes to myself about the fact that people were immersed in media. The note cards gathered dust.

What crystallized the conclusion that I defend here was a parable about a customs official. He goes to work on the border, and just after he arrives on the job, he observes a truck rolling up to his customs booth. He asks the driver some questions, the man answers them, and the guard waves him through. The next day, somewhat to his surprise, the same truck driver pulls up, and this time the guard asks him the same questions, and the driver gives acceptable answers, and he waves him through. The next day the same driver is back. The guard's suspicion is growing. He tells the driver to get out of the cab. He pats him down. He can't find any contraband, and waves him through. The next day the driver is back. This time the guard brings out some equipment. The day after that he brings in another searcher. This goes on for days, it goes on for weeks, it goes on for months, it goes on for years. Eventually the guard is using the most sophisticated X-ray machines, sonar, technical measures hitherto unimagined. Never can he find any contraband. Finally, the guard reaches retirement age, and fast-forward to his last day on the job. Up rolls the truck driver. The official says, "Look, all these years I know you've been smuggling something. For my own satisfaction, please tell me what it is. I can never do you any harm now. I won't say a word. Just tell me, what have you been smuggling?" To which the answer is, of course, "Trucks."

The media have been in the habit of smuggling the habit of living with media.

In the media-saturated way of life, people derive multiple satisfactions from various kinds of experience that they have with media. Surely one reason why people are reliant on media is that powerful and wealthy organizations accrue benefits through the process of making this stuff available, selling it. The attention of customers is the commodity they sell to advertisers. One reason people find the media omnipresent is that a grand effort is made to make them omnipresent. Many are the rewards that accrue to the attention-getting industries that deliver the most attractive goods. The effort of the attention-getters amounts to the supply side of the story of media saturation.

But the supply side doesn't suffice for a comprehensive understanding of what media immersion accomplishes for us, as individuals, as a culture, and even as a civilization—to say nothing of our efforts to make higher education improve the quality of citizenship. While people are surely coaxed, and their preferences molded, in part, by their cultural environment, I cannot accept the notion that people are force-fed with what, after all, gives them pleasure. Americans are by no means exceptional in their reliance on popular culture. It's of some interest that in 1992, when Euro Disneyland opened outside Paris and French intellectuals were signing petitions denouncing it as (in the words of one famous director) "a cultural Chernobyl," *Terminator II* sold five million tickets in France, a nation of fifty million. This didn't happen because Arnold Schwarzenegger stood outside the theater with an AK-47 herding everyone inside. Something is in it for the customers in media saturation: call it the demand side.[2]

It is consonant with our flattering image of ourselves that we go to media in pursuit of information. The technically proficient like to herald themselves as the advance guard of the information society. But what is more important in driving people into the arms of media is that we look to have certain emotions and sensations. We're looking to feel. It seems so self-evident that only decades of scholarship could have missed it. I don't want to say that media experience is uniform, that reading the *Wall Street Journal* is the same as watching *Sesame Street,* or reading *Time* magazine, or viewing *The Simpsons,* or the latest reality show, or the CNN version of the war in Iraq; or listening to a top-ten single on the radio; or sending an instant message; or playing a video game. There are varieties of emotion and sensation attached to all these experiences. But what they have in common, it seems to me, is that they generate emotion or sensation of a type for which we hunger in the modern world: disposable emotion, emotion lite. Deep emotion would incapacitate you for feeling the next. When you're deeply in love, or deeply in grief, you don't resort to a remote-control device of the emotions in search of the next stimulus. You have the feeling, or you are the feeling, and the feeling has you. The kinds of feelings and sensations that we have from television, popular music, video games, the Internet, from most of the media that

are common to us, are transitory, and they are in a sense each a preparation for the next. If we were deeply satisfied, we wouldn't need the next.
But we do need the next—or we feel we do.

Let me just throw out a few numbers to suggest the dimensions of
the sort of relationship that I'm talking about. The figures that follow are
American, but Americans are not that far ahead of the rest of the developed world in our attachments to media. The average American television set is on for more than seven hours a day. The average individual is
in the presence of a television set for about four and a half hours a day.
We have a good study of the media habits of children aged two to eighteen thanks to a solid survey underwritten by the Kaiser Family Fund in
1999.[3] If we look at children ages two to eighteen, we will see that they
spend, in an average day, six and three-quarter hours in contact with
media, not counting homework. Of that six and three-quarter hours,
three-quarters of an hour is spent in reading (not counting homework).
The remaining six are spent with television, recorded music, video games,
etc. More than two-thirds of American children have in their bedrooms
a television set, a tape player, and a radio. Whether you live in a poor or
a rich neighborhood, those figures for the bedroom goods hold fairly
constant. Black kids tend to watch more television, and boys are more
likely than girls to have the equipment in their bedrooms, but the differences are less striking than the similarities. And all of this is to speak
strictly of in-house media: not the mall screens, billboards, Walkman and
iPod modules, car radios, elevator music, and assorted other image displays that accompany the young as they move around their world.

Periodically, far-sighted observers anticipated that a society of this
sort was coming. In the seventeenth century, for example, Pascal worried
that kings would distract themselves from the proper pursuit of God
with women, wine, and gambling.[4] By today's lights, virtually everyone
in the rich societies can live like Pascal's distracted kings. The hunger for
a way of spending time that makes limited demands and relieves one
from the burdens of normal existence—specifically, from the rationality
and utilitarian calculation of everyday life—has become normal.

So much so that to challenge it is considered freakish. About a year
ago, I was struck by the appearance on the front page of the *New York
Times* of an article reporting that a man had been charged with credit
card fraud in New Jersey and sentenced to ten months under house arrest
without a television set. (At the time, he owned seven.) What was this

doing on the front page of the *New York Times*? His lawyers had gone to court arguing that such a punishment constituted "cruel and unusual punishment." The *New York Times* thought this claim not only original but revelatory.

Indeed. The media add up to a machinery of distraction, sensation, and stimulus, and yet institutionally the protections that the media enjoy, their legal and political position in our society, are predicated on a very different model of the purposes and significance of media—namely, one in which the media are carriers of debate for the self-government of a democratic citizenry. The First Amendment, which sanctions the freedoms that have become routine in the domain of the media, is predicated on an eighteenth-century model of political debate in which the media are intended not for steady and unbroken stimulus but for enlightenment. They are for the clarification of the public good.[5]

This is surely one of the purposes of higher education: not only to train a skilled elite but also to bolster the ability of the populace at large to conduct their collective affairs. Yet all educational institutions from the lowest to the highest discover that the official curriculum approved and passed down by school authorities, inscribed in textbooks, tested, graded, and succeeded by other curricula, contends with an informal and largely unacknowledged curriculum, the one that the students bring with them to school—a huge and interwoven set of songs, stories, gestures, terms, tones, slogans, icons, cartoon and celebrity names, figures, and gossip that they have derived from a virtually lifelong immersion in television, recorded music, radio, billboards, video games, and the other media that penetrate their everyday lives. I am not saying that this unacknowledged curriculum is all that our students experience or know. A great deal of thought and imagination is bound up in their lives elsewhere—in the play that they undertake beyond media, their sports, reading, informal home lessons, family contact, religious activity, and so on. But to a large and growing degree, their sense of the world is bound up with media and the emotions and sensations they find in their contacts with media. It is from media that much of their shared vocabulary is drawn. The heroes that bind them are likely to be media celebrities, drawn mainly from the worlds of entertainment and sports.

It is beyond dispute that the informal curriculum of popular culture absorbs much of our students' mental attention. They bring televisions as well as computers and elaborate musical equipment to their dorm rooms. They carry digital phones, with instant messaging and (increasingly) camera adjuncts. They are everywhere in the presence of advertising. This ensemble contributes mightily to the web of social associations that connect them to one another, even if the resulting connections are thin. A welter of items, associations, and fascinations circulate through all the media of our time and then through peer groups, making jingles, themes, names, styles, logos, and so on familiar to them—and not only familiar, but *interesting*.

The sum of nonstop image machinery, the whole nonstop soundtrack— these have been with the young from the earliest ages. As a result, boredom is anathema, whence the media of preference must be speedy and sensational, full of surprises and rapid shifts. Trivia are tailored for weightlessness. "Dead air" is deadly. Movement is all. Sense gratification must be within reach, always. In the visual media, edits come quickly— in music videos and commercials, frequently several per second. Sports are sped up by simultaneous stats, animations, and instant replays streaming across and punctuating the screen, so that even such a viscous spectacle as baseball becomes an explosion of dazzling segments. While human bodies run up against limits in their capacity to race, bend, and otherwise delight, animation does not. Music will be percussive, dominated by rhythmic pulsation. Electronic rumbles and drums drive emotional effects, bass notes producing an aura of menace, strings a whiff of cheer. Stories are conflictful, images kinetic. Many media tales have morals and may kindle a certain order of moral reflection, but usually the morals of the tale emerge quickly and demand rapid resolution.

Much of what streams through the media is funny—often self-consciously so. Jokes come thick and fast, or are supposed to, pitched at the average level of early teens. Physical humor, pratfalls, and goofiness are plentiful. Popular culture serves as the repertory on which popular culture itself draws, so that there is little or no recognition that any more demanding, more difficult, worthier culture might exist. In the last generation, a recognition of the omnipresence of popular culture, as well as its foolishness, is built into popular culture in the form of sarcasm and tongue-in-cheek attitudes. Cartoons that mock the rest of popular culture (most brilliantly in *The Simpsons,* the exception that proves the rule), ads that smirk at other ads, soap-opera characters who selectively disparage popular culture, magazines and Web sites that mercilessly unmask others— these are the common currency. Stupidity is subject to mockery, too, but in a way that suggests that what is wrong with stupidity is that it isn't hip and that those who rise above stupidity are, more than likely, snobs.

This is the condition of the bulk of popular culture, and remains so even if the observer does not sink into a chiding voice. There are of course exceptions where intelligence is not mocked. The best to be said for this culture is that it brings a certain diversity into parochial households, cultivates curiosity, and recommends tolerance. But to expect that expectations of popular culture are tidily put away the moment the student walks into the classroom or opens a textbook is naive—insupportably so.

Casual violence, however misunderstood, is a common value in popular culture. On this score, video games considerably compound the effects of network television, and video games are compounded by videocassettes and DVDs, heavy metal, and rap music. The deeper significance of all the casual violence is not self-evident; of causal links to violence in the real world there is little serious evidence and much counterevidence. My own view is that the importance of media violence lies largely in the sensory experience that it generates, not in the dire behavioral effects popularly attributed to it. The evidence from laboratory studies, limited as it is as a predictor of effects in the outside world, suggests that violent images cultivate both anger and indifference, neither of which is conducive to the intellectual receptivity, disciplined competence, and methodical deliberation that study—or, for that matter, citizenship—requires.

In other words, violence in the media is best addressed as a commonplace feature of the lives that young people actually live, not as a trigger for violence in the actual world beyond media. The replicas of violence constitute a real experience, a part of the life that young people live. It is not an intimation of violence to be performed at some other time or place, it is *already here* in one's daily world. So, while violence in the media pours forth relentlessly without a detectable corresponding uptick in the violence of the actual world, it does desensitize the young and makes their world—*at least the world of human connection with the media themselves,* a world that young people live in for hours a day—casually cruel. In these everyday adventures transposed to the young psyche, empty aggression is the common currency of life.

Violence is only one of the regular crudities. Everyday media are soaked in coarseness of many sorts. Primitive jeers, double entendres, easy jokes about body functions feature regularly in many programs radiated to young people through network sitcoms, MTV, Comedy Central, and other commercial sources, as well as video games (which now outgross movies, in both senses of "outgross") and Internet entertainments. The sexual innuendo of music videos is hard to miss, whence its huge adolescent appeal. Overall, though, probably more prevalent than sexual suggestiveness is the crude style evident in vocabulary, look, gestures—the whole expressive repertory of popular culture. The full range of human emotions is collapsed into the rudimentary alternatives of "love" and "hate," "cool" and "gross." The media take the side of the simple over the complex, the id over the superego, the pleasure principle over the reality principle, the popular over the unpopular.

All in all, then, the media promote emotional payoffs—and expectations of payoffs. The rewards are immediate: fun and excitement. Images and sounds register in the here-and-now. They are supposed to feel good—this is the expectation. They make a cardinal promise: you have a right not to be bored. Yet the media must not feel *too* good for *too* long, because part of their goodness is that they change, yield to the next, and we know it. Accordingly, our students have become accustomed to feel feelings with a particular quality: feelings that are relatively disposable, fast rising and fast fading, excitements and expectations that readily yield (and are expected to yield) to other fast-rising and fast-fading feelings, excitements, and expectations. Young people expect their images and soundtracks not only to cause enjoyment but also to change. They expect jolts of sensation, surges of unexpected (yet, paradoxically, predictably unexpected) feelings. They expect to change the channel—or fast-forward the tape, or search out a different song on the CD—if it does not please them.

Thus, the unacknowledged curriculum readies them not only for sensation but also for interruption. Interruption is a premise of contemporary perception. It is no small part of the experience of media. Interruption—and the expectation of it—is built into the media's own texture. Programs interrupt themselves. There is, in commercials, trailers, and other filler, the interruption of one story by another—expedited by channel switching and the variety of distractions (talking, eating, chatting on the phone, exchanging "buddy messages" on line, and so on) that children build into their media experience.

There is the interruption of one medium by another, deliberately or not, but interruption is even built into content. In the spelling lessons of *Sesame Street* as in the commercials after which it was patterned, in action movies as in video games, in music videos as in disk jockey chitchat, in sportscasting as in news, the young expect split screens, moving logos, and quick cuts, even if some continuity may be supplied by the soundtrack. The acceleration of editing during the past generation is striking, with images jump-cutting to other images in a split second. The contrast with the past is plain whenever one sees a movie more than twenty years old—how static it looks! Finally, within the unedited frame, there is the now normal glide or zoom or, in any case, movement of the image itself, the product of a handheld camera, or one on a dolly or Steadicam. In media, the "story line" turns out to be jagged. The expectation of immediate but disposable rewards has become normal.

Interruption becomes routine. Interference leads to multitasking as the young become accustomed to dividing their attention. Media frequently come to them simultaneously or near simultaneously—and they expect media to come that way. The habit of switching is partly a function of the convenience of switching. Thanks to the remote control device, one of the most underestimated of contemporary technologies, they may conveniently graze between two or three television channels in rapid alternation. They may switch between a video game and a soap opera or sports event, and so on.

For this reason among others, I do not want to argue that when the young attend to the media of popular culture they are necessarily deeply attentive. To the contrary: there is much evidence that they tune out much of the time. They select what they attend to. They retain unevenly. Sometimes they focus and sometimes not. Those who approve of the habit of simultaneous media viewing and listening refer to the cognition this practice demands as "parallel processing." Those who disapprove consider it distraction. But however one evaluates this common condition of half-attention, it is not the focus that is required for intellectual mastery—learning a language, performing a complex computation, grasping the contours of history, assessing rival explanations of a given phenomenon, assessing the moral implications of complex realities. It is not a mood conducive to education—or citizenship.

EDUCATION AND THE VALUES OF CITIZENSHIP

It is against this background—the texture of everyday life in a media-saturated society—that the values of education for citizenship become indispensable, all the more so in an era when higher education has become common.

For students, as for others, popular culture has recreational uses. Escape from rigors and burdens is, after all, its point. But the sheer profusion of popular culture in the lives of the young has a larger implication: the informal curriculum of immediate gratification obstructs education for citizenship—just as it obstructs the analytical work of education across the board.

Education's prime obligation to the public weal in a democratic society is to improve the capacity of citizens to govern themselves. For now, I leave in suspension the question of the degree to which the good citizen is a direct participant in the decisions that affect his or her life—the ideal enshrined as participatory democracy in the 1960s—or, on the other hand, one who (in Michael Schudson's term) "monitors" the decisions of public bodies and intervenes in public affairs only occasionally, in particular when they make decisions that offend ideals or interests.[6] I take it as axiomatic, in either event, that higher education has a distinct and significant part to play in forming and bolstering the capacity for citizenship. The growth of higher education makes colleges and universities steadily more promising—or disappointing, as the case may be— in their potential for public improvement. But colleges and universities can only discharge this duty when they combat the distraction induced by media saturation.

Some would argue that it is an obligation of higher education to mobilize activists. I have long believed that activism is the lifeblood of democracy. I still do. But the mission of mobilization is too important— and distinctive—to be entrusted to institutions that have other primary purposes. Educational institutions ought not to be burdened with the obligation to mobilize—with the important exception of the obligation to mobilize students to register to vote and, subsequently, actually to vote. (As William Galston points out in his chapter, the youth vote has declined precipitously during the past thirty years, as has the percentage of students who read newspapers regularly.) Universities serve bedrock purposes of higher education in a democracy when they spur reasoned participation in politics and the accumulation of knowledge to suit. Toward this end, they are obliged to defend the freedom to teach and the freedom to learn. These academic freedoms are constitutive of the whole educational project, and as such must be explicitly and articulately defended. Such civic services hold no significant downside for the educational mission—to the contrary.

But beyond such fundamental service to democracy, universities ought not to be entrusted with political mobilization. Institutions of learning are forums, not parties. They ought to endorse citizenship, not particular policies.[7] They short-circuit the educational process and damage their commitment to reason when they officially advocate beyond a bare minimum, for the advocacy cuts short the deliberative process that is their proper charge. If they were to mobilize toward particular ends, toward which would they mobilize, and who would decide? What penalties would be prescribed for those who embrace different ends from those embraced by the authorities, or the majority?

No, the arousal and channeling of passions is not the work of colleges and universities. For that there are political organizations, parties, and movements. Education has a more precise responsibility: to cultivate reason and to deepen understanding of the world. No other institution is dedicated to these functions. In fact, the political sphere is dedicated to undermining them, as, in their own ways, are media. Yet reason and understanding, the university's own specialized charge, are imperative. There is no time when this is not so. But a time like the present, with its manifold challenges to humane life and even to life itself, is especially in need of an infusion of knowledge into the political domain. To judge foreign policy, energy needs, terrorist threats to security, ecological problems, questions of economics, and so forth requires not just committed but knowledgeable citizens. Truly America has suffered in recent years from failures of intelligence in more than one sense. Universities should shudder at their history of complacency.

For citizenly as well as strictly educational purposes, then, higher education ought to cultivate a disciplined curiosity about the world and an enthusiasm for careful disputation. Toward these ends, schooling needs to counter the impulsive, hyperkinetic, associational, trivia-centered relation to images and sounds that the bulk of the media offer. Colleges and universities ought to be arenas for robust speech, where students are encouraged not only to reinforce views they already hold but also—knowledgeably and logically—to challenge them. An atmosphere conducive to reflection is one prerequisite for education in civic prerequisites, as also for learning in its own right. Where else in modern life is such an atmosphere to be found, or created, responsive to social needs that are not the needs of the market? If not in colleges and universities, nowhere.

Beyond the specialized crafts, institutions of higher learning exist in significant part to deepen understanding of intellectual traditions—of science, the humanities, and social sciences alike. Toward this end, the spirit of higher learning benefits when students are, for some of their college careers, immersed in a common curriculum. The decisive reason is not that the standard lists of canonical texts deserve to be engraved in granite strictly by virtue of the texts' longevity (a circular argument), or their Westernness (not an argument in behalf of their logic-inducing potential). It is that the student body's shared exposure to central literary and philosophical texts and methods of argument enlarges the community of reason. It widens the circle of shared conversation. It challenges parochialisms of all sorts—including the demographic and subcultural niches preferred by the market as well as the specializations preferred by the professions. Not only does a common curriculum help overcome the intellectual narrowness that accompanies specialization. The core experience also helps cultivate citizens who will be capable of rising above private and group interest to work toward a common good. A core curriculum aerates elites and tends, over time, to substitute meritocratic principle for inherited cultural capital.[8]

So a common curriculum including political philosophy (and thus defenses as well as criticisms of democratic theory) has citizenly as well as intellectual uses. These uses extend beyond the makeup of the curriculum's subjects to the cultivation of reason itself. In particular, the atmosphere of higher education should cultivate an awareness that an argument is different from an assertion or an opinion. An argument is obliged to confront its contraries—engage them, not ignore them or rush past them. An argument ought to confront its contraries at their strong points, not their weak points. An argument is not the simple pressing of a point, as in the shout fests that characterize television punditry. For the arts of argument, evidence and logic are required. Yet for years, teaching at Berkeley, New York University, and Columbia, I have noticed how frequently students have difficulty understanding what an argument is. Many, asked to make an argument on a particular subject, express an opinion—or even an emotion ("I feel that"). Many top high school graduates have come to the university without learning what an argument is. Plainly the whole educational system is in default.

Citizenship requires more than reason, but the public sphere cannot dispense with reason without making a mockery of the democratic idea. Yet, just as the torrent of media washes away the careful sifting and winnowing that reason requires, the conduct of politics today is inimical to the reasoning arts. A reputation for excessive knowledge is "wonkish." A reputation for verbal stumbling establishes the common touch and certifies "likability." The anti-intellectualism of American life, of which Richard Hofstadter wrote forty years ago, has not diminished even as the proportion of the adult population attending colleges and universities and acquiring degrees, even advanced degrees, has grown. The public sphere is, instead, an arena for repetitive expression, professionalized into the imperative of staying "on message." To take but one recent example: Zbigniew Brzezinski, former national security adviser to Jimmy Carter, pointed out in April 2003 that in the eighteen months since September 11, 2001, President Bush spoke the words "either you're with us or with the terrorists" ninety-nine times. The repetition of such remarks is not an argument. It is a declaration meant to stop an argument. So too is the juxtaposition of the September 11 terrorists and Saddam Hussein in the same sentence, again without ever making an argument to the effect that they actually had a significant link.[9] Assuming that the argument had already been made and won and failing to engage any of the counterevidence: This is not debate. This is propaganda.

A measure of the success of a debate is not whether your side has won but whether the protagonists have learned anything in the process. Learning from those whom you defeat can take place under judicious rules in a properly run classroom, where those who hold unpopular views are encouraged to defend them, those who are uncertain are encouraged to understand better the grounds of their uncertainty, and students may experiment with unfamiliar or seemingly outré views.

Finally, for reasons that are cultural or, if you will, spiritual as well as civic, higher education has the obligation to cultivate not only habits of mind conducive to democratic debate but also certain habits of emotion. In an era of high-speed media and transitory experience, it needs to acquaint students with what the art critic Robert Hughes has called "slow art."[10] The greatest work is more likely to elicit depths of pity and terror than lightweight work. The complexity of motives and the torments of unintended consequences hold powerful lessons for public conduct. It is better to study Dostoyevsky than to study *General Hospital*.

There is more to be derived from a production of *Hamlet* than a production of *Married . . . with Children.* Call it the political sublime. A curriculum that credits the sublime cannot be left to the vagaries of popular taste, for popular taste answers to other criteria. In composing a curriculum, the authority of teachers should not be surrendered to the commercial judgments that mold popular taste.

For again: the media's business is to stimulate emotion and sensation that generate instant payoffs. Because their sole criterion of success is market preference, the prime question for them is always whether they can get customers to pay attention. This commitment leaves the realm of emotion impoverished. I can get you to pay attention: I simply have to make a loud noise. But the sensibility of a self-governing society needs more from its collective emotional life than temptation or titillation. It needs to appreciate the sublime. It needs to savor the complex. It needs to instruct in the overcoming of impulse. It needs to teach how to evaluate desire and know the difference between desirability and morality. It needs to teach how to make sense of duties when duties conflict. To glib answers it brings complication, and further questions. To the shallowness of the moment it brings the subsoil of history. To the casualness of everyday talk it brings the discipline of seasoned judgment.

In sum, higher education has the burden of advancing the intellectual side of citizenship. This obligation pits education against the noise of the media and against the pettiness, parochialism, and corruption of politics. It deepens the educational mission. It enrolls higher education in the defense of society's highest values. It is not a mission that can be offloaded onto any other institution. It is partisan only in the sense of a commitment to improve the common life. But that is a partisanship of which we have precious little today. If higher education declines its own authority and swims with popular tides, it will default, and the nation's life will be the poorer in every respect.

NOTES

1. On the other hand, there is also a lively debate over whether the United States, or any nation, can ever be purely civic or political in its identity—whether "values" considered abstractly can ever bind a people as demographically diverse as Americans into a polity that is also capable of a contentious politics. Roger Wilkins argues in his chapter that this is possible, provided, however,

that Americans in our diversity make use of the opportunities afforded by our inherited—if at times contradictory—values and thus reaffirm them. A politics aiming at correcting injustice is itself a form of nation building. Wilkins reminds us that the same elite Founders who passed on racism also bequeathed the institutions and values, the rights and duties of citizens, to combat it, and thus to identity ourselves as politically equal Americans. We may see this sort of political activism as an expression of patriotism, an affirmation grounded in the intellectual side of citizenship for which I argue later in this chapter. See also my *Letters to a Young Activist* (New York: Basic Books, 2003), chap. 11.

2. For an extended treatment of supply, demand, and the place of media in contemporary society, see my *Media Unlimited: How the Torrent of Images and Sounds Overwhelms Our Lives* (New York: Metropolitan Books/Henry Holt, 2002).

3. "Kids and Media @ the New Millennium," www.kff.org/entmedia/1535 -index.cfm (7/16/04).

4. Blaise Pascal, *Pensées,* trans. W. F. Trotter, www.eserver.org/philosophy/ pascal-pensees.txt, sec. 2, par. 142 (7/16/04).

5. See Michael J. Sandel, "Religious Liberty and Freedom of Speech," in *Democracy's Discontent: America in Search of a Public Philosophy* (Cambridge, Mass.: Harvard University Press, 1996), 55–90. See also Cass R. Sunstein, "Political Speech and the Two-Tier First Amendment" and "Deliberative Democracy," in *Democracy and the Problem of Free Speech* (New York: Free Press, 1995), 121–66 and 241–52.

6. Michael Schudson, *The Good Citizen* (New York: Free Press, 1998), 310–11.

7. This case is set out masterfully by Michael Schwartz, president of Cleveland State University and former president of Kent State University, in "The Role of Dissent in Inquiry, Learning, and Reflection," *Peace and Change* 21, no. 2 (April 1996): 169–81. While the university as a whole ought not commit itself to political positions aside from those that bear directly on the conditions for education—especially the defense of the freedom to teach and the freedom to learn—there remains the question of the liberties permitted to individual faculty. What sort of advocacy have they the right to pursue? Is the university obliged to provide for having them challenged in the interests of open debate? See Robert Calvert's chapter 14 in this volume.

8. For a different view of both the meritocratic principle and of inherited cultural capital, see the chapter 14 by Robert Calvert.

9. On Bush administration doubts about any significant link shortly after September 11, 2001, see Thomas H. Kean et al., *The 9/11 Commission Report.* (Washington, D.C.: Government Printing Office, 2004), 334.

10. Robert Hughes, "His TV Series 'The Shock of the New' Changed the Way People Thought about Modern Art," *Guardian,* June 30, 1994, sec. G2, 12.

CHAPTER SIX

Public Spaces and MyUniversity.com

Cass R. Sunstein

My central argument in this chapter is that carriers of culture, including educational institutions, should not be seen as producing an ordinary commodity, properly subject to the forces of supply and demand. In a well-functioning democracy, unchosen, unanticipated exposures to topics and ideas are an important feature of ordinary life. My argument applies to colleges, museums, libraries, historical sites, national holidays, and national wilderness areas, and it applies whether the relevant institutions are publicly or privately owned. Instead of relying on the analogy to ordinary markets, we should use an analogy to public forums in constitutional law. The analogy is not perfect, but it points to some important characteristics, in any society, of those who produce education, art, music, theater, and more. An understanding of the public forum doctrine supports the idea that carriers of culture—including universities—should see their role as involving the cultivation of citizenship.[1]

In rejecting the idea that culture should be treated as an ordinary commodity, I offer three suggestions. The first and most general is that carriers of culture, most prominently including educational institutions, have an important role in shaping preferences and values. They do not simply serve, or cater to, those preferences and values. The second suggestion is that much of the time, carriers of culture do, and should, expose people to experiences that they have not specifically chosen.

Unanticipated, unchosen exposures are indispensable to both politics and education, especially in a period in which "niche marketing," for education and cultural products as for other goods, threatens to place people in gated communities of multiple sorts. The third suggestion is that carriers of culture often provide shared experiences for diverse people. These shared experiences are extremely important, especially in a heterogeneous society. A central purpose of education is to foster such experiences.

To make this argument, I urge that the public forum analogy helps to provide an account of why public institutions need not simply cater to existing tastes. The analogy also raises doubts about the value of a high degree of specialization and sorting in the domain of education and culture. I suggest that the public forum analogy illuminates what cultural institutions should be doing; that it shows the sense in which cultural products are not ordinary commodities; and that it also contains a set of lessons for educational policy and law. If my arguments are convincing, it should be easier to see why educational institutions, museums, and other general-interest carriers of culture will, or should, play a large social role in a period in which it is possible to increase specialization in a dramatic way by providing a multiplicity of offerings specifically suited to individual tastes. If individuals and groups were able to design their own curricula and museums—through a new Web site, for example, under the name Mycourses.com or Mymuseum.com—there would be significant gains, not least because many more people would be able to see cultural offerings that suit their tastes. But much would be lost as well. An understanding of the public forum doctrine helps to explain exactly what would be lost.

THE PUBLIC FORUM DOCTRINE

What is free speech about? And how does the free speech principle bear on democracy and education? In the common understanding, the free speech principle is taken to forbid government (including public educational institutions) from "censoring" speech of which it disapproves. In the standard cases, the government attempts to impose penalties, whether civil or criminal, on political dissent, art, commercial advertising, or sexually explicit speech. The question is whether the government has a legitimate, and sufficiently weighty, reason for restricting the speech that it seeks to control.

This is indeed the focus of most of the law of free speech. But in many free nations, an important part of free speech law takes a quite different form. In the United States, for example, the Supreme Court has ruled that streets and parks must be kept open to the public for expressive activity. In the leading case, from the early part of the twentieth century, the Court said: "Wherever the title of streets and parks may rest, they have immemorially been held in trust for the use of the public and time out of mind, have been used for the purposes of assembly, communicating thought between citizens, and discussing public questions. Such use of the streets and public places has, from ancient times, been a part of the privileges, immunities, rights, and liberties of citizens."[2] Hence governments are obliged to allow speech to occur freely on public streets and in public parks—even if many citizens would prefer to have peace and quiet, and even if people find it irritating, or worse, to come across protesters and dissidents, or artists of one or another sort, when simply walking home or to the local grocery store.

To be sure, the government is allowed to impose restrictions on the "time, place, and manner" of speech in public places. No one has a right to hold rock concerts at 3:00 a.m., to insist that people listen to operas based on readings from Karl Marx, or to monopolize a public park with the work of his favorite artists. But time, place, and manner restrictions must be both reasonable and limited. Government is essentially obliged to allow speakers, whatever their views, to use public property to convey messages of their choosing. The point includes political protesters and would-be educators as well as speakers of any other kind.

Under the Constitution, speakers do not have a general right of access to people and places. If a protester seeks to display his work at a public museum, or for that matter at a private university, the Constitution offers him no help. The free speech principle offers no general "access right." But the public forum doctrine qualifies this idea, for a distinctive feature of the doctrine is that it does create a kind of right of speakers' access, both to places and to people. If an artist wants to display her work on public streets, she is entitled to do so. Another distinctive feature of the public forum doctrine is that it creates a right, not to avoid governmentally imposed penalties on speech, but to ensure government subsidies of speech. There is no question that taxpayers are required to support the expressive activity that, under the public forum doctrine, must be permitted on the streets and parks. Indeed, the costs that taxpayers devote to maintaining open streets and parks, from cleaning to maintenance, can be quite high. Thus the public forum represents one area of law in which the right to free speech demands a public subsidy to speakers.

Unfortunately, the Supreme Court has given little sense of why, exactly, it is important to ensure that the streets and parks remain open to speakers. This is the question that must be answered if we are to know whether, and how, cultural institutions are analogous to public forums. It is possible to make some progress here by noticing that the public forum doctrine promotes four important goals.[3] The first two involve speakers; the third and fourth involve listeners.

First, the public forum doctrine ensures that speakers can have access to a wide array of people. If protesters want to claim that taxes are too high, they are able to press this argument on many people who might otherwise fail to hear the message. The diverse people who walk the streets and use the parks are likely to hear speakers' arguments; they might also learn about the nature and intensity of views held by their fellow citizens. What is true for political protesters is true for artists as well. There may be no simple political message in a painting or a poem, but the free speech principle is not limited to those with political messages. Under the public forum doctrine, those with paintings and poems can appear before others, even if those others would prefer not to see them.

Perhaps some people's views and tastes change because of what they see and hear on streets and in parks. Perhaps they will become curious, even intrigued, enough to alter their interests and to prompt them to do something on their own. It does not much matter if this happens a little or a lot. What is important is that speakers are allowed to press concerns that might otherwise be ignored by their fellow citizens. On the speakers' side, the public forum doctrine thus creates a right of general access to heterogeneous citizens.

Second, the public forum doctrine allows speakers not only to have general access to heterogeneous people but also to specific people and specific institutions whom they wish to reach, or with whom they have a complaint. Suppose, for example, that a critic believes that the state legislature has behaved irresponsibly with respect to crime or health care for children. The public forum ensures that the critic can make his views heard by legislators, simply by protesting in front of the state legislature itself. The point applies to private as well as public institutions. If a clothing store is believed to have cheated customers, or to have acted in a racist manner, protesters are allowed a form of access to the store itself. This is not because they have a right to trespass on private property—no one has such a right—but because a public street is highly likely to be close by, and a strategically located protest will undoubtedly catch the attention of the store and its customers. The same is true for a private university with whom local citizens have a complaint. Under the public forum doctrine, speakers are thus permitted to have access to particular audiences, and particular listeners cannot easily avoid hearing complaints that are directed against them. In other words, listeners have a sharply limited power of self-insulation. Since many cultural protests are directed, in one or another sense, at some private or public institution, the public forum doctrine performs an important function in allowing this kind of specific access.

Third, the public forum doctrine increases the likelihood that people generally will be exposed to a wide variety of people and perspectives. When someone goes to work or visits a park, it is possible that he will have a range of unexpected encounters, however fleeting or seemingly inconsequential. On the way to the office or when eating lunch in the park, people cannot easily wall themselves off from contentions, conditions, or even music and art that they would not have sought out in advance or that they would avoided if they could. Indeed, the exposure might well be considered, much of the time, irritating or worse.

Fourth, the public forum creates not exactly a right but an opportunity, if occasionally an unwelcome one: *shared exposure* to diverse speakers with diverse views and complaints. Many people will be simultaneously exposed to the same views and complaints, and they will encounter views and complaints that some of them might have refused to seek out in the first instance. The central point is that the public forum doctrine tends to ensure a range of experiences that are widely shared—streets and parks are public property—at the same time that it provides a set of exposures to diverse views and conditions.

In these various ways, it should be immediately apparent that the public forum operates on different premises from those that underlie economic markets. In ordinary markets, goods and services are allocated on the basis of private willingness to pay; people receive those things for which they are willing to pay. And of course speech, cultural products, and education operate, to some degree, on market principles. Much of the time, people receive books, art, and education in accordance with their willingness to pay for them. But under the public forum doctrine, the rights of speakers and viewers are not allocated on those principles. Speakers do not have access in accordance with their willingness to pay for it. Nor are they heard in accordance with their ability to persuade viewers to pay for the privilege of hearing them. Speakers have access to audiences for free; the same is true for the access of listeners to speakers. In a sense, this is a benefit for both sides. But for listeners and viewers, at least, it is a burden or a responsibility as well, simply because they will be exposed to materials that they have not specifically chosen. A key idea behind the public forum doctrine must be that involuntary exposures have significant social benefits. In fact we might well see the doctrine as a kind of constitutional celebration of involuntary exposures to ideas and information.

In some ways, the public forum is currently more important as a symbol than as a reality. The most influential communications experiences no longer occur on streets and parks. Much of learning, and most exposure to culture, occurs elsewhere. In any case the twentieth century saw the emergence of "general-interest intermediaries"—newspapers, weekly newsmagazines, commercial broadcasters, and universities, both public and private.[4] These private institutions have served, for better or worse, some of the functions of traditional public forums, by exposing people to topics and ideas that they have not specifically selected and also by creating, much of the time, something like a shared culture. It should be readily apparent that these points have implications for how such intermediaries might understand their social role, and for how they might choose to organize and present themselves. A newspaper, for example, might believe that it is under an obligation to cover diverse topics and ideas, even if most readers are not interested in them in advance. Similarly, a university might decide that it should expose students to a "core" of some sort, both to provide a shared set of background understandings and to ensure that students learn about topics and ideas for which they had, before learning, little enthusiasm. Many newspapers and universities, of course, see themselves very much in these terms. I will return to these points.

SHAPING TASTES

If we take the public forum doctrine as furnishing an analogy, we will have a distinctive understanding of the social role of universities, museums, and other carriers of culture. The most obvious point is that people's tastes are formed and shaped, not merely reflected, by education and by cultural products in general. In fact this is inevitable. Even if producers try simply to cater to existing tastes and do not attempt to influence them, they will affect what people want to see. The public forum doctrine reflects a judgment that market forces are not the only basis on which people's preferences and values should be shaped.

To be sure, there is a market for education and culture. Universities and colleges must compete with one another, and they do so vigorously. The same is true for museums, movie theaters, and much more. In any case a free society does not require students to go to colleges or universities of a certain stripe, or force people to go to museums or to visit historical sites. And because forces of supply and demand will inevitably play a role, producers, both private and public, will inevitably face pressure to cater to existing tastes. But if we are concerned with freedom, we should not celebrate a system in which educational, artistic, and cultural experiences are fully subject to market forces. On the market view, freedom consists in the satisfaction of preferences, whatever their content. But this is an inadequate conception of freedom. It is important to ensure a degree of freedom in the formation of preferences, not only in the satisfaction of preferences. If people's preferences are formed as a result of existing arrangements, including limitations on available opportunities, or of exposure to a limited set of material, then it makes no sense to say that the existing arrangement can be justified by reference to their preferences. We shall soon see that this point has implications for educational practice and in particular for the idea of "consumer choice" in the educational domain.

In any case it is clear that the public's "tastes" with respect to learning, art, and culture do not come from nature or from the sky. They are partly a product of current and recent practices by cultural providers. The relevant tastes are often generated by the market. What people want, in short, is partly a product of what they are accustomed to seeing. If there is a great deal of sexually explicit or violent material, members of the public may well cultivate a taste for more of the same. Tastes are also a product of existing social norms, which can change over time and which are themselves responsive to existing commercial fare. Consider the domain of education. If high school students seek a curriculum of a certain sort, this is because of tastes that have been cultivated socially, and they might well reflect undesirable limitations of various sorts and even forms of unfreedom.

Speaking of the market for culture, Robert Frank and Philip Cook have noted that "free marketeers have little to cheer about if all they can claim is that the market is efficient at filling desires that the market itself creates. . . . Just as culture affects preferences, so also do markets influence culture."[5] They add that existing "financial incentives strongly favor sensational, lurid and formulaic offerings" and that the resulting structure of rewards "is especially troubling in light of evidence that, beginning in infancy and continuing through life, the things we see and read profoundly alter the kinds of people we become." And if markets affect culture in a way that leads to inferior aesthetic experiences, it is appropriate to supplement markets with other mechanisms of supply. Of course it is not easy to explain what makes aesthetic experiences inferior. The only point is that a democratic society does not give markets a monopoly on the dissemination of culture. It adds nonmarket mechanisms.

It might be tempting to respond that the arguments thus far are unacceptably paternalistic, indeed elitist. If individual listeners, viewers, and students prefer fare of a certain kind, how can there be any ground for legitimate complaint? To the extent that I have emphasized the fact that preferences might be formed by limitations on available options, my argument might seem to verge on objectionable paternalism. Certainly people's preferences are not being taken as given. But it is one thing to say that a government should not be authorized to overcome people's judgments when those people are armed with adequate information. It is quite another to say that both public and private institutions should be permitted to take modest steps to promote the operation of a culture in a democratic order by, for example, promoting exposure to diverse views and something in the way of shared experiences. And the charge, indeed the very notion, of paternalism becomes harder to understand when the preferences that are involved are a product of the very system whose legitimacy is at issue.

The general idea here—that preferences and beliefs are a product of existing institutions and practices, and that the result can be a form of unfreedom, one of the most serious of all—is hardly new. It is a long-standing theme in political and legal thought. Thus Tocqueville wrote of the effects of the institution of slavery on the desires of many slaves themselves: "Plunged in this abyss of wretchedness, the Negro hardly notices his ill fortune; he was reduced to slavery by violence, and the habit of servitude has given him the thoughts and ambitions of a slave; he admires his tyrants even more than he hates them and finds his joy and pride in servile imitation of his oppressors."[6] In the same vein, John Dewey wrote that "social conditions may restrict, distort, and almost prevent the development of individuality."[7] He insisted that we should therefore "take an active interest in the working of social institutions that have a bearing, positive or negative, upon the growth of individuals." For Dewey, a just society "is as much interested in the positive construction of favorable institutions, legal, political, and economic, as it is in the work of removing abuses and overt oppressions."

These points underlie some of the most important functions of public forums and of general-interest intermediaries, emphatically including universities, museums, and other sources of public culture. All of these produce unanticipated exposures that help promote the free formation of preferences, even in a world of numerous options. In this sense, they are continuous with the educational system. Indeed they provide a kind of continuing education for adults, something that a free society cannot do without. It does not matter whether the government is directly responsible for the institutions that perform this role. What matters is that they exist.

UNCHOSEN ENCOUNTERS

A central idea behind the public forum doctrine is that it is desirable to create arrangements through which people cannot select in advance all of what they see and hear. The basic claim is that unchosen, unanticipated encounters are desirable for a democratic society. With respect to politics, the point should not be terribly obscure. Gated communities are no friend of citizenship. Suppose, for example, that everyone could easily devise a kind of "Daily Me," ensuring that they were exposed only to topics and points of view of which they approved.[8] This would not be a utopian vision. On the contrary, it would increase social fragmentation, if only because so many people would construct communications universes that were particular to them. Mutual understanding would be more difficult. Indeed the problem might well be worse than that. Social science evidence demonstrates that when like-minded people speak only or mostly with one another, they tend to go to extremes (a point to which I will return).[9] If different groups are sorting themselves into different communications communities, extremism of multiple sorts is to be expected. This is not healthy for a democracy.

The public forum doctrine provides a safeguard here. So long as people are using public streets and parks, gated communities are less likely. People are going to have unexpected, unanticipated encounters with their fellow citizens and also with topics and points of view. And in a period in which streets and parks do not play a dominant role in people's lives, other institutions can pick up the slack. Return to the social roles of the general-interest intermediaries, most prominently daily newspapers, weekly newsmagazines, evening news programs, museums, and universities. These intermediaries do a great deal of filtering, and some of their decisions might be criticized on various grounds. But for present purposes, my point is that they do have many of the functions of streets and parks, especially insofar as they expose people to topics and points of view that have not been selected by individual "consumers" in advance.

Consider here the role of the media. When you read a city newspaper or a national magazine, your eyes will come across a number of articles that you would not have selected in advance. If you are like most people, you will read some of those articles. Perhaps you did not know that you might have an interest in minimum wage legislation, or Somalia, or the latest developments in the Middle East; but a story might catch your attention. What is true for topics is also true for points of view. You might think that you have nothing to learn from someone whose view you abhor. But once you come across the editorial pages, you might well read what they have to say, and you might well benefit from the experience. Perhaps you will be persuaded on one point or another, or informed whether or not you are persuaded. At the same time, the front-page headline or the cover story in *Newsweek* is likely to have a high degree of salience for a wide range of people.

Unplanned and unchosen encounters often turn out to do a great deal of good, for individuals and society at large. In some cases, they even change people's lives. The same is true, though in a different way, for unwanted encounters. In some cases, you might be irritated by seeing an editorial from your least-favorite writer. You might wish that the editorial weren't there. But despite yourself, your curiosity might be piqued, and you might read it. Perhaps this isn't a lot of fun. But it might prompt you to reassess your own view and even to revise it. At the very least, you will have learned what many of your fellow citizens think and why they think it. What is true for arguments is also true for topics, as when you encounter, with some displeasure, a series of stories on crime or global warming or same-sex marriage or alcohol abuse but find yourself learning a bit, or more, from what those stories have to say.

Of course general-interest intermediaries are not public forums in the technical sense that the law recognizes. These are private rather than public institutions. Most important, members of the public do not have a legal right of access to them. Individual citizens are not allowed to override the editorial and economic judgments and choices of private owners. In the 1970s, a sharp constitutional debate on precisely this issue resulted in a resounding defeat for those who claimed a constitutionally guaranteed access right.[10] But the question of legal compulsion is really incidental. Society's general-interest intermediaries, even without legal compulsion, serve many of the functions of public forums. They expose people to information and views that would not have been selected in advance.

My emphasis thus far has been on politics and policy, narrowly defined. But the functions of general-interest intermediaries are far broader. Daily newspapers and weekly newsmagazines cover culture more generally. If you read *Time* or *Newsweek,* you might find yourself learning about a musician, a novelist, or a photographic exhibit in which you expected to have no interest. But the story might capture your attention, and it might direct you to work that you would otherwise have ignored and that you would certainly not have selected in advance. In these various ways, general-interest intermediaries have helped shape tastes; they also produce the desirable effect of exposing people to cultural offerings that they might not have known to investigate.

It is possible to go much further. Many carriers of culture have served similar functions. A prominent museum, for example, might not try to provide the public with what it antecedently wants; it is more likely to provide a range of work, some of it disturbing or even distressing. With respect to their domain, museums are themselves intermediaries, in a sense even general-interest intermediaries. They engage in a degree of filtering designed to provide a selection of material that does not necessarily match what visitors would select in advance. The curators are not doing their job if they simply choose what people "like." Theirs is, in significant part, an educational function. They might well select paintings or other offerings that seem confusing, disturbing, difficult, or even offensive. Part of the experience that they are providing is unchosen and, in some cases, even unwanted. If they are doing their jobs properly, this is both an individual and a social benefit. Universities should be understood in similar terms.

SHARED EXPERIENCES

In a heterogeneous society, it is extremely important for diverse people to have a set of common experiences. Many of our practices reflect a judgment to this effect. National holidays, for example, help constitute a nation by encouraging citizens to think, all at once, about events of shared importance. And they do much more than this. They enable people, in all their diversity, to have certain memories and attitudes. At least this is true in nations where national holidays have a vivid and concrete meaning. In the United States, many national holidays have become mere days off from work, and the precipitating occasion—Presidents' Day, Memorial Day, Labor Day—has come to be nearly invisible. This is a serious loss. With the exception of the Fourth of July, Martin Luther King Day is probably the closest thing to a genuinely substantive national holiday, largely because that celebration involves something that can be treated as concrete and meaningful. In other words, it is *about* something. To the extent that this is newly true, or more true than in recent years, for the Fourth of July, it is because threats to the nation have offered a vivid reminder that ours is, in a sense, one nation and that that nation is worth fighting for.

Communications and culture are of course exceptionally important here. Sometimes millions of people follow the presidential election, or the Super Bowl, or the coronation of a new monarch; and many of them do so because of the simultaneous actions of others. The point very much bears on the historic role of both public forums and carriers of culture. Public parks are of course places where diverse people can congregate and see one another. Large museums provide a set of experiences and memories that can help unify a diverse people.

Why are these shared experiences so desirable? There are three principal reasons.

- Simple enjoyment is probably the least of it, but it is far from irrelevant. People like many experiences more, simply because they are being shared. Consider a popular movie, the Super Bowl, a large event on a college campus, or a presidential debate. For many of us, these are goods that are worth less if many others are not enjoying or purchasing them too. Hence a presidential debate may be worthy of individual attention for many people simply because so many other people consider it worthy of individual attention.

- Sometimes shared experiences ease social interactions, permitting people to speak with one another and to congregate around a common issue, task, or concern, whether or not they have much in common with one another. In this sense the shared experiences provide a form of social glue. They help make it possible for diverse people to believe that they live in the same culture. Indeed they help constitute that shared culture, simply by creating common memories and experiences, and a sense of common tasks.
- A fortunate consequence of shared experiences—many of them produced by the media—is that people who would otherwise see one another as quite unfamiliar, in the extreme case as almost belonging to a different species, can come instead to regard one another as fellow citizens with shared hopes, goals, and concerns. This is a subjective good for those directly involved. But it can be an objective good as well, especially if it leads to cooperative projects of various kinds. When people learn about a disaster faced by fellow citizens, for example, they may respond with financial and other help. The point applies internationally as well as domestically; massive relief efforts are often made possible by virtue of the fact that millions of people learn, all at once, about the relevant need.

How does this bear on democracy and culture? The basic point is that an increasingly fragmented communications system will reduce the level of shared experiences having salience to diverse people. This is a simple matter of numbers. When there were three television networks, much of what appeared would have the quality of a genuinely common experience. The lead story on the evening news, for example, would provide a common reference point for many millions of people. To the extent that choices proliferate, it is inevitable that diverse individuals and diverse groups will have fewer shared experiences and fewer common reference points. It is possible, for example, that some events that are highly salient to some people will barely register on others' view screen.

And it is possible that some views and perspectives that seem obvious for many people will, for others, seem barely intelligible.

This is hardly a suggestion that everyone should be required to watch the same thing. A degree of plurality, with respect to both topics and points of view, is highly desirable. Moreover, talk about "requirements" misses the point. My only claim is that a common set of frameworks and experiences is valuable for a heterogeneous society and that a system with limitless options, making for diverse choices, will compromise the underlying values.

PERSONALIZATION, UNANTICIPATED EXPOSURES, AND MYUNIVERSITY.COM

Now let me turn to the issue with particular reference to education and democracy. I believe that there are important commonalities between education and news and that an understanding of personalization and its pitfalls clarifies those commonalities.

Of course there are many reasons to celebrate freedom of choice. Citizens will inevitably be selective about what they read, and the principal selections should be made by individuals, not by a central authority. At the college level, students should have some room to maneuver, in part because they already know enough to make many informed choices, in part because they are apt to learn more if they are enthusiastic about what they are learning. In any case the power to "personalize" has been increased both by new technologies and by widespread enthusiasm for allowing citizens and students to operate as consumers. That power enables people to learn far more than they could before, and to learn it much faster. If students are interested in issues that bear on public policy—environmental quality, wages over time, motor-vehicle safety—they can use the Internet to find what they need to know in seconds. If you want to design an educational package that is specifically for you, and for no one else, new technologies make it increasingly possible to do precisely that. More generally: if you are suspicious of the mass media and want to discuss current issues with like-minded people, you can do that too, transcending the limitations of geography in ways that could barely be imagined even a decade ago.

But in the midst of the celebration, the public forum doctrine suggests many reasons for caution. Serious risks accompany the growing power of consumers, including students, to "filter" what they see and hear. To be sure, personalization cannot and should not be avoided. Students are allowed to select the colleges and universities they want to attend, and that very selection is a form of personalization. In most institutions, students have a large measure of curricular choice as well. Few sensible people think that higher education should be entirely prescribed for students—that two years or four years of study should be fully selected by educators in advance. Hence the real question is the appropriate *level* of personalization: the extent to which students should be allowed to exclude what they dislike and to include what they like. I will not be able to specify that level here. But I will emphasize certain dangers that accompany personalization in a world in which freedom of choice is the watchword and in which the Internet and other technological developments increasingly enable people to filter in, and also to filter out, information and opinions with unprecedented powers of precision.

Of course, these developments make life much more convenient and in some ways much better. Students, like everyone else, seek to reduce their exposure to uninvited noise. But filtering is a mixed blessing. In a heterogeneous society, institutions of higher education, like democracy itself, should provide something other than free, or publicly unrestricted, individual choices. Invoking the notion of citizenship, I have suggested the importance of unanticipated encounters and shared experiences. Both of these are important in the academic setting.

To explore the issue, let us engage in a thought experiment: an apparently utopian dream, that of complete individuation, in which people, including students, can entirely personalize (or "customize") their universe. Let us imagine, that is, a system of communications and a system of higher education in which each citizen and each student has unlimited power of individual design.

For higher education, we can easily imagine a system in which students are able to use technologies, including the Internet, to select exactly what they would like to learn. If they want to learn only about math or only about English literature, they are entitled to do that. If they want to specialize in South America, that would be permissible as well. If they want teachers of a particular point of view—say, liberals who admire the student movements of the 1960s, or conservatives who lionize former U.S. president Ronald Reagan—they can do that as well. The exchange of ideas with others, or at least with unwanted others, can be avoided, as can encounters with those aspects of higher education that some dislike: football games, clubs, social organizations, and so forth. People can mix and match to the extent that the technology allows it.

At least as a matter of feasibility, our communications market is moving rapidly toward this picture. In terms of news itself, a number of publications allow readers to create filtered versions that contain exactly what they want and no more. For colleges and universities, the picture is similar, with many campuses and institutions increasing students' ability to create individuated learning. MIT professor Nicholas Negroponte refers to the emergence of the "Daily Me"—a communications package that is personally designed, with its components fully chosen in advance by the reader. We can likewise imagine a MyUniversity.com that will enable students to construct their own, personally designed, educational experience. And on many campuses, there is increasing interest in permitting students to do precisely that.

Of course this is not entirely different from what has come before. Not all people who read newspapers read the same newspaper; some people do not read any newspaper at all. People make choices among magazines based on their tastes and their point of view. Students choose many of their courses and professors. But in the emerging situation, there is a difference of degree if not of kind. What is different is the dramatic increase in individual control over content and the corresponding decrease in the power of general-interest intermediaries—the newspapers, magazines, television broadcasters, and educational administrations. For all their problems and their unmistakable limitations and biases, these intermediaries have performed some important democratic and educational functions.

Evaluated with an eye toward citizenship, education itself can be analyzed in the same terms. Completely centralized control over the content of a college or university, excluding student choice, is not desirable. But chance encounters, and even unwanted encounters, are a large part of a good education. A well-designed curriculum, no less than a public forum, exposes people to topics and points of view that they would not have specifically chosen in advance. And a well-designed campus will itself ensure such chance encounters, as students meet people engaged in very different activities and concerned with very different issues. And in conversations with diverse others, students will discover topics that can alter their interests and attentions, even change their lives. Here a campus has crucial advantages over a computer terminal. And insofar as there are distribution requirements that expose people to topics and ideas that they would not antecedently choose, a great deal is to be gained.

In fact, one risk with a system of perfect individual control, on campuses and elsewhere, is that it can reduce the importance of the "public sphere" and of common spaces in general. A key feature of such spaces is that they tend to ensure that people will encounter materials on important issues, whether or not they have specifically chosen the encounter. This point is closely connected to the public forum doctrine.

I have emphasized that in a system with public forums and general-interest intermediaries, people will frequently come across materials that they would not have chosen in advance. For diverse citizens, this provides something like a common framework for social experience. The same point is certainly true for students. But for members of a democratic society, or students in higher education, a system of personalization will change things significantly.

Consider some simple facts. If you take the ten most highly rated television programs for whites and then take the ten most highly rated programs for African Americans, you will find little overlap between them. Indeed, over half of the ten most highly rated programs for African Americans rank among the ten *least* popular programs for whites. Similar racial divisions can be found on the Internet. Not surprisingly, many people tend to choose like-minded sites and like-minded discussion groups. Many of those with committed views on a topic—gun control, abortion, affirmative action—speak mostly with each other. It is exceedingly rare for a site with an identifiable point of view to provide links to sites with opposing views, but it is very common for such a site to provide links to like-minded sites. We can easily imagine personalization having the same consequence for higher education, with like-minded people increasingly congregating together, either virtually or face to face.

GROUP POLARIZATION

We can sharpen our understanding of this problem if we attend to the phenomenon of *group polarization*. The idea behind group polarization is that after deliberating with one another, people in a group are likely to move toward a more extreme point in the direction to which they were previously inclined, as indicated by the median of their predeliberation judgments.[11] Consider some examples of the phenomenon of group polarization, which has been found in over a dozen nations:

- After discussion, citizens of France become more critical of the United States and its intentions with respect to economic aid.
- After discussion, whites predisposed to show racial prejudice offer more negative responses to the question of whether white racism is responsible for conditions faced by African Americans in U.S. cities.
- After discussion, whites predisposed not to show racial prejudice offer more positive responses to the same question.
- After discussion, moderately profeminist women become more strongly profeminist.

It follows that after discussion with one another, those inclined to favor more aggressive affirmative-action programs will become quite extreme on the issue, and that after talking together, those who believe that tax rates are too high will come to think that large, immediate tax reductions are an extremely good idea.

The phenomenon of group polarization has conspicuous importance for personalized education and personalized democracy. The likely result of personalization is that groups with distinctive identities will increasingly engage in within-group discussion. Consider a central problem for democracy. If the public is balkanized and if different groups design their own preferred communications and educational packages, the consequence will be further balkanization, as group members move each other toward more extreme points in line with their initial tendencies. At the same time, differing groups, each consisting of like-minded people, will be driven increasingly far apart, simply because most of their discussions are with members of their own group. Extremist groups will become more extreme. And in fact, group polarization is occurring every day on the Internet. Personalized communications can contribute to the problem. A good system of education should counteract this risk by exposing people to a wide variety of perspectives. And a personalized system of education will fortify rather than reduce the problem. If such a system allows like-minded people to congregate with one another, it will undermine learning itself, simply because such people are likely to move one another to increasingly extreme positions.

CONSUMERS, CITIZENS, AND EDUCATION

Finally, it is important to consider the basic ideal of "consumer sovereignty," which underlies much of the contemporary enthusiasm for personalization in education and elsewhere. Consumer sovereignty means that people can choose to purchase, or to obtain, whatever they want. For many purposes, this is a worthy ideal, and it animates economic markets themselves. But the adverse effects of group polarization show that in communications and education, consumer sovereignty is likely to produce serious problems for individuals and society at large—and that these problems will occur by a kind of iron logic of social interactions. Education is not an ordinary commodity, in part because it should shape preferences and values, not merely cater to them. People are citizens, not merely consumers, and education, properly conceived and operated, is a breeding ground for citizenship. A system of personalization threatens to undermine that ideal. The issue can be sharpened in the educational setting. For many students, a valuable part of higher education comes from classes and experiences that are widely shared by diverse people. These shared experiences are prized both at the time and in retrospect. If a campus is simply a collection of diverse groups lacking such experiences, the process of education will seriously suffer.

What are the particular implications of these points for education or for democracy? I cannot spell them out in this space. The most general point is that a well-functioning system of communications does not focus only on consumer sovereignty; it seeks to promote the conditions for deliberative democracy. Hence it tries to ensure that people do not live in gated communities of any kind. With respect to education, the implications involve both admissions and curriculum. A sensible system of admissions attempts to ensure not merely excellence but also diversity of many different kinds. A university that has students from many states and countries, for example, will to that extent provide better learning, simply because students will have a much broader stock of experiences on which to draw. A diverse array of students, or for that matter faculty, will by itself provide a set of unanticipated exposure to topics and ideas.

In terms of curriculum, an appreciation of the public forum analogy suggests the sense of the old idea of compulsory courses, designed to provide shared experiences for diverse students and at the same time to expose them to materials that they would not have selected in advance. A general recognition to this effect does not require any specific kind of design. It certainly does not suggest that the best choices can be found in the standard core curricula. Perhaps some of them reflect sensible decisions; undoubtedly some of them can be greatly improved. Nor have I suggested that total prescription is a good idea. The only claim is the modest one: freedom of choice is not an appropriate foundation for a system of education, just as it is an incomplete basis for a system of communications.

WELL BEYOND PERSONALIZATION

I have urged that complete personalization creates risks to both democracy and institutions of higher education. I have not emphasized the standard reason for concern: that students often lack the information that would enable them to make fully informed choices. That point is correct, but my broader claim is that both a well-functioning democracy and a well-functioning system of higher education require that people be exposed to unanticipated, unchosen encounters and that people share a range of common experiences. When a democracy or a campus is working well, these two requirements are met.

I have argued here that the provision of culture should be seen not only in terms of free markets but also in the light of the public forum doctrine. The reason is that people's values and tastes are produced by cultural offerings, not simply reflected by them. This point certainly does not mean that government should be permitted to mold tastes as it sees fit. Efforts of this kind would be palpably unconstitutional (and futile to boot). But it does mean that in a properly decentralized system offering a range of offerings and opportunities, it is proper for both private and public institutions to have aspirations and goals that produce offerings that diverge, some of the time, from people's consumption choices.

I have suggested that the public forum doctrine provides a helpful way of thinking about democratic principles and about education for citizenship. This is especially so insofar as it promotes a range of shared experiences and also exposes people to materials that they would not have specifically chosen in advance. A democratic society does not value gated communities, in which people use a kind of MyChoices.com to see exactly what they like and to filter out everything else. Of course such a society prizes freedom of choice, which has a large place in any social order that claims to be democratic. But such an order also prizes institutions and arrangements that expose people to materials that they would not have chosen in advance, not because it rejects freedom, but because it wants to ensure it.

NOTES

1. This argument should be seen as a development and extension of the argument in Cass R. Sunstein, *Republic.com* (Princeton, N.J.: Princeton University Press, 2000).

2. *Hague v. CIO,* 307 US 496 (1939). For present purposes, it is not necessary to discuss the public forum doctrine in detail. Interested readers might consult Geoffrey Stone et al., *The First Amendment* (New York: Aspen, 1999), 286–330.

3. See the excellent discussion in Noah D. Zatz, "Sidewalks in Cyberspace: Making Space for Public Forums in the Electronic Environment," *Harvard Journal of Law and Technology* 12, no. 1 (Fall 1998): 149.

4. For elaboration, see Sunstein, *Republic.com.*

5. Robert H. Frank and Philip J. Cook, *The Winner-Take-All Society* (New York: Penguin Books, 1996), 243.

6. Alexis de Tocqueville, *Democracy in America*, ed. J. P. Mayer, trans. George Lawrence (New York: Harper & Row, 1988), 317.

7. John Dewey, "The Future of Liberalism," in *Dewey and His Critics: Essays from the Journal of Philosophy,* ed. Sidney Morgenbesser (New York: Journal of Philosophy, 1978), 695, 697.

8. For detailed discussion, see Sunstein, *Republic.com.*

9. See Roger Brown, *Social Psychology,* 2nd ed. (New York: Free Press, 1985).

10. See *Columbia Broadcasting System v. Democratic National Committee,* 412 US 94 (1973).

11. See Cass R. Sunstein, *Why Societies Need Dissent* (Cambridge, Mass.: Harvard University Press, 2003).

SEVEN

The Culture of Expedience
Liberal Education Meets
the "Real" World

JAMES B. STEWART

R ichard Rescorla was at his desk on the forty-fourth floor of Two
World Trade Center when he heard an explosion rock the complex.
His first thought was that it was a bomb, perhaps another truck bomb like
the one that exploded in 1993. Then, as head of security of Morgan
Stanley Dean Witter, he had overseen the evacuation of all the firm's
employees. But he had been expecting such an attack for the past eight
years. Indeed, he and his best friend, Dan Hill, a former army colleague
whom he'd hired as a consultant on antiterrorism measures, had prepared
a written report warning that Islamic fundamentalists would never rest
until the World Trade Center, which they believed to be the "towers in the
sky" described in the Koran, was destroyed. They warned that the most
effective means to do so was by flying a plane into the towers, preferably a
large cargo plane loaded with explosives. The Port Authority of New York
and New Jersey, which owned the complex, had ignored the report.

Rescorla grabbed his suit jacket and bullhorn and headed toward the
stairwells. Out the large windows he could see the flames pouring from
tower 1, papers and debris falling from the upper floors. Unlike many,
Rescorla had remained vigilant during the intervening years, designating numerous deputies and requiring elaborate evacuation drills. Morgan

Stanley was the largest employer in the trade center, with 2,700 employees in the south tower. Now they dutifully organized on each floor and began the descent through the stairwells to the forty-fourth floor sky lobby, where Rescorla greeted them. Although Port Authority officials were using the public address system to order people to remain at their desks, Rescorla countermanded the order. As he told Dan Hill on his cell phone, "Everything above where that plane hit is going to collapse, and it's going to take the whole building with it. I'm getting my people the f—— out of here."

This is how I described the scene on the forty-fourth floor after interviewing Kathy Comerford, an event planner for Morgan Stanley.

Suddenly a huge blast shook the building. Bulbs in the chandeliers exploded, all lights went out, and the floor plunged into darkness. Comerford was blown out of her sandals and thrown hard against the marble surface that surrounded the elevator doors. She heard a tremendous rush of air in the elevator shaft, as if an enormous vacuum had been released. She staggered to her feet, her shoulder throbbing, and noticed Rescorla trying to regain his footing next to her. But it was hard to stand. She couldn't find her shoes. The floor was undulating in huge waves, as if she were on a roller coaster. She felt the entire tower lean precariously. Suddenly it snapped back to vertical, again throwing people to the floor. People started running to the stairwell, pushing and trampling one another. But that stairwell had filled with smoke. People were beginning to panic. Comerford felt her heart pounding.

Then Comerford heard Rescorla's voice. "Stop!" he commanded. "Stay calm. There's another staircase." His tone was measured, but there was an element of steel in it that made people obey. The crowd fell silent. "The lights are going to come back on momentarily," he assured them. Then, as if by a miracle, the emergency generator began to function, and lights did appear. People looked around, dazed. Rescorla spoke continuously through the bullhorn in soothing, repetitive tones. "Be still," he said quietly. "Be silent. Be calm." No one spoke or moved. It was as if Rescorla had cast a spell. One of Rescorla's staff appeared. "Is it clear?" Rescorla asked.

"Yes," he answered.

"OK, everyone," Rescorla said. "The northeast staircase is clear." He pointed in that direction. "Let's move. Stay calm. Watch your partner."

Two by two, they evacuated. Rescorla was seen by the last to leave on the tenth floor. Then, he began to climb the stairs again. He never returned. Tape recordings of the final communications between fire-fighters in the moments before the tower collapsed indicate that he reached a group of people, still alive, who were trapped on the seventy-eighth floor.

My telling of the Rescorla story, first in the *New Yorker* and then, much expanded, in my book *Heart of a Soldier*[1] took some readers by surprise, since much of my best-known work focuses on scandal, cor-ruption, and personal greed, featuring characters who are the antithesis of a Rick Rescorla or a Dan Hill. My most recent story for the *New Yorker*, "Spend, Spend, Spend!"[2] recounts the rise and fall of Dennis Kozlowski, the chairman and CEO of Tyco International, who, in a year in which he was paid $190 million in compensation, nonetheless felt compelled to evade several million dollars in sales taxes on multimillion-dollar art purchases and was subsequently accused of looting the company of approximately $400 million. Or Michael Milken, the former junk bond king and main character in *Den of Thieves*,[3] who paid himself a bonus of $750 million in 1987, much of it extracted from soon-to-be defunct sav-ings and loans, while publicly maintaining that he "was never interested in money."

And yet all of these works focus on critical moments of moral deci-sion making, in which people face a clearly defined choice between self-interest and the interests of a broader community. In many instances, these interests can be quantified: in the Milken case, for example, the choice between vast personal wealth and the billions in losses suffered by investors as a consequence. Or Kozlowski's choice between personal gain and the interests of Tyco shareholders and taxpayers. Rescorla, too, faced a stark choice between self-interest—indeed, self-preservation—and the interests of the community he served, in this case, workers in the World Trade Center. What interests me as a writer and a reporter is not just the choices these people make, but why.

For these motives, in any story of complexity and nuance, are hardly self-evident. In the financial cases, you might say the obvious motive is money. Yet we are not dealing with a Jean Valjean in *Les Misérables*, steal-ing a silver candlestick to buy a loaf of bread. Milken, Kozlowski, and others were already wealthy, vastly so. They had no rational need for greater wealth. Rescorla, too, had no need to return to the stricken tower. He had gotten almost all of his people safely out of the building. He was not a policeman, he was not a fireman; his job description did not require him to continue to risk his own life. He would surely have been lauded as a national hero had he simply left with his employees and returned to Susan, the wife he loved so much and had met only three years before. Why did he go back?

The decisions on which these stories turn, besides being highly dramatic, are also extremely focused and clear-cut. They do not occur in the shifting sands of moral ambiguity. They would be ill suited for issue-spotting exercises on bar exams and in ethics courses. The moral choices, the difference between right and wrong, are as plain as day, not just to observers like myself, but to the participants themselves. Many of the wrongdoers, like Milken, not only pleaded guilty to felonies but, both by subsequent admission and by their actions at the time, clearly knew that what they were doing was wrong. It is impossible to know exactly what was in Rescorla's mind when he made his fateful decision, but it is clear from his last conversation with Hill that he was acting out of a sense of a purpose that transcended the value of his own life. As Hill put it, had Rescorla not gone back into the tower, his sense of honor was such that he would have had to commit suicide. Thus, the characters in these stories act out of a clear sense of purpose, not negligence, confusion, or inadvertence. This gives their stories an unambiguous moral dimension.

Finally, and especially apropos our theme at this symposium, all of these decisions, by their very nature, not only transgress or reaffirm existing community standards. They call into question the very existence of a community in any meaningful sense, since the idea of community implies that there are values that take precedence over self-interest. A conscious decision to break the law takes on a very different connotation when moral authority and enforcement have collapsed and "everyone is doing it"—the most common refrain on Wall Street in the 1980s and in corporate boardrooms during the past few years.

As a result, all of these stories also hold up a mirror to our own life and times. It is perhaps just as troubling that the behavior of a Rescorla would be deemed so extraordinary as that the felonies of a Milken or the alleged misdeeds of a Kozlowski would be seen as commonplace.

Before exploring in greater detail the motives and the broader implications of some of the characters in my work, I should mention something that is probably already obvious, which is that in contrast to other participants in this distinguished symposium, I am not an academic and do not bring formal academic training to my observations. My work often touches upon many academic disciplines—psychology, economics, political science, history, the sciences, and, of course, literature. But I claim no particular expertise in any of these fields. I do share the academic commitment to truth, and to the best of my ability, my observations and writings, my stories, are true.

Perhaps my status carries an inherent advantage, in that I come from what students like to describe as "the real world." It may be true that my status in that world is somewhat suspect: journalists as a group are accorded little respect by the public at large, and I drift through that world with a peculiar license to ask questions and interrupt people going about their business. I am often chided by friends for not having a "real" job. Still, I can attest that the moral dilemmas that seem somewhat abstract from the perspective of the classroom do in fact occur almost constantly and often in the least likely places. I have written lengthy stories, even books, not just about public figures like President Clinton and Hillary Clinton, Milken and Ivan Boesky, but also about an assembly-line worker in Detroit, an accountant in Harrisburg, Pennsylvania, a piano saleswoman in New York City, and a doctor from my hometown of Quincy, Illinois, who turned out to be a serial killer.

In nearly all of these examples, I have been fascinated by the role that education has played in the development of character and personality and the degree to which their academic experiences help explain their subsequent fateful decisions. This was especially true in the case of Rescorla, since not only were his moral choices the opposite of many on Wall Street, for example, but so was his education: he lacked a college degree (until he earned one relatively late in life) and was largely self-taught; many of those ensnared by scandal not only occupied highly paid positions carrying immense prestige, but they also boasted glittering academic résumés: Milken was a graduate of Berkeley and the Wharton School at the University of Pennsylvania; Martin Siegel, head of mergers and acquisitions at Kidder Peabody, who went to prison for insider trading, earned bachelor's and master's degrees at Rensselaer Polytechnic Institute and graduated with distinction from Harvard Business School; Robert Wilkis, a conspirator with Dennis Levine who also went to prison, graduated with honors from Harvard and Stanford Business School. Kozlowski graduated from Rutgers and later served as a trustee of both Rutgers and Bennington College; and even Ivan Boesky, though he hid the fact that he never graduated from college, boasted an impressive résumé: the Cranbrook School, the University of Michigan, and membership on the Board of Overseers of the Harvard School of Public Health. He acquired his overseer position through lavish donations to Harvard, which also secured him membership at the Harvard Club of New York City. The club's distinguished McKim, Mead and White quarters on West Forty-fourth Street proved to be the setting for some of Boesky's most brazen insider trading activities.

Boesky's concern about the appearance of education, if not the reality, was a trait shared to varying degrees by nearly all the Wall Street felons I wrote about, including many who had actually earned their prestigious degrees. Their educations seemed little more than another notch in the belt of "success," a way station to high-paying, powerful jobs that in turn led to greater wealth and influence. Indeed, for the most part, they exhibited a disdain for colleagues who were actually sidetracked by the substance of their educations, and they were particularly contemptuous of academics, including their own professors, even as they assiduously courted and flattered them in their quest for high marks.

These attitudes were particularly evident in the case of Dennis Levine, whose massive insider trading and wide-ranging conspiracy eventually led to the downfall of Boesky, Milken, and ultimately the firm where he worked, Drexel, Burnham, and Lambert. I can claim no clairvoyance here, but I thought Dennis Levine was a phony the moment I met him, and he insisted on constantly putting his arm around my shoulders and clapping me on the back. A revealing anecdote, I learned, was that at the age of thirty he was made head of mergers and acquisitions at Drexel, Burnham, a post for which he was manifestly unqualified. And his boss called him in for his first bonus review, and said, "Dennis, I'm going to make you very happy, your bonus this year is a million dollars." At which point Dennis said, "That's an insult," and walked out. The only thing more amazing to me about that is that the tactic worked, and he got more than a million dollars as his first bonus. At any event, as Levine so memorably put it, "Only morons would work for $50,000 a year"—at the time, I might add, the average salary of a tenured professor.

Levine did not have impressive academic credentials or an Ivy League degree, something that obsessed him. He grew up in a middle-class neighborhood of Queens, had rarely left the metropolitan area, and had compiled an undistinguished record at then-tuition-free Baruch College, a part of the City University of New York. At a time when many students were protesting the Vietnam War, Levine sought to distinguish himself by wearing a coat and tie to school every day. He avidly courted his teachers, certain he would need them as "contacts" later in his career. The only book that seems to have made an impression on Levine was called *The Financiers.*[4] He later showed a dog-eared copy of the book to Bob Wilkis, his coconspirator, whom he met when both were working in low-level jobs at Citicorp. He had highlighted in yellow those passages that described the bankers' lifestyles: their incomes, their Savile Row tailoring, their cars and estates. He seemed indifferent to what they actually did, which was to help others by rendering a professional service, in this case, to raise capital.

Levine alternately flattered and mocked Wilkis's Ivy League credentials. "You really went to Harvard and yet you'll talk to me?" he asked Wilkis at one of their early meetings. But he also routinely referred to Wilkis as a "left-wing pinkie commie." "You know your problem, Wilkis?" he asked. "You worry too much about the gray areas in life. That's where we're different. I have clear-cut goals. You don't."

Wilkis soon left Citicorp for a job at an international investment bank that was starting a unit to finance development projects in Third World countries. Levine was contemptuous. "I don't understand you," he said angrily. "You want to help the niggers and the spics? Why do you want to do this Third World crap?" Then Levine's tone shifted. "Bob, you're my friend. I only want you to do well. You're so naive. Wall Street is going to eat you up. No one cares about this left-wing shit of yours. They'll use you. You've got to think of yourself, your family. You've got to do more to help your mother."

Levine earned glowing performance reviews from his superiors for being "aggressive," "hungry," someone who wanted to "move fast." But just as the substance of Levine's education in fact meant nothing to him, so was he indifferent to his work. He shrewdly enlisted other employees to mask his deficiencies at basic math and accounting, and emphasized the trappings of success, such as the bright red Ferrari Testarossa he drove down Fifth Avenue. He was as contemptuous of clients as he was of his teachers. He often denounced his work as boring. The workplace was simply a stage on which he could enjoy playing the part of an investment banker. His "clear-cut goal" about which he boasted was to earn a fortune from insider information, and one of his first acts was to open a secret Swiss bank account. As he confided in Wilkis, "I knew after I was bar mitzvahed that there was an inside track and information was the key."

Wilkis did not immediately succumb to these blandishments, but Levine had already found a weakness in Wilkis's moral shield: the nagging belief, no doubt shared by many, that the values inculcated by his education, first at a private Hebrew school in Baltimore that stressed ethics and then at Harvard and Stanford, existed in some rarefied parallel universe to the one that he actually occupied. (I should say that this attitude is not all that uncommon among some of my students today at Columbia, and there have been rare cases where some have admitted, after failing essentially to perform any of the tasks I have assigned them, that they only enrolled in my course because I have a reputation for "contacts" elsewhere in the media and because some of my former students have landed enviable jobs.)

Back to Wilkis, on a later walk in Central Park, Levine asked Wilkis point-blank for confidential information about takeovers that were pending at Lazard Freres, where Wilkis was now working. Levine would trade on that information, but no one would suspect anything because Levine had no obvious connection to Lazard. Levine would in turn pass information to Wilkis about deals at Smith Barney, where he was employed. "It's easy," Levine told him. "All you need is the right setup. You could get rich, get out of Wall Street. You could go to Nepal, become a Buddhist monk. Isn't that what you want?"

"It's illegal, Dennis," Wilkis replied. "I'm scared." But for the next few weeks, Wilkis thought of little else. Wilkis's rationalizations were in fact quite sophisticated. Everyone on Wall Street seemed to be turning confidential information to their own advantage. What was the real harm? Didn't the legitimate work he was doing often enrich the investment bankers with little or no corresponding social good? Perhaps the ill-gotten gains would liberate Wilkis to pursue the work he believed in, if not to become a Buddhist monk then perhaps to teach in an inner-city school.

I could repeat variations on this exchange in numerous contexts. Wilkis did in fact join Levine's scheme and was eventually sentenced to eighteen months in a federal prison. To me, Wilkis, the corrupted, is an even more fascinating character than Levine, the corrupter. Levine was committed to crime at an early age. Wilkis wrestled with his decision over weeks and months. Wilkis also explicitly acknowledged that he knew his actions were wrong and illegal, yet he succumbed to temptation. It would be tempting to say that Wilkis's education had failed him, but I don't believe it is so simple. I think it would be more accurate to say that his native intelligence, his powers of analysis, and his broad education had been twisted to serve a sinister purpose. Nor was this uncommon. Often in my reporting I have discovered that the qualities cultivated by a liberal education—powers of insight, analysis, and communication—can as easily serve immoral or illegal purposes as honorable ends. It isn't enough simply to be aware of community standards and the reasons for their existence; it requires a commitment to them that transcends perceptions of immediate self-interest.

Of course I suppose I should also mention the obvious, which is that these calculations of self-interest in the case of Levine and Wilkis turned out to be wrong. Their impulse to achieve short-term gains by breaking the law landed them in prison. It effectively destroyed their careers, not to mention their future income potential. But I think ultimately if the question becomes simply a sophisticated measurement of risk—and let's face it, there are probably people who accurately calculate that and are not, as Levine and Wilkis were, caught—if it has come to that, if there is no moral underpinning, then the education has already failed.

Human motivation is of course an enormously complicated subject: the influence of family, friends, religious figures, and others should not be discounted, nor can educational influences be weighed in a vacuum. And yet I have found the educational parallels among wrongdoers, at least the affluent, highly educated white-collar criminals who have been the subject of much of my work, to be striking. So, too, is their contrast to someone like Rescorla.

Rick Rescorla was born just before World War II in Hayle, a Cornish seaport whose iron and copper industries had long ago fallen to marginal status. He grew up in an unusual family situation, believing that his grandparents were his parents. In fact his "sister" was his mother, and he never learned the identity of his father. No one in Hayle ever mentioned this to him, and he learned the truth only after he had immigrated to America, when his grandfather was near death.

Though the family had modest means and lacked university educations, the young Cyril (his given name, which he hated) was encouraged to read, often doing so under the kitchen table. His performance on standardized tests earned him a place at Penzance grammar school, where he commuted by train. Having had a somewhat romantic view of English schools, I was somewhat surprised to learn that a grammar school education in Britain in the 1940s was no better than in America, and may have been worse, characterized by unruly behavior, frequent corporal punishment, and indifferent teachers. Rescorla's love of music and literature, so pronounced in later life, can hardly have been incubated in Penzance. The music teacher, after distributing recorders still damp from the previous class, sternly lectured that if anyone made a sound without permission, the instruments would be confiscated. One of the boys promptly emitted an ear-piercing shriek from his recorder, and that was the last of the class's music education. Rescorla auditioned for the choir, but his effort was halted after three notes of "Do, Re, Mi." The only required works of literature were Swift's *Gulliver's Travels*, Chaucer's prologue to the *Canterbury Tales*, and Shakespeare's *Romeo and Juliet*.

Rescorla excelled at athletics, especially rugby. But at sixteen, even though he passed the so-called O-level examinations, which entitled him to two subsequent years of a preuniversity curriculum, Rescorla was apprenticed to the post office and attended a local technical college one day a week. To escape his provincial origins, Rescorla, like many before him, enlisted in the British military and in 1957 was assigned to a British intelligence unit then fighting a communist-backed insurgency on the Mediterranean island of Cyprus.

Dan Hill met Rescorla in 1960 in what was then the British colony of Northern Rhodesia. In the intervening three years Rescorla had completed his tour in Cyprus and joined the Northern Rhodesia police force. In those years he had somehow completed a remarkable course of self-education. Soon after they met, and Hill moved in with Rescorla in the British barracks at Kitwe, Rhodesia, Rescorla read aloud to Hill the short story by Rudyard Kipling "The Man Who Would Be King," a story destined to have a profound impact on their lives. Apart from the unusual role that literature played in Rescorla's life—I found it remarkable that he would initiate what turned out to be a lifelong friendship by reading aloud from a work of fiction—Rescorla also kept the entire set of the Harvard Classics on his barracks shelf and told Hill that he had read all of the volumes.

The fifty volumes of the Harvard Classics were once as familiar as the *Encyclopaedia Britannica* and were compiled in the early twentieth century by then Harvard University president Charles W. Eliot.[5] A reading course "unparalleled in comprehensiveness and authority," as they were described, they were thought to constitute the essence of a liberal education. They made such an impression on Rescorla that he later gave a set to Hill, which he still proudly displays at his home in St. Augustine, Florida. Today, forty-three years later, Hill is still trying to read his way through them.

Although the notion that certain "great books" lie at the heart of a liberal arts education has fallen from favor (though it lives on at a few places like Columbia and St. John's), the idea still lurks somewhere in most college curricula, and vestiges of it live on in the form of graduation requirements. I daresay that few of us today have read most of these works in their entirety: not just classics like Homer, Plato, Aeschylus, Sophocles, Plutarch, and Virgil, as well as all the major writers covered by Professor Calvert in my own college course in political theory at DePauw, but also extensive passages from the Bible, the Buddha's teachings, the Bhagavad-Gita, the Koran; the *Autobiography* of Benjamin Franklin and *Some Fruits of Solitude* by William Penn; three volumes of English poetry; and *On the Antiseptic Principle of the Practice of Surgery* by Joseph Lister. By today's standards, of course, it is a curriculum preserved in amber. No women are represented, not to mention minorities. If Rescorla actually read all fifty volumes of these works, he must have had ample free time during his tour of duty on Cyprus and then in Africa, but to my skepticism Hill insisted that Rescorla could quote passages from nearly any of these works that came up in conversation, and they frequently did.

Still, the writer who made the most profound impression on Rescorla, and subsequently Hill, was Rudyard Kipling. I don't know how Rescorla discovered Kipling; once the most widely read author in English, the recipient of a Nobel Prize, he had largely fallen from favor by World War II and had been dropped from the standard curriculum, even in England. But Churchill was a great admirer, and Rescorla in turn revered Churchill: his *History of the English-Speaking Peoples* also adorned Rescorla's shelves. In any event, it was Kipling whom Rescorla chose to read aloud to Hill.

Far from the academy, it is unlikely that Rescorla's reading of Kipling would have been colored by the stain that has darkened Kipling's reputation: that he was a racist apologist for colonialism. In 1964, the Methodist Church dropped from its hymnal what is arguably Kipling's most famous poem, "Recessional," on the grounds that the poem contained, according to the Methodists, "an unmistakable racial slur."

Another of his most famous works, "The White Man's Burden," has been widely reviled on similar grounds, and of course there is his famous aphorism, "East is East and West is West."

Growing up in colonial India, then at boarding school in England, Kipling was undeniably shaped by his times, which were the heyday of Queen Victoria and the British Empire. By today's standards, many of his word choices are inappropriate or even insulting. But in my view, Kipling's stature seems long overdue for a serious reappraisal, a point made by David Gilmour's recent biography of Kipling, *The Long Recessional*,[6] though Gilmour himself, a British biographer and former Oxford fellow, doesn't really supply it. Having reread both "Recessional" and "The White Man's Burden" recently myself, I could make the case that both are in fact bitter cries against colonialism, all the more remarkable given the prevailing norms of Kipling's time. Consider in light of current events this passage, from "The White Man's Burden": "Take up the white man's burden—and reap his old reward: The blame of those ye better, the hate of those ye guard." But in any event, neither of these poems figured in Rescorla's reverence for Kipling.

The works that he turned to again and again were "The Man Who Would Be King" and the poem "If." I think "If" is worth reading in its entirety, but these famous stanzas had a profound impact on Rescorla:

If you can force your heart and nerve and sinew
To serve your turn long after they are gone,
And so to hold on when there is nothing in you,
Except the Will which says to them: "Hold on!"

If all men count with you, but none too much;
If you can fill the unforgiving minute
With sixty seconds' worth of distance run,
Yours is the Earth and everything that's in it,
And—which is more—you'll be a Man, my son.

Condensed into a very few phrases are some of the most important aspects of Rescorla's character: his strength of will; his generosity of spirit toward his fellow man, of whatever race, nationality, or economic status; the notion that every minute in life counts and should be filled with the utmost exertion; and, finally, that this is the essence of what it is to be human, which is ultimately its own reward: the Earth and everything that's in it.

Like Woodrow Wilson before him, Rescorla always carried a copy of "If" in his wallet. He gave a copy to Dan, who came to have somewhat more ambivalent feelings about the poem after he in turn gave a copy to a young protégé who was killed in Vietnam. Hill worried—he still worries—that the poem's celebration of boundless effort led the young man to his death. But Rescorla himself never wavered.

"The Man Who Would Be King" warrants somewhat more discussion, and I spent considerable time on the story in the text of *Heart of a Soldier* as it appears in the context of Rescorla's and Hill's lives. In fact, in terms of foreshadowing, I felt I had all but hit readers over the head with a sledgehammer. And yet only one reviewer, Janet Maslin in the *New York Times*, made any reference to the story and the amazing degree to which it anticipates the lives of Rescorla and Hill.

The story's two main characters, Peachey Carnahan and Daniel Dravot, of indeterminate but humble origins and adrift on the fringes of the British Empire, choose as their prospective kingdom the province of Kafiristan (in reality Nuristan) in northern Afghanistan. The key to their plan is to take with them a case of 450 Snider rifles and use them to organize a fighting force. "In any place where they fight, a man who knows how to drill men can always be a King," Peachey tells the story's narrator. "We shall go to these parts and say to any King we find, 'D' you want to vanquish your foes?' and we will show them how to drill men; for that we know better than anything else. Then we will subvert that King and seize his throne and establish a Dynasty.'" They sign a contract to rule as equals, to forswear alcohol and women, and "to conduct ourselves with Dignity and Discretion, and if one of us gets into trouble the other will stay by him."

In Afghanistan they do become kings, first Dravot and then, after the region is subdued by their infantry, Peachey as well. They are worshipped as gods and direct descendants of Alexander the Great, whose troops passed through in 300 B.C. and whose blue-eyed descendants still inhabit Nuristan. Dravot is beloved by his people; Peachey, feared. Someday, Dravot promises, when everything was "shipshape," he would bow before Queen Victoria and surrender his crown to British authority. "And she'd say, 'Rise up, Sir Daniel Dravot.'"

It all ends badly. Breaking their contract, and in defiance of local custom, Dravot insists on taking a wife. When the terrified girl is presented for his approval and he asks for a kiss, she bites him, drawing blood. Local tribal leaders are shocked by this evidence that Dravot is as human as they are. His authority collapses. His troops mutiny, and his weapons are turned against him and Peachey.

They flee but are trapped by advancing troops in the rugged mountains. Dravot turns to Peachey. "'I've brought you to this,' says he. 'Brought you out of your happy life to be killed in Kafiristan, where you was late Commander-in-Chief of the Emperor's forces. Say you forgive me, Peachey.' 'I do,' says Peachey. 'Fully and freely do I forgive you, Dan.' 'Shake hands, Peachey,' says he. 'I'm going now.'"

Dravot walks onto a rope bridge precariously spanning a deep ravine. "'Cut, you beggars,' he shouts, and they cut, and old Dan fell, turning round and round and round, twenty thousand miles, for he took half an hour to fall till he struck the water, and I could see his body caught on a rock with the gold crown close beside."

Peachey is captured, crucified, and left for dead. Horribly disfigured, he makes his way back to India, where he finds the narrator and manages to tell his story. Dismissed as deranged and incoherent, he is taken to an asylum, soon to die. As Peachey is led away at the end of the story, he sings an odd song:

> The Son of Man goes forth to war,
> A golden crown to gain;
> His blood-red banner streams afar—
> Who follows in his train?

I find "The Man Who Would Be King" to be a great short story, certainly one of Kipling's best (the movie version, starring Sean Connery and Michael Caine, has an avid following). Counter to the Kipling stereotype, I find it difficult to interpret it as anything but a denunciation of colonialism. Peachey's crucifixion and parting song clearly invoke the bloody history of the Crusades and the madness of religious warfare.

And yet we sympathize with the characters' grand ambitions despite their illusions. Rescorla said explicitly that he saw himself as Dravot and Hill as Peachey. Surely not because they embarked on an ill-fated, neo-colonial conquest, even with benign motives, but because of their fierce determination to better themselves, their courage and fearlessness, and the depth of their loyalty and friendship. I found it extraordinary that the story unfolds in Afghanistan, where Dan Hill, a convert to Islam, would later fight with the Mujahadeen against the Soviet invaders (in the province of Nuristan, no less), and the very country engulfed in war as a result of the attacks on September 11. And I was haunted by the image of Dravot's fate, his surreal descent of "twenty thousand miles," when I pondered Rescorla's fall from high in the World Trade Center into—what?

The parallels are so striking that I have often had to wonder how much Rescorla and Hill consciously modeled their own lives after the characters they experienced through literature, especially Peachey and Dravot. I sense they did so to a remarkable degree. Not only did they lead lives worthy of a Kipling or a Conrad, but they lay awake at night in the jungles of Vietnam discussing the American Constitution and the role of the military in a democracy. They came to oppose the U.S. war effort in Vietnam, and in a remarkable interview recorded on videotape several years before he died, Rescorla warned of the dangers of terrorism, the threat of unconventional war, and the seeds of anti-Americanism being sown by the arrogant economic exploitation of other countries and cultures by American-led capitalism. Rescorla was a consistent and vocal opponent of racism and prejudice. His much-admired top deputy, Wesley Mercer, was African-American and gay, and he followed Rescorla to his death. And if you think such tolerance can be taken for granted, even today, consider the fact that Morgan Stanley would not allow Mercer's domestic partner to sit with other family members of victims at the memorial service at St. Patrick's Cathedral. Heartbroken, his companion stayed away.

Beyond the obvious literary dimensions of their remarkable lives, Rescorla and Hill absorbed a capacity for moral judgment and analysis, an appreciation of nuance and ambiguity and foresight, that are surely among the most estimable goals of education. I find it significant that despite his extensive military training and experience, on September 11 Rescorla saved thousands of lives because he defied rather than followed the orders of his superiors at the Port Authority, owners of the World Trade Center. At the same time, it would be unrealistic and a disservice to suggest that Rescorla had no flaws. He was hardly an ideal parent. He had strained relations with his two children, especially his son, Trevor. He was dismissed as a coach of his son's soccer team and then expelled from matches altogether for what was deemed inappropriately aggressive behavior. His relations with women were sometimes awkward. He grew up in a world that was largely segregated by sex. And the only women on his staff were low-level administrators or clerks. But when tragedy struck, it was as if everything in Rescorla's education and experience had prepared him to rise to this one, extraordinary, occasion.

It is of course impossible to know with any precision what was going through Rescorla's mind when he made the decision to go back up into the tower to search for survivors. But his last cell phone conversations make clear that he knew his life was at risk: Hill told him that tower 2, his tower, would be the first to collapse and that catastrophe was imminent. Rescorla's final words to his wife Susan—"I want you to know that you made my life"—suggest an awareness that he would not return. The writing in his diary in the weeks before his death also suggests a powerful sense of duty to his fellow man and an overriding need to redeem the deaths of his men that he experienced in Vietnam. Whatever the precise motives, he must have acted with the knowledge not only that he was risking his own life but also that he was leaving behind his wife and best friend, forgoing the joys of their companionship, and leaving them to lives without him.

This was something that proved extraordinarily difficult for Susan, and for Dan as well. As Susan finally confided in Dan, "What's really difficult for me is that I know he had a choice. He chose to go back in there. I can understand why he went back. What I can't understand is why I was left behind. I'm afraid he didn't love me." Dan did his best to comfort Susan by explaining that this was Rick's nature, and that was why she loved him in the first place. But even Dan has wrestled with Rick's loss. As he told me in a letter,

> Kipling wrote that "all men should count with you, but none too much." I failed there. Rick counted as the world to me. Somebody cautioned that if a person or thing means the world to you, and you lose that person or thing, then you have lost the world. I lost the world when Rick died.

In writing Rescorla's story, I often had occasion to think of a passage from the book *From Dawn to Decadence*, by Jacques Barzun. In this recent cultural history of Western civilization, Barzun seems to suggest that the traditional epic disappeared in the modern era:

If, as critics seem to agree, *epic* means heroic, the Italian attempts at the genre must be called failures, or else classified under some other rubric. . . . Their authors knew but disregarded or misunderstood Aristotle's dictum that the source of interest in epic is character in the sense of "person of character." The hero must be firm in danger and undeviating from the line of duty. Achilles' defection at the opening of the *Iliad* is part of a struggle for power, and Aeneas is not afraid to boast: "I am the faithful Aeneas," meaning faithful to his mission—and therefore unfaithful to Dido. This artistic principle excludes the self-indulgence of the lovelorn. To be sure, there are love passages in the *Odyssey* and the *Aeneid,* but they are few, brief, and shown as hindrances, not priorities. In the 8C *Song of Roland,* the only mention of a woman in love—Roland's betrothed Aude—is half a stanza about her death from grief at his being killed. In the Italians' would-be epics the women are finer, stronger characters than the men—another sign that the tone of the poems was up to date. . . .

Reasons for the eclipse of a classic are not easy to find. . . .

[T]here is the ever-watchful Boredom, ready to pounce and destroy what has been too often tasted and touted. And when the really new is abundant, as it was in the Romanticist period, it swamps the old by sheer weight of numbers. Finally, there is the pressure of social evolution. The sequence of dominant genres during our half millennium has paralleled the march of the Individual toward equality; it runs: epic, tragedy, the lyric speaking for the self, and the novel and the play in prose criticizing life. This is to say that it goes from the hero of a whole people to the great hero of tragedy, to the common-man hero, to the anti-hero.[7]

I think another way of putting this is that modern society simply lacks the defining standards of community that would yield a cause that would be worth dying for.

Recently I saw a production at the Metropolitan Opera of Berlioz's *Les Troyens,* which in operatic form tells Homer's epic the *Aeneid,* the story of Cassandra's warnings about the Trojan horse, Aeneas's flight to Carthage, his love for Dido, and finally his decision to leave her behind in order to found Rome. The parallels to Rescorla are obvious—his unheeded warnings, the solace he found in his love for Susan, and his decision to leave her behind in the pursuit of a higher purpose. Were the gods whispering in Rescorla's ear, as they did in Aeneas's?

So I think Barzun was wrong, or at least premature. Such stories, now as in centuries past, handed down from one generation to another, are the underpinnings of community. This is not simply because they tell the story of a hero, someone who embraces duty over self-interest—it is because the hero's act of selflessness in and of itself is both born out of and transcends the wickedness, depravity, and indifference to suffering that would otherwise make life intolerable.

I think Rescorla knew this, knew that if he died, it would be in a moment that would honor all of those characters, real and fictional, that he so admired and that had shaped his life. In stark contrast to the wrongdoers I have so often written about, what he and Hill absorbed from their wide readings was never at one remove from their identities, something to adorn their résumés. It had become the essence of who they were.

As writers and educators, we could hardly hope for more.

How can this kind of education be instilled at America's colleges and universities today? We live in a vastly more complex and morally ambiguous society than did prior generations. Homer lived at a time when he could take for granted that his audience would recognize Aeneas's heroism in his decision to leave Dido and pursue his duty to found Rome. We live in a time when many revere Osama bin Laden as a hero. Many others grow queasy at any invocation of the notion of heroism. After all, heroes arrogate to themselves the right to make moral judgments that will affect the lives of others, something that flies in the face of unbridled individualism. Even Rick's wife, much as she admired him, would have preferred him to stay alive and come home, as have countless women in history who have lost their husbands and lovers to military combat. Heroism is small comfort in the face of loneliness and loss.

Conversely, the notion of villainy requires shared moral standards that have eroded or disappeared. Hence, the continuing admiration for Milken.

But one need not judge these characters in order to learn from them. As educators, we cannot throw up our hands because moral choices are not easy in today's society. Indeed, the goals of a liberal arts education strike me as even more important because our students cannot expect widespread praise and recognition for making the right choices in life. This is never easy in a youth culture that often favors a compliant conformity. Our students will need to be self-reliant even as they become more compassionate toward their fellow man.

There is obviously no easy formula for success. The skills, as opposed to the values, cultivated by a liberal education can be used for good or ill. But we can expose our students to the process of moral decision making, and one way to do this is to share with them and discuss the stories—the narratives—that history has bestowed upon us. Like all of us, students have the capacity, if not always the motivation, to live vicariously and, by doing so, to absorb a context for moral decision making that will both enrich their own lives and contribute to the common good. This is what Rescorla and Hill managed to do on their own, without assignments, without grades, without any diploma. How fortunate our students would be to have the benefit of an academic community devoted to nurturing those qualities. I am a fervent believer in a liberal arts education, however acquired. There will always be some for whom it proves to be all but meaningless, simply another entry on a résumé. But for many its seeds will take root and grow in ways we may not be able to foresee. I know that in some it will eventually yield those moments that transcend individual lives and self-interest and define both our potential as human beings and our notions of community. Those will be the stories that future generations turn to for moral education, and we must not shy from them. For as individuals we will all die eventually; humankind will live on.

NOTES

1. James B. Stewart, *Heart of a Soldier: A Story of Love, Heroism, and September 11* (New York: Simon & Schuster, 2002). [Editor's note: This was named by *Time* magazine the best nonfiction book of 2002.]

2. James B. Stewart, "Spend, Spend, Spend!" *New Yorker,* February 17–24, 2003.

3. James B. Stewart, *Den of Thieves* (New York: Simon & Schuster, 1991).

4. Michael C. Jensen, *The Financiers: The World of the Great Wall Street Investment Banking Houses* (New York: Weybright & Talley, 1976).

5. The Harvard Classics were published from 1909 to 1917, by P. F. Collier.

6. David Gilmour, *The Long Recessional: The Imperial Life of Rudyard Kipling* (New York: Farrar, Straus & Giroux, 2002).

7. Jacques Barzun, *From Dawn to Decadence* (New York: HarperCollins, 2000), 152–53.

EIGHT

Education and Character in an Age of Moral Freedom

ALAN WOLFE

HEROES AND THE SOURCES OF CHARACTER

In *Heart of a Soldier*, James B. Stewart recounts the life of Rick Rescorla, a man whose actions on September 11, 2001, seemed to belie every generalization about how the United States had become a nation of selfish individualists more concerned with the satisfaction of personal needs than a willingness to sacrifice for others. Not only did Rescorla put the safety of others before his own life, he led the evacuation of the World Trade Center with such calm confidence that people who might have lost their lives in panic found their way out of the tower. Rescorla's heroism seems almost otherworldly in retrospect. "The lights are going to come back on momentarily," he assured the near panicky at one point. As Stewart writes, "Then, as if by a miracle, the emergency generator began to function, and the lights did appear."[1] Rescorla, Stewart makes clear, was not just a character in a book; he was a man of character. As such, he stood out in a society noticeably lacking the attributes that make for virtuous behavior.

If Rick Rescorla's life and death are to have meaning for us in the world after September 11, they should contain lessons about how good character can best be cultivated. Yet there is little in Rescorla's biography that conforms to much of what we hear about the cultivation of character in

America. For one thing, Rescorla was not (originally) American; he was born and raised in Great Britain before becoming an American citizen. Like many Brits, moreover, he received little if any religious training in his upbringing, although religion, we are told repeatedly, is a central ingredient in the teaching of good character. Rescorla's knowledge was not imparted to him by mentors—he never knew his own father—but came through his self-motivated perusal of Harvard Classics. He demonstrated his courage under fire in Vietnam in the Ia Drang valley, yet he had doubts about the war, and, although he never joined protest movements at the University of Oklahoma after his tours of duty ended, he did describe the American effort as a "quagmire" and told his friends that "political wars are a mistake."[2] Anyone who associates good character with unquestioned devotion to family, God, and country cannot account for the extraordinary life of Rick Rescorla.

Because Rescorla was such an unusual man, we might conclude that his story is too unrepresentative to be useful for any didactic purpose. But I do think that there is a lesson to be drawn from Stewart's moving account of his life. Rescorla teaches us that the relationship between character on the one hand and religion and education on the other may be more contingent than we at first might wish to acknowledge. When it comes to character, we have a tendency to look at those institutions such as families, churches, and schools that form individual personality and to emphasize the central role they must play in directing individuals away from their selfish instincts and toward communally chosen goals. Yet as important as institutions may be in socializing people, they are also, when all is said and done, less important than the choices individuals make—often for reasons we cannot begin to understand. The bottom line when it comes to character may be this: you have it, or you lack it, because of who you are. Your life can be shaped by all the right things and you can turn out to be a coward or a tyrant. And you can be less than perfect in your upbringing and surprise everyone around you when the situation calls for leadership.

There are good reasons to examine the question of whether character is shaped by institutional requirements or individual choices, for we live in an era when institutions are becoming palpably weaker and the range of decisions made by ordinary people continuously expands. I have called this an era of moral freedom to make the point that contemporary Americans frequently find themselves turning inward to their own values rather than outward to others when they have to answer fundamental questions involving right and wrong or good and bad.[3] If one believes that strong institutions make for strong character, an age of moral freedom will not make for good citizens. But if one believes that rules cannot work unless they take account of individual needs and that individuals can and do play a role in determining what the rules are, then the prospects for character are not so bleak, although the task of cultivating character in an age of moral freedom will be daunting.

To illustrate my argument, I will turn from the life of an individual like Rick Rescorla to the transformations taking place in an institution I have come to know and respect: the Roman Catholic Church and, in particular, the colleges and universities that exist within its tradition. Religion has long been concerned with the process of character formation. And of all religions, Catholicism has been the West's most institutionally organized church, one that emphasized God's truths accumulated over centuries and transmitted authoritatively through a hierarchy charged with earthly responsibilities. Because of its particular nature, Catholicism historically has stood in sharp contrast with the idea of moral freedom. Now, given the ubiquity of moral freedom in contemporary America, it is no longer clear that it does. And if it does not, there may be lessons to be learned about education and character in the conflicts that frequently emerge between the church and the culture in which it finds itself. And if the relationship between education and character has changed in the direction of greater moral freedom in the Catholic Church, one of the institutions most committed historically to an older theory of character formation, then surely the change in America's other institutions of both faith and higher learning is even greater.

INSTITUTIONS, CHARACTER, AND MORAL FREEDOM: THE PROTESTANTIZING OF AMERICAN CATHOLICS

After a long period in which they were dismissed by non-Catholics as hotbeds of intolerance, sexism, and dogmatism, America's Catholic colleges and universities are widely admired by people of all faiths for their determined efforts to retain a religious nature while pursuing academic excellence. How they do so, of course, varies from one institution to another. At my own university, Boston College, theology remains a required course (although substitutes can be found), a spirit of social justice pervades the entire campus, volunteerism and community service are emphasized, and retreats and other introductions to Ignatian spirituality are offered to students both Catholic and non-Catholic. There may not be many crosses on classroom walls but there are some; if you visit Boston College, you know fairly quickly that you are visiting a Catholic institution.

For some, such as Fr. James Burtchaell, the former provost of Notre Dame, the religious life of a university such as Boston College is all but dead; Father Burtchaell is convinced that Catholic colleges have become indistinguishable from secular ones, just as Protestant institutions like Northwestern or Emory have.[4] (It occurs to me that I have chosen examples from the Methodist tradition, in part because students these days generally do not know the roots of these institutions; indeed many students do not know that Southern Methodist was once Methodist. It also occurs to me that I did not include DePauw; I leave it to you to decide whether Francis Asbury would or should be proud of what his efforts wrought.) To non-Catholics like myself, on the other hand, Boston College's Jesuit heritage is evident in nearly all aspects of campus life, including even the way our primarily non-Catholic department of political science structures a curriculum heavy with political philosophy and noticeably lacking in fashionable rational choice modeling. There is, however, one way in which Father Burtchaell's story of how the light of religion has been extinguished at Catholic colleges is correct. Over the course of the past half century, Boston College has experienced dramatic changes because American Catholicism is not the same as it once was.

Particularly its Boston component, American Catholicism was, from the moment of the arrival of the first wave of European immigrants from countries such as Italy and Ireland, primarily an urban religion. In order to prove that they belonged in their new land, Catholics invested heavily in the construction of monumental church buildings. Obligated both by the rules of their faith and by custom to attend Mass at their local parish, Catholics were far less likely than those of other religions to flee to the suburbs with the first available opportunity. Even if Catholics wanted to leave the city behind, moreover, not that many of them could. Rates of college and university attendance among Catholics lagged behind the rates of other religious groups. Of course some Catholics, most famously the Kennedys, achieved great wealth. But most were tied to working-class jobs and to the ethnic, ghetto-like lifestyles that came with them.

Because of their urban way of life, Catholics throughout the 1930s and 1940s led lives connected to institutions. Many belonged to labor unions; even as the growth of unions began to slow down, the head of the AFL-CIO would invariably be Catholic. It was Catholics who took the lead in organizing their political life through parties, sustaining the machines made famous by Boston's James Michael Curley. Government was another institution central to Catholic life, either because so many of the faithful found employment in city agencies or because some were still dependent on governmental assistance. Catholics, alone among America's religious groups, had their own system of schools, eventually including colleges and universities, which not only taught their children but also provided employment. They organized their social lives institutionally, in organizations like the Knights of Columbus. And no roll call of institutions important to Catholics could leave out the family. Strictures against divorce were taken seriously during these years, and when Catholics, especially women, prayed to the Madonna—the other Madonna, that is—or to Our Lady of Perpetual Help, they prayed for the protection of their family.

As a result of this strong emphasis on institutions, Catholics developed an appreciation of the importance of loyalty. "Go West, young man," Horace Greeley advised Americans, and they have been fleeing established institutions ever since. But Catholics did not go west, not even, at first, to such Boston suburbs as Weston or Wellesley, let alone California or Texas. Institutional loyalties were not to be so casually disregarded. There was a Catholic ethic in America just as much as there was a Protestant one. American Catholics were attracted to the kinds of virtues that stand out in the life of Rick Rescorla. Like him, they were predisposed to work for institutions, such as the military or the police, that required men to wear a uniform, stressed the importance of solidarity with one's coworkers, and considered themselves somewhat alienated from the more hedonistic and self-interested corners of American life. Those institutions, moreover, were ones that put lives at risk; if there is one picture with which every American Catholic is familiar, it is that of the funeral in which the policeman's or firefighter's bravery is celebrated in the homily offered by the priest as the bereaved wife and uncomprehending children listen and weep. There once was a decidedly

Old World feel to the lives led by American Catholics. The sociologist Herbert Gans captures that feel in his portrayal of Boston's Italians; they were, in Gans's terms, "urban villagers," more committed to what sociologists call the gemeinschaft values of close ties than to gesellschaft requirements of impersonality and advancement based on merit.[5]

Central to the cultivation of this particular kind of character were the institutions Catholics created to teach their young. In parochial schools, academic subjects were accompanied by, and sometimes took a backseat to, respect for authority, including clerical authority. Taught primarily by nuns who sacrificed personal income for the sake of the next generation, Catholic schools placed importance on discipline and were guided by the same approach to religion that characterized the Catholic faithful in general. Sins were clear-cut and unambiguous, divided into the mortal and the venal. Expiation was to be achieved through confession to a priest. Priests in turn were under the authority of bishops, who in turn looked to cardinals, who in their turn elected the pope. It is not just that Catholic schools were religious institutions that was important to the conception of character they emphasized. It was also that Catholicism was a distinct form of religion, one that placed a relatively low priority on an individual's own search for spiritual truth in favor of the idea that religious truth was handed down by duly authorized individuals whose special mode of selection and theological expertise enabled them to guide and lead others to God.

When academically achieving students graduated from these kinds of parochial schools, their parents would, if they had the means and desire, send them to Catholic colleges and universities. These institutions were decidedly countercultural in the world of American higher education. More so than secular institutions, they were segregated by sex. Their faculties were not chosen on the basis of research and its meritocratic priorities; instead, lay Catholics and priests occupied most teaching positions. Boards of trustees contained few laypeople and considered their institutions under the jurisdiction, formal or otherwise, of the local archdiocese. Academic freedom was less valued at these institutions than religious mission. As a result, few if any Catholic institutions made it into the highest ranks of academic prestige, although many were known for their athletic teams. (These were the days when even urban Fordham was a football power, producing none other than Vince Lombardi, the National Football League's most celebrated coach.) The values emphasized at Catholic colleges and universities were shaped by, and shaped in turn, the values emphasized by most American Catholics. If they produced people who landed jobs with the FBI, stayed sober, married and raised children without scandal, attended church frequently, and participated in the life of the local parish, they were doing their job.

To the students in my classes at Boston College now, the world I have just described is foreign and unrecognizable, although they sometimes hear about it from their grandparents. My students are overwhelmingly the product of suburban upbringings. No longer confined to the Boston area, they come from every corner of the United States. They include females alongside males; like other institutions of higher learning BC has to practice a certain amount of affirmative action with respect to gender or else, were merit the only criterion, have 60 percent or 70 percent of the freshman class be female. Their fathers, graduates of Boston College in the 1970s, tend to be successful executives or professionals. Their mothers work. Either their parents defy papal teachings and use birth control or they avoid sex, because the number of siblings my students have is around the national average. Some have divorced parents. Others have one parent who is not Catholic. Many have attended the well-known prep schools made famous by previous generations of Protestants. Even those who attended Catholic schools tend to be graduates of suburban academies that resemble Groton more than Monsignor O'Reilly. Sociologically speaking, American Catholics no longer live separate lives. With the exception of Hispanics, and there only some of them, they have become fully as much of the suburban middle class as any other ethnic or religious group.

As a result, my students, although regular church attenders in their youth, know little about their own faith; I frequently find myself, neither Catholic nor religious, teaching them about the fundamentals of their own tradition. In this, students at Boston College are typical of young Catholics around the United States. Consider the views of Mary Mallozzi, who was interviewed by a group of sociologists interested in the religious views of young American Catholics. Mary is the kind of Catholic for whom the church ought to be grateful. A cradle Catholic, she was raised in the institutional church and, as a thirty-year-old, remains very loyal to it. "Church is a very big thing to me," says Mary. "I need to belong to a parish that is going to nurture me along and offer me the tools in the areas that I need." Fortunately for her, she found such a parish in Blessed

Sacrament, where she met her husband, Jim. Both remain extremely active in parish affairs, yet although Mary regularly attends Mass, she does not believe that she is obligated by her faith to do so. "I hate rules, such as 'you have to go to Mass,'" she adds. "I try to reframe it and say, 'It's part of our growth as religious people.'" Her Catholic identity is as strong as Catholic identity can be, and she says proudly that "I don't think there is anything that would drive me out of the Church." Yet she will make up her own mind on whether priests should be allowed to marry and whether birth control is permissible.[6]

People like Mary Mallozzi are most likely in the minority among American Catholics between twenty and forty. Far more typical are individuals like Robert Wilkes, a twenty-seven-year-old graduate student. Asked whether he will be a lifelong Catholic, Robert, who has no interest in switching to any other religion, answers "Definitely." But he does not view himself as a lifelong parishioner. He once found a parish in which he felt comfortable, particularly because the priest encouraged lay participation and an active concern with social justice. When the local bishop stepped in and stopped any experimentation, Robert dropped out and decided to keep his faith to himself rather than to find another parish in which to worship. Unlike Catholics who retain only an ethnic identity with the church, Robert is a believer and considers himself loyal in his own way. But unlike those active in particular parishes, he would like to see the Catholic Church alter what to him are outdated hierarchical and authoritarian forms of organization. His kind of Catholicism, however different from his faith in the past, may well come to represent his faith in the future, especially in the aftermath of the pedophilia and cover-up scandals that rocked the church in 2002.[7]

A study of a Catholic parish in a large southern city undertaken in 1951 examined church teachings among active parishioners and found that their "Catholic mind" was "about two-thirds Catholic and one-third pagan."[8] One can only wonder what the author of this study, Fr. Joseph Fichter, would make of today's Catholics. An example is provided by one of the more controversial recent attempts by the Vatican to define a doctrinal point central to Catholicism's understanding of itself: *Dominus Iesus*, Cardinal Joseph Ratzinger's September 2000 declaration attacking relativism, which was widely interpreted as a defense of Catholicism as the one true faith. When Cardinal Ratzinger writes that "the Catholic faithful *are required to profess* that there is an historical continuity—

rooted in the apostolic succession—between the Church founded by Christ and the Catholic Church,"[9] today's younger Catholics are likely to reject any such formulation suggesting that non-Catholic Christians have the wrong doctrinal ideas. What does it mean to be a good Catholic?, one young person was asked. "I just feel as long as you live a life without harming others or yourself and . . . you are just really living a good, decent life, then you really are living the way God intended you to live" was his response.[10] This decidedly nondoctrinal sentiment is more and more the norm among contemporary Catholics; only a minority among post–Vatican II Catholics believe that the Catholic Church is the one true church, and 45 percent say that they could be just as happy in some other religious tradition that was not Catholic. "It's *my* one true religion," another believer responds when asked if the Catholic Church is the one true church. "For me and for my children and my family, it's the one true church. But to God, I don't think it's the one true church. . . . I really believe that the God that I think is out there isn't really going to care that the Episcopalians do things one way and Catholics do it another way."[11] As the authors of a recent survey of young Catholics conclude, "Significant numbers of young adult Catholics today no longer see the Roman Catholic Church as unique or essential, the pope as necessary, the Church's structures as important, or tradition as a source of objective truth."[12]

What is true of doctrine is also true of ritual. Historian Robert Orsi has written of the "intense devotional creativity and improvisation in American Catholic culture" that characterized the religious life of his parents' generation,[13] but in today's world, one study found 61 percent of religiously active Catholics never pray with a rosary, 76 percent never engage in the novena (nine consecutive evenings of prayer), 44 percent never participate in the stations of the cross, and 53 percent never attend benediction.[14] Another survey discovered that far more Catholics pray privately (77 percent) than say devotions to Mary or other saints (29 percent) or finger the rosary (20 percent).[15] And among younger Catholics, the figures are even more striking; more of both Latinos and non-Latinos said that they had participated in a meditation group or meditated on their own in the past year than had attended a eucharistic adoration or benediction.[16]

Declining interest in, and practice of, the devotions has been accompanied by a decrease in the practice of the sacrament that for an earlier generation most seemed to characterize the faith: confession, or, as it is called after Vatican II, the sacrament of reconciliation. According to one estimate, 38 percent of American Catholics said that they attended confession once a month in 1965, compared to 38 percent who, in 1975, said that they never went at all.[17] It is not hard to understand why. One very devout younger Catholic speaks of her dislike of "walking into a dark, quiet church and going into a booth." Her parish had gone over to Lenten services with general confession, and she loved it. "There were so many young people it was wonderful. To me it was a whole different experience, going to confession. I really liked it. It was collective, but then you could go by yourself to a priest. . . . It was a way to feel welcome into the whole thing, calming you down before you go up to confession."[18] Many Catholics share this believer's distaste for the confession box. In his account of St. Brigid's, a thriving Catholic church, the journalist Robert Keeler interviewed many older parishioners who viewed confession as "the scariest sacrament: a sweat-inducing ordeal in a dark, closetlike box, where the sinner kneels and waits for the sound of a small panel to be slid back, revealing behind a screen the fuzzy outline of a priest who may or may not act with compassion."[19] Against the warmth that contemporary religious believers expect, traditional confession, associated as it is with the dark and the dismal, does not stand much of chance.

I could go on multiplying examples—these, and many others, come from my recently published book, *The Transformation of American Religion*—but I think the point has been made.[20] Young American Catholics these days, even those who are proudest of their faith, treat their religion in more individualistic, personalistic, and privatized ways than did their parents and grandparents. Indeed it is not a stretch to claim that the huge differences that once divided Protestants and Catholics are increasingly disappearing in the United States as Catholics increasingly adopt Protestant-like ways of practicing their faith. No wonder, then, that my students cannot tell me what a novena is or do not know that the body of Catholic teachings is called the magisterium. Ethnically, they are proud to be Catholic. But in terms of religion itself, their faith has blended in with the culture around them. Catholic colleges are no longer countercultural. They retain a religious mission, but otherwise they have become part of the mainstream of American higher education.

MORAL FREEDOM AND THE AMERICANIZATION
OF CATHOLIC EDUCATION

In the winter of 2002–2003, Thomas Monaghan, best known as the founding CEO of Domino's Pizza, decided to donate a significant portion of his personal wealth to the creation of a true Catholic college. "God has been good to me, and now I want to pay back," Monaghan said in announcing that he had chosen the area around Naples, Florida, as the site of his new venture. "I'm devoting the rest of my life to Catholic education and Ave Maria University." The goals of the new institution were best formulated by the former commissioner of baseball Bowie Kuhn. "As Christians, we are always searching for God," Kuhn pointed out. "The sad thing today is that the search for God not only has been abandoned, it has been eliminated from universities. If God is excluded from universities, how can they possibly, possibly seek truth?"[21] Although neither Monaghan nor Kuhn said so explicitly, the reason for their new initiative has much to do with what takes place at institutions like Boston College. These men want an alternative for the faithful, an institution that sets itself up intentionally to run against the grain of American culture and to restore the days when Catholic colleges made religion central to their purpose.

Personally, I hope that these gentlemen succeed in their venture; there ought, in my view, to be many different kinds of institutions of higher learning pursuing many different goals. If they were to succeed, moreover, there would be created a kind of laboratory experiment designed to shed light on the question of faith, education, and character. Would students who were the product of a more traditional religious education be likely to become people of better character than students who attend an institution like Boston College that has blended into American culture?

I could begin to provide an answer by taking something of a cheap shot. Across the street from Boston College can be found St. John's Seminary, the major training ground for priests in the area and the home of Boston's archbishop. When Bernard Cardinal Law made St. John's Seminary his home, he presided over a Catholic church that was overwhelmingly dominated by products of Old World American Catholicism. And they, of course—products of the best schools, trained in the sacrifices of the priesthood, faithful to the hierarchy, dedicated to the life of the church—acted in the most reprehensible, if not downright immoral, ways in which human beings can act. I do not mean by this rather strong comment to call attention to the remarkable number of sexual predators that existed among them, although one cannot overlook them. The greater crime, in my view, is that, when faced with the pain and suffering caused by wayward priests, the hierarchy united, as if it were one person, in covering up hints and scandal, paying off families on condition of confidentiality, and then, most venal of all, transferring sick and degraded men to new parishes where they could cause future havoc. So deep was the scandal that Cardinal Law could not survive it; not only did he resign, close to unprecedented for a church that does not run its affairs through public opinion polling, but also he was followed by a Franciscan, Bishop Sean O'Malley, who took a vow of poverty, moved to inner-city Boston, and sold Cardinal Law's palatial mansion to Boston College for roughly the same amount owed to the victims of sexual abuse.

I have called my decision to bring this matter up a cheap shot, but is it really? Strong institutions have many attractive features: they encourage people to put the needs of others before their own, they help make organized social life possible, and they transmit teachings from generation to generation. Yet the scandal in the church makes plain to all what happens when institutions go wrong. Their communal norms transform themselves into cover-ups. Their emphasis on loyalty discourages whistle-blowing and promotes incompetent people to positions of responsibility. Protection of the institution takes priority over protection of people. And, most serious of all for an institution with a religious mission, leadership, faced with a crisis, loses all touch with spiritual purpose, sounding for all the world to hear more like a politician or businessman under investigation or indictment than a church responsible for salvation and good works.

Because of the kinds of transformations in religious practice taking place among younger Catholics, the American church, once the headlines of the scandal have faded, will never again be the same. Indeed, one of the most striking sociological features of American Catholicism today has been the gap that has opened up between the way ordinary parishioners understand their religion and the way a more old-fashioned hierarchy insists that the religion be practiced. As American Catholics become used to questioning authority, the church insists on its authoritative teachings, including teachings on sexual morality in which most American Catholics no longer believe. An increasingly affluent membership has come to accept Vatican II's stress on the active participation of "the people of God" in the liturgy, meaning people much like themselves, but not all church leaders share their enthusiasm. Catholics searching for a religion that speaks to their own needs make a distinction between their faith, which is personal and intimate, and their religion, which is bureaucratic and organizational, but this, of course, is anathema to those for whom the church is the hierarchy. To the extent that Catholics identify with the institutional structure of their religion, moreover, they increasingly tend to look to their local parish rather than to the archdiocese or Rome. It is not the job of religious leaders to hire sociologists and survey researchers to find out what their members want (although some religious institutions, such as Protestant megachurches, frequently do). But smart church leaders will keep their ears to the ground, slowly changing themselves to adjust to new realities even as they insist on the importance of tradition or ritual.

Fortunately for American Catholicism, worshippers who love their church have stepped in to preserve the institution in areas where the hierarchy has failed. The largest organization working in this capacity— founded in the upper-middle-class suburb of Wellesley, to which many Boston Catholics have moved—is called Voice of the Faithful. Careful not to take positions on women's ordination or celibacy, which would lead to needless polarization, VOF is parish based, moderate in its calls for reform, and staffed by dedicated believers, men and women, who clearly speak for the conscience of American Catholicism. At times, VOF has been pushed by the seriousness of the scandal toward relatively confrontational tactics; it encourages Boston Catholics, for example, to bypass the archbishop's office and to contribute funds directly to such organizations as Catholic Charities. But through its seriousness of purpose and its demeanor, Voice of the Faithful has demonstrated the possibility that the best forms of moral character can lie outside established religious organizations and can instead be found in the ordinary acts of ordinary people.

Students at a Catholic university such as Boston College were given a fairly clear choice as they observed the scandals surrounding their neighborhood and church. One finds at BC very few, if any, students who defended Cardinal Law. (An invitation to the cardinal to speak at the college, extended before his resignation, was quietly withdrawn.) When I discuss the crisis with students in my classes, their instincts take them directly to the positions adopted by Voice of the Faithful. True, like many college students, they rarely involve themselves in civilly engaged activities, including those of VOF. But they know that the Catholic Church of the past is not for them, and they hope, often with an edge of desperation, that the church will change sufficiently so that they can be proud of their membership in it. Boston College has taken the lead in offering to students and to the public a series of lectures, seminars, and discussions devoted to the crisis in the church. Students attend in surprisingly large numbers—or at least surprising to those who view today's students as apathetic—and their attendance and questions are motivated by a strong desire to see their church reform itself.

Because of the crisis in the church, as well as because of the response of groups such as Voice of the Faithful and Boston College students, I do not believe that a return to a more traditional Catholic education will produce students with better character. There are certainly voices calling for such a return, and, during the election campaign of 2004, some of them succeeded in persuading a few American bishops to announce that they would deny communion to Catholic politicians, such as John F. Kerry, if they took positions on abortion and other social issues that seemed to go against the teachings of the church. Should such traditional Catholicism ever return to the United States (which, in any large numbers, I doubt), it would be more likely to produce believers who would turn their eyes away from the kinds of immoral acts we have recently witnessed. Before the scandal, Boston College administrators expressed considerable doubt that they were doing moral formation in the right way. Like many Catholic schools, Boston College has a drinking problem. Sex is another word for dormitory life. Sporting events draw larger crowds that academic events. As not only a faculty member but also as the father of two BC undergraduates, I share these concerns. The culturally conservative part of me would love to see the place get serious about curbing undergraduate drinking and partying.

Still, it is striking that when an issue as serious as the crisis in the church arose, so many BC students had exactly the right moral instincts. To me, this suggests that whatever Boston College was doing to encourage moral formation among its students, something was working. And I have a hypothesis to offer about what that something might be.

Before any particular crisis had developed to expose its internal working to the media, Boston College had decided, on its own and without significant outside pressure, to reform the way it carried out its business. Becoming coeducational was part of that process; women cannot be priests, but they can major in theology at Catholic colleges and contribute to the teachings of the church in many capacities. Once governed by a board of trustees that was entirely Jesuit, Boston College now has a lay board. Unlike Georgetown, which recently hired a layperson to be its president, all of BC's presidents have been Jesuits, but neither the academic vice president nor any of the major deans is. As J. Donald Monan, the chancellor of Boston College and its former president, is fond of pointing out, the transformation of the college into an institution with a Catholic identity that functions in the secular world is a good model for the church as a whole.[22]

By adapting to the changes in society while holding onto a Catholic identity, Boston College implicitly sends a message to those who study and work there that the institution is both rooted in a tradition and responsive to change. In that way, it reacts to the complexities of the contemporary world by working with, rather than by resisting, the kinds of lives its students lead. To avoid becoming an institution that stands for nothing, it has retained its Catholic character. But to avoid a stance so hostile to the modern world that its resources would be spurned by contemporary students, it incorporates ideas about gender equality, individualism, and compromise that do not quite fit Catholicism's historic conception of itself. The result displeases many, including traditionalists hoping for something along the lines of Ave Maria University, as well as those non-Catholic and nonreligious students who think it should be more like Boston University down Commonwealth Avenue. But its often awkward and sometimes incoherent compromises please others, including myself, who do not believe that there are any easy answers to the question of how to lead a good and meaningful life under conditions of moral freedom.

THE MORAL FREEDOM OF STUDENTS AND THE MORAL RESPONSIBILITY OF UNIVERSITIES

I am not suggesting that most of my students at Boston College, should they ever—God forbid—find themselves in a situation like the one that faced Rick Rescorla, would react as he did, although I hope that some of them would. None of us until a moment of crisis appears upon us know how we would act in an extreme situation. But I do know that my students are decent human beings whose instinct is to do the right thing. This need not necessarily be taken as a compliment. In his book *The Closing of the American Mind*, Allan Bloom characterizes his students with the word "nice"—and he does not mean it nicely.[23] Students, in his view, should be educated and cultivated, not necessarily pleasant and accommodating. I often find myself as frustrated as Bloom was by the casual attitude my students take toward great ideas. But I also find their niceness admirable. I much prefer it to snobbery, close-mindedness, and arrogance, all of which are terms that might well have characterized college students of previous eras.

My conclusion should thus be obvious: if we are to use education and faith to cultivate good citizens, we cannot do so by yesterday's methods. The fact that our students live at a time of moral freedom increases the moral responsibility of the role of the faculty. No longer will a college capstone course in moral philosophy, nor compulsory chapel or ROTC, nor religiously inspired vocational counselors do the trick. We must instead trust our students to use the freedom they have to find, with our guidance, moral responses that resonate with their own experiences. There are no guarantees that we can do our job; there have never been guarantees that human beings will act morally. But an age of moral freedom is an exciting time to be a college professor. It is up to us—in the books we select for students to read, the topics we choose to study with them, and the writing and speaking we do as public intellectuals such as the symposium at DePauw—to help our students not only understand the world but also act as responsibly formed moral creatures within it.

NOTES

1. James B. Stewart, *Heart of a Soldier: A Story of Love, Heroism, and September 11* (New York: Simon & Schuster, 2002), 258.

2. Stewart, *Heart of a Soldier*, 151.

3. Alan Wolfe, *Moral Freedom: The Search for Virtue in a World of Choice* (New York: Norton, 2001).

4. James Tunstead Burtchaell, *The Dying of the Light: The Disengagement of Christian Colleges and Universities from Their Christian Churches* (Grand Rapids, Mich.: Eerdmans, 1998).

5. Herbert J. Gans, *The Urban Villagers: Group and Class in the Life of Italian-Americans* (New York: Free Press, 1962).

6. Cited in Dean R. Hoge et al., *Young American Catholics: Religion in the Culture of Choice* (Notre Dame, Ind.: University of Notre Dame Press, 2001), 80–84.

7. Hoge et al., *Young American Catholics*, 184–86.

8. Joseph Fichter, *Southern Parish: Dynamics of a City Church* (Chicago: University of Chicago Press, 1951), 270.

9. www.vatican.va/roman_curia/congregations/cfaith/documents/rc_con_cfaith_doc_20000806_dominus-iesus_en.html (7/19/04).

10. Hoge et al., *Young American Catholics*, 171.

11. Hoge et al., *Young American Catholics*, 223–24.

12. Hoge et al., *Young American Catholics*, 221.

13. Robert A. Orsi, "'Mildred, Is It Fun to Be a Cripple?': The Culture of Suffering in Mid-Twentieth Century American Catholicism," in *Catholic Lives, Contemporary America,* ed. Thomas J. Ferraro (Durham, N.C.: Duke University Press, 1997), 47.

14. Joseph Gremillion and Jim Castelli, *The Emerging Parish: The Notre Dame Study of Catholic Life Since Vatican II* (New York: Harper & Row, 1987), 45.

15. William V. D'Antonio et al., *American Catholics: Gender, Generation, and Commitment* (Walnut Creek, Calif.: Alta Mira, 2001), 60.

16. Hoge et al., *Young American Catholics*, 156.

17. James O'Toole, "Empty Confessionals: Where Have All the Sinners Gone?" *Commonweal*, February 23, 2001, 10–12.

18. Hoge et al., *Young American Catholics*, 82.

19. Robert F. Keeler, *Parish! The Pulitzer Prize-Winning Story of a Vibrant Catholic Community* (New York: Crossroad, 1997), 78, 83.

20. Alan Wolfe, *The Transformation of American Religion: How We Actually Live our Faith* (New York: Free Press, 2003).

21. www.thewandererpress.com/november28.pdf (7/19/04).

22. Personal discussions with the author.

23. Allan Bloom, *The Closing of the American Mind: How Higher Education Has Failed Democracy and Impoverished the Souls of Today's Students* (New York: Simon & Schuster, 1987), 82.

CHAPTER NINE

Democracy, Character, and the University

LEROY S. ROUNER

My thesis is that the health of American democracy is dependent on people of a certain character, that that character has a religious dimension, and that it is one of the "secular" university's responsibilities to produce such people.

DEMOCRACY

So, what holds American democracy together? On the face of it, it shouldn't work because it pits two opposing political principles against each other. One of these is our vaunted individualism, and the credo of freedom that undergirds it. The other is our common identity as Americans, an identity that has enormous prestige with us. That sense of community is not built on the thick traditional bonds of blood, land, language, caste or class, and religion—the bonds of a traditional society that give places like India and China their cultural depth and density. In comparison with these ancient traditions, the modern American sense of community is thin and fragile. America is not a culture in the conventional sense; it's a creed, as Carl Friedrich of Harvard pointed out some years ago, the constituent elements of a shared *political* culture. One could almost say that America is not so much a place as it is an adventure, because freedom is only a starting point, the condition for the fulfillment of potential. Perry Miller, the historian of American literature, said that its common theme is the question "What does it mean to be an American?" Note, however, that the answer to that question is based in what Robert Bellah first called American "civil religion."[1] This is a loose collection of beliefs and values: freedom, individualism, equality, the willingness to sacrifice for the common good, trust in divine guidance, and hope for the future. At its best it gives America its capacity for doing self-sacrificial good in the world; in its specifically "civil" dimension, it promotes also that patriotic self-sacrifice we associate with republican citizenship reflected in the Pledge of Allegiance, and with that charitable welcoming of immigrant-strangers into our midst. At its worst it can descend into jingoism and a steely, near-demonic self-righteousness that can be enormously destructive both at home and abroad. In itself American civil religion is neither inherently good nor bad, it is only inherently necessary. The reason for that is that liberal democracy per se has only minimal moral grounding. After you have celebrated the freedom of the individual, there isn't much more to say. In his Farewell Address George Washington was at pains to point out the significance of religion for the political life. His illustration was the validity of oaths in courts of law, and his point was that if you don't have the Bible to swear on, how can you be sure that witnesses will tell the truth?

Europeans, largely separatists from the Church of England, came to a New World previously untouched by European cultures, announcing that they would build a "city upon a hill" for all the world to see.[2] So, from the beginning America was a theological adventure that became transmuted into a political vision. That "political" theology went from a brief, unhappy experiment with Calvinist theocracy, through the republican era of Revolution and Founding, to the dreamy transcendental truths of Emersonian Unitarianism, but the strong underlying theme was always that we were a special people, "endowed by our Creator with certain inalienable rights," prepared to make sacrifices for a transcendent good, and celebrating that myth of the American dream with extraordinary enthusiasm and conviction. That myth downplayed the traditional identities of blood, region, language, caste or class, and religion. You didn't have to belong to a particular one of these traditional groups. In fact, they didn't matter anymore.[3] If you adopted the creed and trusted the dream, *anyone* could be an American. Our heroes were the Andrew

Carnegies, who arrived on our shores with only a dollar in their pockets and became obscenely rich, and Abe Lincoln, the rail splitter who determined he was not going to make his living by working with his hands, who read books by firelight, and who grew up to be president. One was now free to take advantage of limitless opportunity, so the dream went. The early promise of religious freedom was eventually expanded into its political counterparts, constitutional guarantees of freedom of speech, freedom of the press, freedom of movement, and freedom of political belief and action.

The naive enthusiasm for this romantic vision made Americans the teenagers of world political culture, constantly in search of themselves. endearing in their optimism, obnoxious in their refusal to heed the experienced wisdom of the Old World they had left behind. At our best, we were generous and creative, fashioning the Marshall Plan and the Peace Corps. At our worst, we were slaughtering and being slaughtered in Vietnam, constantly thinking up increasingly unpersuasive arguments for why this was what America was really all about. But the Vietnam War and the civil rights movement together were a turning point in recent American history. The combination of those two events sobered the teenager in us and helped us grow up a little. What we learned from those twin defeats of our corrupted idealism was that we had been lying to ourselves about a number of important things. When we said that "all men are created equal," we forgot about blacks, and Jews, and women, who were excluded from the marketplace, and the rights of children, to mention only a few. Our critics are right to call us phonies on those and related issues. What they and we tend to forget, however, is that the myth was not about what we have accomplished, it's about what we value, what we intend to be, what we hope for. The American celebration of freedom does not mean that Americans are freer than others; it means only that we want it badly enough to make it central to our self-understanding.

Now, this qualified idealism runs against the grain of American pragmatism and utilitarianism, which stress particular and practical results and eschew romantic dreaming as wispy, wimpy, and inconsequential. But pragmatism is only a good guess as to what may work today, and it has never had clear-cut criteria for what long-term "workability" really means. If you drain the oil from your car's engine and then try to start the car, will it start? Yes. And if you put it in gear, can you drive down the street? Oh, yes. So is it working? Sure, for a couple of minutes, until you smell that awful death exhalation and hear that grinding death rattle that tells you your engine is now a metaphysically lost cause. Utilitarianism is equally vulnerable because it operates on the impossible assumption that there is some rational way to calculate what would be "the greatest good for the greatest number" over a reasonably long future. What can that mean in the Iraq war, for example, when the law of unforeseen consequences still lies lurking in wait for us? There's no really serious way to know what the greatest good for the greatest number might ever be.

But that's not the point. The myth is about what we believe and who we want to be. Americans are those people who both built a better mousetrap and dreamed a grander dream, and while the dream may be a thin, vague, and fragile bond, it is not wispy or wimpy. It has, in fact, been an agent of change. In race relations, for example, as we gradually realized that we had been lying to ourselves about the equality of blacks and whites in America, things began to happen. One of my father's great points of pride is that he was minister of a church in Brooklyn and Branch Rickey was a member of his church when he hired Jackie Robinson to play second base for the Brooklyn Dodgers, the first black man in either of the major leagues. Check your rosters today. Racism still exists in America, but we have come a long way from Jackie Robinson's day. The reason is that, at our best, a critical mass of us knew that that is what America is supposed to be about.

To be sure, our democracy does not run on fragile dreams alone. Jean Elshtain and I have Augustine and Reinhold Niebuhr in common. Reinhold Niebuhr—who was one of the keenest observers of what he called "the irony of American history"—often commented that "the good in men makes democracy possible; the evil in men makes democracy necessary." His point about irony is that the best thing about us—our dream—is too often the source of the worst things that we do. Romantic dreams, especially self-serving ones about how good we are, and self-confident ones about what is best for other nations, are too easily corrupted by self-righteousness, a sense of Manifest Destiny and occasionally downright warmongering. So the genius of democracy is partly in the system of checks and balances, where no branch of government has absolute power, where legislative leaders can always be voted out, and where imperial presidents, praise God, are always no more than eight years away from private life. But Niebuhr knew that while corruptibility of the dream is always a clear and present danger, it is American idealism that moves us forward.

What we now call multiculturalism was always incipiently a part of the American dream. James Madison celebrated early American religious diversity by noting that Presbyterians, Episcopalians, Baptists, and even Mennonites were living in harmony together. Not a diverse crowd by present standards, but a beginning. Jean Elshtain cites statistics about proportions of religious folk in the American community. Today there are more Muslims than there are Presbyterians in the United States; Hindu temples abound, and Buddhist groups are major players in ecological and peace movements.

What has this done to the old idea that America was essentially a Protestant Christian nation, with an acquiescing subculture of Catholics and Jews, as explored in Will Herberg's influential book *Protestant, Catholic, and Jew* in the mid-1950s?[4] It has recognized that the old idea is gone. But there is a residue from that old idea that is still alive and well, and that is American civil religion. It isn't really a religion in any formal sense. It is the dimension of depth in human experience, it is the visceral core of the American dream that gives the dream its substance. Bellah traces the message from Lincoln to Kennedy—the message that we have been particularly blessed by a gracious God with this good land and have been called to a life of commitment and sacrifice in the cause of freedom. "Ask not what your country can do for you. Ask what you can do for your country." But you don't have to go back to Lincoln's Second Inaugural or John Kennedy's famous address. American civil religion is celebrated in small towns and large cities every year on Memorial Day and the Fourth of July. You hear the same message all over again. This is who we are; we are the people who hold these values, and that's what defines us as Americans.

Now, there are, of course, alternative views, especially the one that says that American democracy is held together by common economic commitment. This assumes that economic success makes loyal Americans—the idea that the dream meant a good job, a nice house, and a bunch of kids who all went to college and did better economically than their parents. But we know that this isn't necessarily so. We hear of "successful" Americans whose loyalty to their country is conspicuously absent as they surrender their citizenship in order to avoid paying taxes. On the other hand, many who have not been economically advantaged have nevertheless clung to the American dream that they belonged to a specially blessed people. They sport bumper stickers on aging and perpetually muddy pickup trucks throughout the country announcing that they are "Proud to be American." And, even those radical militia groups, whose idealism is about as corrupted as it can get, are nevertheless profoundly committed to *their* America, the America of the old frontier, where you ruled your own homestead and there wasn't any government to speak of.

CHARACTER

Which brings us to the question of character. The popular image of America's founders is one of distinguished Renaissance characters like Thomas Jefferson and Ben Franklin, John Adams and George Washington, men of vision who wrote well, thought clearly, and drew on rich cultural backgrounds; and then those stalwart New England Puritan families with awesome energy, dignity, and faith, half of whom died in the first winter in this country with a prayer on their lips, and the rest of whom soldiered on, bereft but believing, building their homes, their churches, and a little college in Harvard Square so that "when our present ministers shall lie in the dust, the church may not be left with an illiterate ministry." In the meantime, however, those regarded as hoi polloi included a large alumni contingent from the best prisons of Europe, and this new community of folk who announced that they were all "created equal" had to face a developing divergency in cultural background, education, and moral sensibility. Undaunted, however, and with unbridled confidence that the chemistry of their new community could corrode the bad history of their previous lives, and with audacious confidence that they could perpetuate the moral and spiritual inheritance of those aristocrats from the era of Washington and Jefferson, Franklin and Adams, Americans since have reached out to the "tired and poor," the riffraff of Europe, asking only that they should "yearn to breathe free."

The sages of the "old Europe" must have thought them mad. Even today, in retrospect, it seems wonderfully audacious. But here we all are, after generations of immigration, literally getting more diverse by the minute, and yet still somehow not only hanging in with each other but also making some sort of common cause. And our question now is, what ensures this "common cake of custom"? And what do you and I embody as a characteristic that makes that commonality effective in our national life?

On one level it's an easy question. What America needs is what any nation needs—good citizens. And what makes good citizens is loyalty to a common cause and to the community, or, as Josiah Royce once rather mystically put it, "loyalty to loyalty." But our "nation" is not like other nations, bound together by ties of blood, race, or even, increasingly, religion. If you have a seriously polyglot community—forget Madison's cultural pluralism of both Methodists and Mennonites—and not only from Europe, but now also from the Middle East, southern and east Asia, Latin America, and so on, how do you claim some sort of common value for this common cause? How can you possibly throw your arms wide to the "tired and the poor," especially if your community is based on some sort of "religion," since we are now increasingly pluralistic in our religious life? We really have two problems here. One is relating Muslims to Hindus, to Buddhists, and all the rest. The other is finding a common creedal basis among all these groups that gives them their American identity.

John Wilson at Princeton has argued that American civil religion has been dependent upon America's *common* religion, and now that America is no longer a "Protestant nation," our civil religion is in jeopardy. He has a point. We find it increasingly difficult in this country to have a rational debate about much of anything because we have less common ground than we had in the days before urbanization and immigration made us so radically diverse. At the same time, however, these folk are all Americans. And American Buddhism, for example, is a far cry from, say, Buddhism in Sri Lanka. I spend time regularly in Sri Lanka, and let me tell you, some of those guys are no fun. American Buddhism has a New Age tinge to it. It is about spirituality and meditation, whole-earth ecology, world peace, maybe hugging a tree or two as you go along. In Sri Lanka, however, the Buddhist priests are hardliners in the war between the Sinhalese-dominated government and the Tamils in the north and east.

The development of a distinctively American Buddhism is an example of how all religions are changing as a result of their interaction with one another, but it also illustrates the continuing vitality of American civil religion. For example, several years ago I was giving a lecture on human rights at an East-West philosophy conference in Honolulu. My friend Tai Unno was there. Tai is a Buddhist priest who taught in the religion department at Smith College. In a discussion after the lecture I couldn't resist needling him, so I said, "Tai, I don't understand how you

Buddhists can support human rights because the individual self is the bearer of rights in the human rights tradition, and you have a no-self doctrine." He replied with some passion, "Of *course* I believe in human rights. *I'm an American!*" That is about as philosophically incorrect for a Buddhist as you can get, but it's real, and it's happening not only to Buddhists, it's also happening to Christians in America, and all sorts of others. So what is this quintessentially American character? We go back to Robert Bellah: trust in our blessing by a transcendent power, willingness to make sacrifices for our defining ideal of freedom, hope for the future, generosity, and a fundamental decency.

The significance of this last virtue was illustrated by a dramatic event, which most of you won't remember, but I do vividly, during the McCarthy era when Senator Joe McCarthy was holding hearings investigating the U.S. Army. The lead lawyer for the army was one Joseph Welch, a Boston Brahmin who wore tweed suits and a bow tie and looked for all the world like the grandfather you wished you had had. This was the early 1950s and it was one of the first national television events in the postwar era. At first glance Joe Welch, with his proper Bostonian manners and demeanor, seemed no match for the wily street fighter from Wisconsin and his sleazy sidekick, Roy Cohn. At one point, however, McCarthy started assassinating some opponent's character without any evidence whatsoever, except that blank sheet of paper he had in his hand and waved, and said, "I have here in my hand a list of all the communists," so on and so forth. That was his usual modus operandi. And Joseph Welch, trembling with righteous indignation, said, "Have you no sense of decency, sir, at long last? Have you left no sense of decency?" I was an undergraduate at Harvard. I saw that on television. "Have you left no sense of decency?" And that's the day McCarthyism died. After those hearings he was revealed for the alcoholic demagogue that he was. His power was broken by a man who believed in the power of decency in the American character.

Implicit in the foregoing is what must be the operative answer to the age-old problem of American unity amidst diversity, the problem of *e pluribus unum.* Our solution must be a growing emphasis on the "civil" in American's civil religion, a concentration on those elements of our shared political culture—liberty public and private, equality, the sanctity of the individual, and the rest—which, though ultimately rooted in the Protestant Christianity I have alluded to above, has now come to permeate our civic sense of what it means to be an American, has come to be the only "national identity" we can legitimately claim.

THE UNIVERSITY

So what responsibility do our universities have in the shaping of the American character? The earliest ventures in higher education were religiously motivated, and a great many of our private colleges and universities were "church related," so character shaping was high on their agenda. Today most of these institutions have been effectively secularized, and there is considerable debate about whether the university as such has any appropriate role in the character formation of its students. Yet some of our most secularized institutions are still committed to character formation. One example is Harvard, where I went to college and then stayed on to coach crew and spend a couple of years as an assistant dean of freshmen. And during the early 1980s I was chairman of the board of ministry there. I went in to see Derek Bok, who was then president, about the responsibilities of this board. My appointment said that the "Board [was] responsible for the religious life of Harvard University," and I told Derek that I hadn't known that Harvard University had a religious life anymore. What the conversation focused on, however, was a plan he had for sending Harvard undergraduates to live and work in a Third World country for a year before graduation. He said, "Most of these kids are going to be movers and shakers in the world, and they don't have any idea how poor the rest of the world is." That program took a long time to get off the ground, but now, two presidents later, it is part of a new proposal to sharpen the conscience, and thus shape the character, of these highly privileged kids.

The university is not a church, it's not a hospital, and it's not a family, although universities incorporate significant moral values, have a responsibility for the good health of the university community, and have a care for each other. Paul Weiss, the Yale philosopher, was fond of saying, "I do not think we should love our students, I think we should leave that to their mothers," but anyone who knew him and his students knew that he did indeed love many of them, and was much loved by many of them, and that this love played an important role in the effectiveness of his teaching. He taught them to learn what they loved rather than what they thought was going to get them ahead in the world. We also do well to keep in mind that the tradition of education as character building goes back to classical Greece, where it had much to do with transcendent values, although little to do with formal religion. Plato's dialogue *Protagoras* is, I think, the best thing ever written on the philosophy of education. It begins at something like three o'clock in the morning when a young friend of Socrates comes beating on his door, full of excitement because the famous Sophist teacher, Protagoras, had just come to Athens, was staying at the house of a rich friend, and had agreed to tutor a select group of wealthy young men—for a substantial fee—and this young friend of Socrates, one Hippocrates, wanted to get into that group, even though he knew that Socrates was not enthusiastic about the Sophists because they were philosophical relativists, and they charged large fees for their teaching, which Socrates regarded as prostitution. So Socrates asked his young friend, "If you study with Protagoras, what will he make of you?" The kid wasn't sure he understood the question, so Socrates elaborated: "Well, if you studied with your namesake Hippocrates the physician, what would he make of you?" "A physician." "And Protagoras is a Sophist, so what will he make of you?" Well, the kid knew that answering "A Sophist" was not going to make Socrates happy, and anyway he didn't want to be a Sophist, he wanted to learn rhetoric, which my teacher Jack Randall at Columbia said was the art of how to get elected without really knowing anything. Randall added, with characteristic liberal scorn, that they were all the Richard Nixons of their time who were great debaters but didn't really have a philosophical position. Anyway, the kid played it safe: "I don't know." So Socrates said, "Well, let's go ask him," and that's how the dialogue begins on the problem of teaching virtue.

When we are asked whether universities can properly engage in a kind of character education, the answer is that character education is inevitable. We don't have any choice. What's happening in college is that you feed an adolescent in one end, and four years later you get a young adult out the other. The kid has matured, developed new interests, new ideas, new values, and his or her teachers have been instrumental in shaping this emerging character. Now, an argument can be made that while this is indeed what is happening, the university should not take direct responsibility for this development because it is properly the responsibility of the individual students, since they are now adults. The students love this argument, because they love the new freedom of college life, don't want any of this in loco parentis stuff, especially when it comes to having beer parties and having girls or guys in their rooms overnight. Coming from faculty, however, the argument is not very persuasive, especially those who have teenagers at home and are keenly aware of the difference between a late teenager and a young adult. In their heart of hearts they know that teenagers are just that. Morally speaking, they are not yet ready for prime time. But faculty are having a hard enough time getting tenure, and most don't really want to worry about character formation in students, even if they could figure out what sort of character they should be trying to form, and even though they love them dearly and spend a lot of time trying to help them through the difficult and threatening experience we call education. Which brings us back to multiculturalism, colonialism, and intercultural understanding.

There is a carefully reasoned argument abroad that distinctive cultural groups are incommensurable in relation to one another. The most sophisticated version of this argument is the "communitarianism" of Alasdair MacIntyre, in which he struggles with and rather laments the difficulty that one cultural group (he's in the philosophical tradition of Aristotle) has in understanding and empathizing with the culture of others.[5] In fields like cultural anthropology the incommensurability argument is used to object to the "colonialist" attitudes of the dominant Western culture toward cultures it labels "primitive" and therefore less valuable than its own. And in fields dealing with "marginalized" people such as women, blacks, and Asians, the political argument is sometimes made—as in Elisabeth Schüssler Fiorenza's study of women in the New Testament, *In Memory of Her*[6]—that the only people who are qualified for participation in the discussion are not only "X"s but "X"s who share the author's understanding of the meaning of "X-ness."

That's a pretty severe epistemology, analogous to arguing that the only truth is a tautology, where the subject and object are the same thing. Not only does this condition guarantee that all of your interlocutors are on the same page, it also guarantees that they have nothing new to say to each other. And what we have seen in recent years are numerous highly regarded books and essays by followers of different ideologies in which the views of the founders were celebrated, occasionally elaborated upon, but, alas, seldom advanced.

Countering that argument is a recent essay by Wendy Doniger of the University of Chicago, who is a scholar of Hindu mythology. She has been attacked for writing about Hinduism because she is not a Hindu.

She counters, in part, that her Western perspective has always been as advantage in objective assessment of Hindu texts, and that is indeed a point to be pondered.

The ideology-driven views cultivate their own camp but do not connect with any outside camp, which the ideologues are trying to persuade. When these outsiders discover that conversation with the ideologues is not possible because they do not belong to group X, they turn to conversation with those who want to talk with them and not at them. This leaves the ideologues even more marginalized than before, and because marginalization is what they want most to overcome, they eventually tend to soften their stance in search of conversation partners.

The nonideological uses of the incommensurability argument are more persuasive, but they are dependent on subtle and rather academic arguments. Within the university the question of character shaping often gets bogged down in these academic subtleties. The Buddhist views of self are different from the Western views, the Chinese don't honor human rights, so what to do? Well, yes, but before we get to these matters, we have to ask ourselves, What's the moral foundation of the university as we understand it? What is our function as a university based on? And where might we go from there?

The fundamental issues are general values that are shared by people of very different religious and cultural backgrounds, such as honesty in one's academic work. A colleague of mine once said that "plagiarism is the sin against the Holy Ghost in the academic community." If you're going to cheat, you don't belong. That's right, and it's a universal principle of universities everywhere, as far as I know. Don't cheat. That principle is understood a little differently in different places, but it is essentially as true at the University of Calcutta as it is at DePauw. Lower-caste students at Calcutta feel socially disadvantaged, but in the central life of the university a rational argument still trumps social status as a basic value, as it does here. And the values of civility are the necessary context for any rational argument. Again, scholarly conversations in South India are louder than they are in Greencastle, and the first time you hear them, you think people are mad at each other, but the ground rules of civility still apply. So, honesty, rationality, and civility are values built into the idea of a university.

And now I have to tell you about my dog. When I deal with a question of rationality with my philosophy students, I always point out that the definitive characteristic of human rationality is not the ability to figure things out, it's the capacity of self-transcendence. It's the ability to stand off from yourself and look at yourself and say, "I was wrong," or "I was right." It's the capacity to reflect upon the past, to plan for the future. That's something that has a certain kind of mystical quality to it, and it is transcendent in the sense that it puts us in touch with certain values that are not immediate if we keep to the question of rational discourse as simply figuring things out. Now, my dog was very good at figuring things out. Maya was a German shepherd. She lived until she was fourteen. I took her to the office, I took her to class. The students loved her, and so I would say, "The difference between me and Maya is that I know I'm a man, and she doesn't know she's a dog." The students didn't like that, because they liked Maya, and they figured I was putting her down. So, the conversation would go something like this: They say, "How do you know she doesn't know?" And I say, "Well, if she knew, she would have said so." And then we have a long discussion about language and rationality, and then some smart kid who's into dolphins says, "How do you know she isn't saying so, and you're just too dumb to get it?" At which point I change the subject. I'm the professor; I can change the subject if I want to. But you see my point. She's very good at figuring things out. She figured all sorts of things out, but she didn't have this human rational capacity for self-transcendence, and it's that capacity that puts us in touch with our deepest values. And it's not the result of figuring things out. If you've read Plato and studied the Platonic dialogues, you know that dialectic, in Plato's philosophy, only gets you so far. It's an underbrush-clearing operation. You get rid of bad arguments. And you say, "Well, no, justice isn't this, and it's not that, and it's not the other, and so forth. Okay. What is it really?" Well, Socrates had two answers. One was, "I don't really know; I mean, I'm just here to ask you questions." On the other hand, he had a positive answer, and that is that it's what Wilhelm Windelband, the great historian of Western philosophy, called a "synoptic intuition."

Socrates said that this insight was "a gift from the gods." My argument about a real understanding of rationality in the university is not that all universities should be Christian, or Buddhist, or whatever, but that everyone should be open to this transcendent dimension of human rationality in which synoptic intuition plays such a critical part and where true insight into the nature of the most important things in our lives can well be described as a gift from the gods.

So, a university is a cultural institution. Arguments abound over which culture we should be representing. There is no question that most American universities have suffered from cultural provincialism. In my own discipline of philosophy, scholars are still publishing books called *The History of Philosophy* that take you from the pre-Socratics to Bertrand Russell, as though the philosophies of India and China don't count. I started teaching Indian philosophy in India in the early 1960s, and I've been teaching it at Boston University since 1970. It is part of our task to help shape good citizens, so it is our responsibility to look around us, ask what kind of a world we are living in, and the classical tradition of Western culture is where I believe that we ought to begin, almost obviously, because that's who we are. This would include in our own case an intensive study of how the religions in America have so critically informed our deepest political principles, giving us paradoxically a religion-based political culture that is also tolerant of religious diversity. Learning about the great cultures of India and China is, however, crucial cultural catching up on our part. We need to keep broadening the horizons of our student citizens, but we need to do it selectively and with a little humility, because we can't do everything. And once again the ideologues—those modern barbarians—are clamoring at the gates, insisting that if we don't focus on *their* concern, we are just proving what colonialists, racists, chauvinists, or whatever we really are.

So the question before us comes down to this: Can we conceive of an undergraduate education, with self-transcendence and synoptic intuition its daily fare, such that universities might aid today's students in developing a better understanding of themselves *as citizens*? How might we help better equip them, by what they are asked to study, to understand with detachment themselves, their particular cultures, and their nation itself? And how can we also help to enable them to bring together, to synthesize, the otherwise bewildering confusion of their world into an understanding of it that will "make sense" to them *as citizens*? More than this, however, how can we encourage them to *act* on their understandings, to test them with others in the actual work of citizens?

In the light of all this our greatest responsibility is, through our students, to help teach a nation that has forgotten how to have an honest, rational, and civil debate, how much we need people of character who know how to have that kind of serious engagement with each other.

NOTES

1. Robert N. Bellah, "Civil Religion in America," *Dædalus* 96, no. 1 (Winter 1967): 1–21.

2. John Winthrop, "A Model of Christian Charity," ed. Alan Heimert and Andrew Delbanco, *The Puritans in America: A Narrative Anthology,* (Cambridge, MA: Harvard University Press, 1985), 91.

3. At a point early in my life my friend Jack Carazella and I were in Latin class together. And our Latin teacher said, "Of course, Carazella"—Jack was second-generation Italian—"has an advantage over you guys because he's Italian." And Jack said, "Don't look at me." He said, "I don't know any Italian." He said, "My parents won't let me speak Italian. They want me to be an American." For generations this was the familiar immigrant story.

4. Will Herberg, *Protestant, Catholic, Jew: An Essay in American Religious Sociology* (New York: Doubleday, 1956).

5. Alasdair MacIntyre, *Whose Justice? Which Rationality?* (Notre Dame, Ind.: University of Notre Dame Press, 1989).

6. Elizabeth Schüssler Fiorenza, *In Memory of Her* (New York: Crossroads/ Herder& Herder, 1994).

How Do We Talk?
God Talk and American
Political Life

Jean Bethke Elshtain

In the matter of the entanglement of religion with American political life, the salient question is not "whether" but "how." "God talk" at least as much as "rights talk" is the way America speaks. American politics is indecipherable if it is severed from the interplay and panoply of America's religions, most importantly Protestant Christianity. America remains an overwhelmingly Christian nation in its religious identification. The breakdown currently, for those who like statistics, is 82 percent Christian, 1 percent Jewish, 1 percent Muslim, 2 percent other, 1 percent atheist, 2 percent agnostic. About 8 percent said they had no particular religious identification. Moreover, the percentage of Americans who claim belief in God is 95 percent or slightly less, depending on the survey, and over 70 percent claim regular membership in a religious body.[1]

American democracy from its inception was premised on the enactment of projects that were a complex intermingling of religious and political imperatives. The majority of Americans were religious seekers and believers who saw in communal liberty the freedom to *be* religious as they saw fit rather than freedom *from* religion.[2] It is, therefore, not surprising that such a huge chunk of American juridical life has been devoted to sorting out the often inaptly named church-state debate. In a less religious society this would be a far less salient issue.

RELIGION, PUBLIC NOT PRIVATE

Although church and state are kept separate—ours is not and never has been either a theocracy or a nation with an official civic religion—religion and politics have always mutually constituted one another in ways direct and indirect. This is a theme advanced by Alexis de Tocqueville in his masterwork, *Democracy in America*. Tocqueville proclaimed that the religiously formed and shaped democratic optimism and egalitarianism and the associational enthusiasm he witnessed when he toured these United States during the Jacksonian era were something new under the political sun.[3] Remember that Tocqueville's own experience of this issue was either the alliance between throne and altar characteristic of France's ancien régime or, alternatively, the horrific and violent assault on faith and its replacement by an *official* civic religion during the bloody French Revolution. Tocqueville saw the enervating effect of this wrenching, this violent assault on faith.

By contrast, in the American democracy, the action of religion on politics, and vice versa, put into play a number of important categories: the believer and the citizen, the church and the state. The terrain in which they met, most of the time, was, Tocqueville observed, in that realm of institutional and associational life we call civil society. It is important to note here at the outset that we make a rather major mistake if we map the legalistic terms of the church-state debate as juridical concepts onto the far more fluid, complex, and nuanced world of religion and politics. Church-state and religion-politics are *not* identical.

That church and state are separate—ours is a secular government—does *not* mean that ours is a thoroughly secularized society. It isn't now. It never has been. In March 2000, the ninety-sixth American Assembly, a by now venerable effort that goes back over half a century and is designed to bring together citizens to confront honestly major issues of public life, met to consider religion and American political life and civic culture. As one of the leaders of this assembly, it was my job to gain the widest possible representation of America's religions and to help to steer our diverse group toward a statement we could all agree to, and sign on with, on the role of religion in American political life. Fifty-seven men and women representing sixteen different religious orientations attended. Here are four key sentences from the document that we produced at the culmination of our intense three-day meeting:

> We reject the notion that religion is exclusively a private matter relegated to the homes and sacred meeting places of the faithful, primarily for two reasons. First, religious convictions of individuals cannot be severed from their daily lives. People of faith in business, law, medicine, education, and other sectors should not be required to divorce their faith from their professions. Second, many religious communities have a rich tradition of constructive social engagement, and our nation benefits from their work in such varied areas as social justice, civil rights, and ethics.

These conclusions suggest a logic for engagement in the civic realm that clashes with a dominant strand of argument in the academy and some jurisprudential circles that, as we shall see, touches not at all on how people actually talk and act and react "on the ground." I refer to the work of the philosopher John Rawls and his insistence that, if you are religious, your convictions need to be translated into a strictly secular civic idiom if you are to take part in political deliberation.[4] You make this translation or you'd best remain silent. Part of Rawls's complex argument (although that neo-Kantian argument yields a few pretty simple dicta) is that there is a single vocabulary of political discussion. This argument has made its way into jurisprudential thought and logic, but it hasn't made much of an inroad into our politics as this takes place concretely in the world of American civil society—a world that includes day-to-day civic life, including political parties.

Rawls's argument is part of a tradition I call *liberal monism*, for its roots lie in one strand of liberal political philosophy. I will have more to say on this as we go along but, for now, let me just note that this position cuts against the grain of American political history and civic culture. The U.S. Constitution, unlike, for example, the terms under which Jewish residents of the nation were admitted into the polity in France as citizens, had not required that Jews give up the communal dimensions of their faith that found expression in and through Hebrew schools, communally enforced dietary rules and regulations and dress, and the like, as the price of civic admission. Instead, *confessional pluralism* and *social pluralism* were linked in the American polity as religious differences were afforded public markers and forms of communal identification. One reason that America's religious institutions remain the heart of American civil society lies in the fact that religion in America was never required to go into hiding and to privatize itself—despite some efforts in that direction over the years.[5]

Some historic backdrop might be helpful at this point. For the first 150 years of the American Republic, primary responsibility for religious rights and liberties was lodged in the states. Attempts to create a national law on religion applicable to the states and enforceable in the federal courts were defeated. The federal government got into the act in a big way only over the last half century. A constitutional position emerged that might be called "strong separationism." Like Rawlsian philosophy, it, too, is an offshoot of liberal monism. Although this position, one that pushes to strip public life of religious symbols, signs, markers, and even speech, never held consistent sway, it figures in the thinking of those who, whether in law or out, not only assume church-state separation but also seek a thoroughly secularized society in which religion must be invisible to public life.

Within this position there is an animus against the determination by faith communities to sustain their own networks of schools, social provision, civic advocacy groups, health care institutions, and the like, and to see these activities as both religious and civic. A strong separationist finds the idea of public religion both oxymoronic and anathema across the board, not only in cases where possible receipt of any public moneys in support of broad-based activities might be at stake. Strong separationists hold that religion is by definition private and must needs be so: thus public religion is oxymoronic. As well, "public religion" is an aggressive threat to civic life as religious believers deep down want to sacralize the public sphere; hence, public religion is anathema.

Let's be clear about liberal monism at this juncture. I am not referring to some broad-based critique of liberal political philosophy across the board; rather, I refer to a position that holds that all institutions internal to a democratic society must conform to a single, representational authority principle; a single standard of what counts as reason and deliberation; a single vocabulary of political discussion. Within this position, religion is routinely discounted as irrationalism, or special pleading, or a search for epistemological privilege.

It follows that Christians, Jews, Muslims, anyone with a faith commitment, is not permitted, when speaking as a citizen, to give reasons for his or her support or dissent from a public policy measure in language that incorporates an explicit religious reference. Citizens who are also believers are obliged, as I noted with Rawls's argument, to translate every view supported by their religious beliefs into a purportedly "neutral" civic language. Only in this way, claims liberal monism, can America achieve a workable civic consensus. If one refracts these concerns from the standpoint of religious belief, however, "the problem" looks quite different: *what becomes evident is a problem with narrowing the purview of politics rather than with bringing religious commitments to politics.* Nevertheless, it is religion that is put on the defensive consistently, nowhere more so than in discussions and assumptions that prevail in many of our institutions of higher education, especially the elite academy.

In his book *The Dissent of the Governed*, the distinguished constitutional scholar Stephen Carter reminds us that tolerance "is not simply a willingness to listen to what others have to say. It is also a resistance to the quick use of state power . . . to force dissenters and the different to conform."[6] As an example of this phenomenon, Carter points to pro-life protest and the ways in which attempts to quash this form of public advocacy have proceeded apace with the blessing of the courts in applying RICO racketeering statutes to pro-life dissent. Whether one accepts this example as valid or not, Carter's more general point is that if we set up as paradigmatic the view that the nation must be morally more or less the same, plurality is denied and community autonomy is eroded. All of this is traceable to the old notion that human beings cannot embrace simultaneously dual (or more) loyalties that may, at times, conflict.

This was an explicit worry in the work of such important social contractarians as John Locke and Jean-Jacques Rousseau, especially in Rousseau, and it is a worry that carries forward even now. Rather than thinking of our many loyalties as enriching us, the thought is that dual loyalties—to our church and to our polity—threaten to undermine political loyalty. If you thought this canard was dead, just consider some of the disturbing arguments mounted in the run-up to the Iraq war with vague notions circulating that Jewish Americans, given their loyalty to a faith that extends to concern with the fate of the state of Israel, were, for religious reasons, pushing America into war. What is this but a demand that our loyalties be monistic, not plural?

HOW SHOULD WE TALK?
THE MONIST DEMAND

The position I call liberal monism, and from which I trace both Rawlsian restrictions on God talk in political life and strict separationism in jurisprudence, views religion as a set of comprehensive, authoritative, and total claims. Because the claims of law and politics are similarly authoritative and comprehensive, there is bound to be tension; likely to be a clash. Something's got to give. For if the writ of each extends to all aspects of human life and makes total claims, each aspires to take up "all" the space, so to speak. The upshot? Well, if you want liberal politics, the upshot, having characterized matters in this way, is that the one, law and politics, may decide that it can, and should, accommodate the other—if the other behaves itself, more or less. This all goes forward under the name of "toleration."

The modern regime of religious toleration derives in large part from John Locke's justly famous *Letter on Toleration* in which Locke draws up a map separating soulcraft, the world of religion, from statecraft, the realm of government. A person could be a citizen of each so long as religion meant primarily freedom of conscience rather than strong institutional loyalty to a religious body that engaged the society in all its aspects. Locke argued that under such terms all religions, save atheism and Roman Catholicism, were to be tolerated. Atheists couldn't be tolerated as they would not take an oath on the Bible, hence were untrustworthy; Catholics did not fit within the terms of the tolerance regime because they had that dangerous double loyalty—they were loyal to a strong church as well as to the polity, but, given their loyalty to church, their political loyalty was bound to be suspect or tepid at best. It was the institutional presence and authority of the Catholic Church that seemed to unhinge Locke on this question.[7] So: a strong public presence and witness for religion, no. Private freedom of conscience, not only tolerated but infinitely superior to any other mode of religious expression: yes. In the words of one of America's leading constitutional lawyers on the free exercise of religion, Michael McConnell: "Locke's exclusion of atheists and Catholics from toleration cannot be dismissed as a quaint exception to his beneficent liberalism; it follows logically from the ground on which his argument for toleration rested. If religious freedom meant nothing more than that religion should be free so long as it is irrelevant to the state, it does not mean very much."[8] Yet this, McConnell insists, is precisely what the regime of liberal toleration pushes toward and, under the terms of strong liberal monism, requires.

The "Rawlsian requirement" or variant on liberal monism strips persons religious of religious speech when they enter the political realm. I won't rehearse this position yet again; rather, let's turn to religious responses to it. There have been several. The first holds that the fullness of religious belief, commitment, and witness must enter the public sphere and precisely on religious terms. This has nothing to do with the legal establishment of religion. It has to do, rather, with the conviction that religion is undermined if persons with religious commitments are compelled to engage in any translation of these commitments into a civic idiom. In an essay on the subject, I tagged this the *full-bore Christian politics* position.[9] It assumes that a full display of religious reason-giving is appropriate and may even be necessary on every political issue.

By contrast, there is a position that, at first glance, looks similar but is, in fact, quite distinct: the prophetic-witness position. Within this frame, no one pushes for an undiluted "Christian politics" nor seeks Christian saturation of ordinary everyday political discourse and action; rather, persons religious respond to extraordinary situations from the fullness of religious commitment. One thinks here first and foremost of Martin Luther King and his great speeches, which were also sermons. It would be an act of the most severe restraint on speech to require of King retroactively that he drop all religious references to Scripture in his speech. The speech wouldn't exist without the cadences and specific references—indeed, basic text—drawn from the prophet Amos.

Whether full-bore Christian politics or prophetic witness, however, the requirement from the direction of liberal monism would be that these positions are unacceptable or suspect as public discourse because they mount arguments that are critically unassailable, being based on "private" or special revelation. But this is a misunderstanding of religious argument. Religious arguments are epistemologically incorrigible in large part because the Christian tradition is one of contested interpretations. For every "Christian position" on public policy x or y there is another "Christian position" that differs. To be sure, many Christians forget this, but when they do they are more likely to chide those who disagree with them for being lousy Christians than terrible citizens.

A third religious response to the demands that religious speech be "cleaned up" before it goes out in public is more or less along these lines:

well, if that's the way they want it, we'll retreat into our own enclave and live out a faithful life as Christians in a community of faith. Citizenship is downgraded or even considered potentially idolatrous because it invites loyalty and faithfulness to something other than church. I call this position *radical dualism.* It is, in its own way, an even stronger dualism than that effected by the regime of liberal tolerance, but it is self-imposed rather than being state mandated. The keen observer will note that the radical dualist posture is a negative mirror image of full-bore Christian politics. One example of this radical dualism in practice is the argument mounted recently that the Christian, in particular the Catholic, understanding of marriage is the quaint property of a few believers and should not, therefore, affect how the civic world construes marriage. So why not open marriage up to any and all—whether gay marriage, or (one presumes) polygamy, or some other arrangement? This is what I mean by a robust withdrawal from public debate.[10]

There is, finally, a fourth option and my preferred alternative. This position is internally complex. It calls upon citizen-believers to offer a nuanced assessment of the ways in which religion enters civic discourse depending upon the nature of the issues involved—What are the stakes?—and depending on what arenas or spheres of human social existence are affected and how—Who are the key players? How should those implicated in any given situation address the issues at stake and go on to express their concerns to their fellow citizens? Perhaps the best tag for this position is *contextual engagement.*

My working assumption is that, in a pluralistic society such as our own, with its politics of modulation, negotiation, and compromise, most often the engagement of religious believers with politics does not present an earth-shattering dilemma. The lines are not drawn in the sand. I also assume that it is not the task of Christianity or any religion in a society premised on nonestablishment and free exercise to underwrite any political ideology, agenda, or platform. Indeed, when and where the issues call for a sharp, decisive break of Christianity with secular power, politics as usual is likely to have already disappeared.

On nearly all issues, Christians—with other citizens, whether of religious commitment or not—are obliged to continue the argument, to participate in discourse, to find ways to find common ground. Most of the time. This means that, most of the time, the fullness of religious reason-giving in political life is neither required nor desirable. Suppose that I support protection of endangered species because of the Creation doctrine—God created the earth and all its wonders. Am I obliged to lay out an exegesis of Genesis in order to indicate my support for a bill extending protection to endangered species? I doubt it. There are other ways to make the case. Do I think it would be wrong, unacceptable, to speak of the Genesis account, as the Rawlsian requirement would have it? No. But it might not be the best politics.

There are, however, other issues—euthanasia, abortion, capital punishment, cloning, and the stem-cell debate—that may require going "all the way down" in one's argument. One may be obliged in such circumstances to offer the fullness of religious reason-giving, including the theological anthropology at work in one's stance. If you are committed to the dignity of the human person and a certain understanding of human rights on theological grounds—not exclusively theological grounds, but these are the very heart of the matter—it strikes me as a draconian and prejudicial demand for you to be obliged to excise the depth of your beliefs from the reasons you proffer publicly for the stance you take.

There are times when Christians, and other persons religious, will want to make it absolutely clear where they stand, and why, but these moments are likely to be rare in a democratic society. It is also the case that public policy is not attached to a moral mandate with superglue. Persons with religious convictions may agree on the rightness or wrongness of something but disagree on how that can best be expressed in law and policy. The key moral questions are likely to be: Who is inside or outside the boundary of moral concern? Is this a common good question? And so on.

Let's turn next to my new reflections prompted by the questions put to me, as to all speakers, to guide us in writing our presentations.

How We Talk? Or, Let's Get Real

Democratic politics most of the time is a pretty rough-and-tumble affair. There is a complex dialectic at work at all times that never arrives at some grand synthesis. Citizens, variously located, engage one another through a culture of democratic argument, sort things out, as people tend to do, in an untidy way. The resort to the courts, or to moral philosophers, for that matter, should be a last resort, not the first move made in this dialectic. Issues of religious and political importance that can be worked out informally become far more difficult to sort out if one group or another brings a test case seeking a controlling precedent. In such cases, battle lines harden. Similarly, to hew strictly to the terms of liberal monism, to insist that there is some metalanguage of democratic deliberation stripped of particularity where religious belief is concerned imposes an artificial and unacceptable constraint on political argument and its rules of engagement.

Most of the time, as I've already suggested, total claims are not at stake in these matters from the religious side but, rather, an attempt to promote or to defend a religiously derived vision of social justice, or protection of all persons without distinction, as part of a normative vision *for* civil society rather than as one item of a particularistic credo that the believer wants to map in a total way over all of society.

This makes it all the more important that civil authorities not circumscribe the boundaries of discursive rules of engagement in severe and a priori ways. The goods at stake are best understood not as totalistic religious goods versus some contrary set of total goods, but as competing understandings of a public good, variously derived. In a reasonably decent and well-ordered civil society such as our own, the rare case is one in which religious conscience and society's values as manifested in the rule of law comprise opposite ends of a spectrum. The far more common case puts belief and law, religion and politics, together and finds them tussling until some modus vivendi is worked out.

Why, then, has the Rawlsian requirement proved to be so attractive to academic scholars in philosophy and jurisprudence alike? Here's a suggestion: contemporary distrust of organized politics and public religion often go hand-in-hand. Both involve public expression; collectivities of persons involved in a shared enterprise; rules and convictions; sometimes hard-hitting encounters. That we seem not to have the stomach for either suggests that our capacity for democracy is growing anemic. A preference for getting things tidied up both in argument and through the courts is a distaste for politics itself. To me this suggests that we are not doing a very good job of social, political, and, yes, religious formation: preparing citizens for a world in which there are disagreements and there are decisions to be made and you cannot and should not tell people of religious conviction to keep it to themselves. Religion, in all its complexity and plurality, plays a major role in asking and in answering the most important questions: What kind of people are we? What sort of place is this? What do we hope for?

Let's turn the usual way of framing this question around. The usual way of framing it is, remember: How can or should politics "accommodate" religion? What is acceptable and not acceptable from the political side where the public presence and voice of religion is concerned? Do we permit religion to play a robust role? Ought we? As theologian Robin Lovin has argued recently, there is a very hypothetical and abstract quality to this way of putting things. Instead of looking at how things actually play themselves out, we move to a metaplane and ask what is required in order that a cleaned-up democratic discourse can go forward. Lovin asks us to frame these matters, for a change, from the point of view of religion: What sort of politics does religion require in order to play a role that religious commitments demand? Perhaps the problem in the discussions I have been analyzing and criticizing is a too-narrow understanding of politics rather than a dangerously intrusive religion.

I cannot do justice to Lovin's complex argument here, but, to summarize, he does something quite refreshing. He asks us to look at how people actually talk when they "go public." Is there really some language of "public reason" that properly functioning citizens in a democratic society advert to in political discussion? If you go this route, you find that our political discussions are as various as are our political participants. All manner of identities, commitments, and particular concerns are brought forward. On issues of unusual gravity and moment, nearly everyone, without exception, speaks of a public good or commonweal, religious and nonreligious persons alike.

Everyone who goes public embraces a set of practical concerns, unless his or her purpose is prophetic witness to a sin of great magnitude at a moment in a country's history when calling attention to something seems more important than incremental change. How can I best advance my case? Who can I persuade and how? What am I prepared to compromise on? What is rock-bottom and I'll not be budged? Religious and nonreligious citizens alike do this. Within a framework associated with Augustinianism and, more recently, Reinhold Niebuhr, the person religious "sees the interaction of religion and politics as a continuing tension, in which religious judgments are always in danger of being dismissed, ridiculed, or even persecuted, but in which religion nevertheless provides the critical self-limitation that keeps a political system from overreaching and overconfidence."[11]

A desire to be politically effective means that one rarely offers religious reasons as the exclusive reasons for one's stance. Lovin suggests that he hasn't yet done this work, but if one were to go through and go over the ways in which religious bodies, through their primary documents and entreaties, enter the political arena, one would find them addressing themselves to all citizens without distinction as well as to their coreligionists. Those who are best equipped to do this are Roman Catholics with their venerable tradition of natural law and common good arguments, but also all persons religious, save for certain fundamentalists or Pentecostals who, at least historically, tended to eschew politics for the most part.

The upshot is that the demand that religious persons clean up their act is largely unnecessary—because most persons religious offer a panoply of reasons for why they favor or oppose some policy or anticipated course of action, not all of them religious. Indeed, most of the time, most of the reasons are not exclusively religious. In addition, the demand is unfair— because it places a burden on over 90 percent of the American population to strip themselves of their religious convictions in the course of participating in some highly rarefied realm of "public reason." Lovin suggests that any survey of the terms on which religious people enter the public square suggests interactions between "religious reasons" and "public reasons" that are not apparent in hypothetical cases designed to test the limits of public discourse. Real people not only bring religious arguments into public discourse. They also bring a religious evaluation of the discourse itself. They have religious reasons for public choices, and they have religious ideas about how the public chooses. Those ideas about how the public chooses help them to decide how, and whether, to relate their religious reasons to public reasons.

The realm of political life is political, not religious. One enters it as a citizen. But one may be a citizen with religious convictions, so these convictions go along with you as you stride into the public square. Just as the fact that you are black or white, male or female, with or without children, able-bodied or with a disability, from Mississippi or Minnesota, like rock and roll or revile it, on and on, go with you as well. These particular facts about us help to determine who we are, how we think, what we care about, how we argue. That is as it should be in a democracy.

The implication of my argument for civic and liberal education is that it makes absolutely no sense to reduce "diversity" to gender, race, or ethnicity and to view strongly held religious convictions as a threat rather than as an intrinsic part of American pluralism in all its messy glory. I have had many experiences over the years, some of them recent, in which I was told in rather hushed terms that this or that student group on campus should really not be included in a list of RSOs—recognized student organizations—because they were religious in nature and used their meetings to actually try to "convert" people.

How did they try to do this, I would ask? Did they tie people down and read Scripture verses to them twenty-four hours a day, with bright lights glaring in their faces, and food and water withheld? No, they did what we all do: they used speech and force of argument and example. That's what is done in student government, in student political organizations, in student branches of Amnesty International or People for the Ethical Treatment of Animals, or . . . well, the reader may complete the list. The purposes and aspirations of American democracy are not parochial because they are based on a set of universal principles open in principle to all without exception. But people react to these principles in a variety of ways. Among these precious freedoms is not only the freedom to believe but to try to persuade others of your beliefs. We should practice what we preach—on college campuses as well as in the wider civic world.

How do we talk? Just listen. The endless varieties, intonations, accents, harmonies, atonalities, punctuations, and pauses of American speech are extraordinary. Civic education is, in part, a way to help us become aware of these multiple idioms, including their religious variety, and to appreciate them all, with few exceptions, as ways of living complex human lives, particularly and even idiosyncratically, while at the same time articulating visions of how it is we can come to know a good in common that we cannot know alone. This is how we do talk and it is also, I believe, how we should talk.

NOTES

1. These are the results of a survey conducted in February and March 2002 by the Pew Research Council. www.adherents.com/rel_USA.html (6/9/05).

2. The First Amendment, of course, speaks to both senses of religious freedom—with a lot of dispute ever since over what they mean.

3. Tocqueville's analysis of religion in the United States will be found in *Democracy in America,* ed. Harvey C. Mansfield and Delba Winthrop (Chicago:

University of Chicago Press, 2000), esp. vol. 1, pt. 2, chap. 9, and vol. 2, pt. 1, chaps. 5–7.

4. See John Rawls, *Political Liberalism* (New York: Columbia University Press, 1993), especially lecture 6.

5. Here I think it important to distinguish between *secular* life and *secularism* as an ideology. The secular is earthly life as such, derived from the Latin, *saeculum*. It simply means earthly existence between creation and the end-time. Secularism, however, is an explicitly antireligious ideology with its several "manifestos" that proclaims the illegitimacy and irrelevance of any "transcendent" reference point. The upshot is that it would be foolhardy to fight against "the secular," as we all live in it, so to speak. But secularism as an ideology that would strip civic life of all symbols, markers, remembrance, and terms of a religious sort is something else altogether.

6. Stephen Carter, *The Dissent of the Governed* (Cambridge, Mass.: Harvard University Press, 1998), 85.

7. Locke put it this way: "That Church can have no right to be tolerated by the magistrate which is constituted upon such a bottom that all those who enter into it do thereby *ipso facto* deliver themselves up to the protection and service of another prince. For by this means the magistrate would give way to the settling of a foreign jurisdiction in his own country and suffer his own people to be listed, as it were, for soldiers against his own Government." John Locke, *Treatise of Civil Government and Letter Concerning Toleration,* ed. Charles L. Sherman (New York: Appleton-Century-Crofts, 1937), 212.

8. Quoted in Paul J. Griffiths and Jean Bethke Elshtain, "Proselytizing for Tolerance," pt. 2, *First Things,* November 2002.

9. Jean Bethke Elshtain, "How Should We Talk?" *Case Western Reserve Law Review* 49 (199): 731–46.

10. This is not the time and place to begin an argument about marriage between homosexuals. I use this as one recent example made by those who believe that believers should lurk behind a cordon sanitaire, practice their quaint beliefs, and let the civic world go on its merry way.

11. Robin Lovin, "Consensus and Commitment: Real People, Religious Reasons, and Public Discourse," forthcoming in *Theology, Morality, and Public Life*, ed. Kenneth Grasso and Celia Rodriguez Castillo, in the series *Religion and Public Life,* ed. Jean Bethke Elshtain and John Carlson (Grand Rapids, Mich.: Eerdmans).

CHAPTER ELEVEN

Plato's Dogs
Reflections on the University after 9/11

STEPHEN HOLMES

U nblushing members of "the military-industrial-academic complex,"[1] universities make an indisputable contribution to America's
daunting power to do good or ill in the world. The principal question
facing the authors of this volume is: What contribution can these same
institutions of higher learning make to the wise use of America's formidable power? How can our universities help us respond intelligently to
the unprecedented perils and challenges of the new century? What politically important role can universities play in this new, complex, changing, and turbulent world?

To pose this question is already to suggest that American universities
are not now playing the role that they could and should play, that they are
not, for example, doing a creditable job helping produce the educated
public that we so manifestly lack and need. That more than 50 percent of
Americans apparently still believe that Saddam Hussein had a hand in
9/11 provides an unflattering, if not shameful, commentary on the educational preparedness of this country's opinion-making elite. So why
have we fallen into this miserable state? Some of the cultural critics
included in this volume claim that our institutions of higher education are
betraying us politically because they have been suffused with commercial

values.[2] Whether persuasive or unpersuasive, this charge is anything but new. In 1918, for instance, Max Weber wrote:

> The American's conception of the teacher who faces him is: He sells me his knowledge and methods for my father's money, just as the greengrocer sells my mother cabbage. And that is all. To be sure, if the teacher happens to be a football coach, then, in this field, he is a leader.[3]

According to their more recent and perhaps less humorous admonishers, U.S. universities have now succumbed to the market conception of freedom, oriented to the satisfaction of individual desires, and have thereby irresponsibly shed the civic conception of freedom, which (at some unidentifiable historical moment) involved intense public debate about common purposes. I cannot say that I understand this claim very well, especially given the prominence and persistence of faculty tenure, an antimarket institution par excellence. But, of course, I appreciate as much as anyone the irony of professors who earn money by selling books in which they showcase their dislike or distrust of the market.

Those who focus on the continuing commercialization of higher education, admittedly, are not simply self-deluded. Derek Bok, for example, has helpfully drawn public attention to the way the pharmaceutical industry is endangering the independence of biochemical research.[4] Moreover, critics are right who argue that universities, to play a positive role in our political life, must be shielded to some extent from the pressing demands of the private economy. They must not be turned into wholly owned subsidiaries of for-profit corporations. It is reasonable, therefore, to ask universities to disentangle themselves somewhat from the most robust and dynamic part of society, that is to say, America's large and immensely influential profit-making enterprises. But is it realistic to ask universities, as some of my colleagues have done, to attach themselves *instead* to a political culture of democratic "participation" and deliberation that does not, in fact, exist?

"Commercialization," if the truth be told, is a rather rarefied charge. It is much more common to hear politically tinctured complaints. For instance, right-wing critics of U.S. universities deplore what they perceive as disloyalty, that is, a lack of patriotism. Left-wing critics, by contrast, lament student apathy, that is, an absence of engagement. The two charges have some things in common, but they sound more similar than they actually are. The former is genuinely pernicious, for instance, while the latter is merely frivolous.

I want to postpone my discussion of patriotism versus disloyalty for a few pages, so let me now say a few words first about engagement versus apathy. To begin with, "participation" is a very sixties word. It emits a strong aroma of nostalgia for the days of student protest against the Vietnam War. There is nothing wrong with the ideal of participation, in fact, except its ineradicable ambivalence. Participation is good or bad depending on the knowledge, habits, skills, motives, psychoses, and antipathies of the participators. To say that universities should foster greater and more intense participation is therefore nonsensical; and no one who says it actually means us to take it seriously as a platform for university reform.

There is no point trying to supervise other professors' theorizing, to be sure. But I would suggest that, given the scarcity of time and the urgency of the need, we refocus, not on how a reformed university might conceivably promote the most demanding personal and social ideals, but, instead, on the urgent political and social problems that we can help solve with the materials at hand. There is no use proposing a remedy, however, before we have a clear understanding of the disease from which the patient is suffering. So we should start with diagnosis.

If the essential predicament of our universities were excessive privatization, marketization, and political apathy, then perhaps an appealing and appropriate solution would involve promoting participation and civic virtue. But what if the essential problem were something quite different, namely a combination of *anachronism* and *parochialism*? Such ailments would call for quite different cures.

Universities first emerged in a social context that has, in the interim, evolved unrecognizably. Social change is highly uneven, and it is quite normal for institutions with a degree of formal autonomy—for instance, where currently employed personnel have a free hand in selecting successor cohorts—to maintain themselves in their original form long after the surrounding society, whose needs they were originally designed to meet, has been utterly transformed. An instructive example is NATO, created to defend the West against the USSR but continuing to lead a Don Quixote existence, tilting at windmills, fifteen years after the USSR vanished from the map. NATO survives by sheer inertia, that is, because it is

188 | CHAPTER 11

an inherited institution populated by influential individuals with careers, homes, salaries, and so forth to protect.

Something similar, it seems to me, can be said about American universities. After World War II, our major research universities were swept up in the Cold War. I am not speaking only of the hard sciences here, although they certainly illustrate the point I want to make.[5] I am also referring to political science, Slavic studies, economics, and so forth, all of which were imbued with the ideological atmosphere of the time. Opposition to Soviet-style communism was widely shared, providing a core of common assumptions shared by the right and the mainstream left. McCarthyism aside, this underlying consensus did not stifle critical voices. On the contrary, many conservatives understood that conspicuous tolerance of left-leaning critics made the West look good in its worldwide struggle with Marxist totalitarianism.

When the pyramids began to crumble, in 1989, some important fields of university research became unhinged. Simultaneously, some of our leading intellects, to put it mildly, seriously lost their bearings. (To name names would be both impolite and useless.) Soviet studies provides only the most clamorous example. What this historically conditioned disorientation suggests is that our universities are more like NATO than we might have suspected. Universities adapt, to be sure, but not as fast as the world around them changes. They were built, after all, to preserve and transmit accumulated knowledge. No surprise, therefore, if they have a serious problem keeping up with the accelerating pace of historical events. One problem is that they are populated by individuals who have, as individuals, invested years of effort becoming experts in subjects and methods that, to universal shock, can become irrelevant virtually overnight. It is only natural that mature professors resist a supple adaptation to new realities, since rapid adjustment would entail their own marginalization and replacement by younger scholars less burdened by passé knowledge. In other words, the incentives facing the entrenched professoriat, armed with the power of choosing successors, are not well aligned with the public interest.

In modern times, universities were founded to reproduce the elite cadres of homogeneous nation-states. (The handful of universities founded in the Middle Ages were eventually co-opted, nation by nation, into the same cause.) Today's universities retain this function in part. There are virtually no international universities in the world because universities, to amass resources and attract personnel, must draw upon the energy and purpose of a relatively coherent polity. Separate states, with flags and armies and a pretense to "sovereignty," are still major actors in the world, and they still have a large incentive to invest in the selection and training of their future leaders and innovators. Nevertheless, in a larger sense, the original context in which universities arose has now vanished. U.S. universities are caught today in an unprecedented situation. They have to absorb ethnic diversity within while confronting globalization without. This is a tension-filled and difficult place to work and not one that universities were originally designed to occupy. The relative homogeneity of their student bodies and their relative detachment from the rest of the world were two essential attributes of American universities until the 1960s if not later. This provides yet another reason to doubt those who tell us that universities are being ruined by "modern market values" and have to be saved by a retrieval of "civic virtues." The moralizing contrast of corrupting markets versus civic virtue provides no guidance at all to those who must face the difficulties and opportunities of ethnic diversity inside and globalization outside. The problem is not loss of the past and overadaptation to the present, but the contrary. Far from overadapting, universities have underadapted and seem unable to teach a highly diverse group of young people what they need to know in order to live responsibly and fruitfully in a world without walls.

To those who say at this point that low and decreasing voter turnout is a sign that American democracy is floundering, I make no objection. And I also heartily concur with those, such as Benjamin Barber above, who add that individual rights can never be reliably protected in a society where citizens are mostly passive and inert. But the problem that Barber and his colleagues accurately describe was not created by universities and cannot be solved by universities. We are faced here with massive tectonic shifts in the social landscape that cannot be reversed by pep talks or institutional engineering. As William Galston mentions in his chapter in this volume, economic development undermines traditional social solidarity by giving individuals the means—namely, money—to purchase the cooperation they require, relieving them of the need to rely on normatively obligatory reciprocity among neighbors. Solidarity is necessarily eroded as economies prosper and wealth is more widely distributed. No amount of sermonizing can turn back the clock. Only an unimaginable economic catastrophe would resurrect the helping-hand society lamented by communitarians.

Analogously, the emergence of high-tech weaponry means that privileged social groups are now less dependent on ordinary citizen-soldiers than they were when civic republicanism was a dominant ideal. As we have recently seen, our political rulers can now conduct a massive military campaign without resorting to conscription, and therefore without stimulating fierce public criticism and protest. The technological possibility of war-making without conscription explains why there will be no return to the Vietnam-era campus and its puerile idealizations of "participation." It also explains the fatuity of attempting to revive, in today's world, old-style "republicanism," that is, a political form built around the pivotal role played by citizen-soldiers.

Crudely speaking, democracy refers to a system in which those who are affected by political decisions have some capacity to influence the decision makers, in the ideal case by voting them out of office. The growing unreality of democratic ideals in the light of contemporary trends should be clear from this definition alone. Today, the whole world is directly affected, often in immensely negative ways, by decisions taken in Washington, D.C. Since we are not moving toward a system in which the entire adult population of the globe can vote in U.S. elections, our increasingly interdependent world is becoming palpably less democratic. We can and should lament this development, but we cannot reverse it.

Political decision making is becoming increasingly global. But there are no global political parties capable of losing global elections and no global lawmakers elected and ousted by global voters. The densely populated civil society underlying liberal-democratic polities has no counterpart on the global level. This is not a psychological or moral-emotional problem, therefore, rooted in weak character or a lack of personal commitment. Nor is a new upsurge of democracy being held down by bad theories. Citizens in democracies and semi-democracies around the world are increasingly alienated from civic engagement because civic engagement is often a sham. Brilliant professors writing inspirational treatises will in no way affect this secular trend. Nor will universities play an important role in some dubious attempt, against the tide of times, to democratize global politics.

The left-wing complaint that universities are not doing enough to promote civic engagement is a lighthearted counterpart to the right's much more sinister complaint that universities are not doing enough to promote patriotism. I now turn to that more urgent and disturbing theme. According to Fox News, some American professors have been overheard doubting the proposition that "America is the greatest country that has ever existed." That such doubts sound scandalous to well-funded and highly visible right-wing ideologues brings us to the title of this chapter, namely to Plato's conception of patriotism and its relation to the life of the mind. The real threat to the university lies here, not in commercialism but in the vulgar jingoism of a few anti-intellectual conservatives who have shown what fatal influence they can wield over an uneducated public in an age of panic induced by terror.

Conservative hostility to the university is not new, as a glance at McCarthyism reveals. But during most of the Cold War, as already mentioned, critical minds were protected somewhat from charges of lack of patriotism by the nature of the enemy. Soviet communism was universally associated with censorship and a lack of intellectual freedom. As a result, tolerance of a free-thinking and critical professoriat was widely viewed, including by many conservatives, as an important weapon in the anti-communist arsenal. But, in a development that has yet to attract the attention it deserves, this powerful reason for conservatives to respect the intellectual independence of universities ended along with the Cold War. As a result, the charge of professorial disloyalty may yet prove more effective today than it did in the early 1950s. It all depends on the gravity of future attacks on the United States and the rationality of our government's response. There are obviously reasons for concern on both accounts.

Here we come to Plato's "dogs." No polity can survive this dangerous world, Plato explained, without soldiers who are keen observers, swift pursuers, and brave fighters. They must be high spirited, that is, fearless and unconquerable in the face of the greatest dangers. The problem is to make sure that such fierce young men never turn their terrifying ferocity on each other or their fellow citizens. They must be "gentle to their friends and harsh to their enemies."[6] This sounds at first like an impossible combination, Plato says, but then he adds, "You surely have observed in well-bred hounds that their natural disposition is to be most gentle to their familiars and those whom they recognize, but the contrary to those whom they do not know."[7] This analogy between soldiers and guard dogs contains, in condensed form, Plato's theory of patriotism. His core idea is that patriotism, that is to say, instinctive fondness for fellow citizens and xenophobic aversion to foreigners, is inimical to thought. A guard dog has no need for highly developed cognitive faculties. His brain shrinks to the size of a pea and his sole mental function is to distinguish friend from foe: "The sight of an unknown person angers him before he has suffered any injury, but he will fawn upon an acquaintance though he has never received any kindness from him."[8]

These are important passages to keep in mind when we listen to the shouts of American GIs as they storm leather-booted into the houses of Iraqi civilians shouting, "Get on the fucking floor!" to women and children who presumably know no English. This is what Plato meant when he said, apparently euphemistically, that effective soldiers had to seal their eyes to foreign charms. The only "wisdom" that good soldiers need is the ability to distinguish Americans from non-Americans.

That this is not the kind of wisdom that should preoccupy institutions of higher learning does not need saying. The virtues that we hope to cultivate in our students are not the same virtues that we strive to inculcate in our soldiers. That the timeless truths of mathematics are accessible to all human beings, regardless of the specific community to which they belong, was one of Plato's principal ideas and does not need to be defended here. But it may be worthwhile to recall Julien Benda's splendid *j'accuse* against rabidly nationalist intellectuals who betrayed their obligations to truth and knowledge in order to worship pieces of cloth nailed to sticks:

> Here we come upon one of the great impieties of the moderns: The refusal to believe that above their nations there exists a development of a superior kind, by which they will be swept away like all other things. The ancients, so completely the adorers of their States, nevertheless placed them beneath Fate.[9]

An even more cutting rejoinder to America's latest generation of extreme nationalist writers, including especially the so-called neoconservatives, is the verse allegedly displayed at a World War I cemetery to express the posthumous sentiments of those buried there: "If they ask you why we died/Tell them that our fathers lied." So far, almost two thousand American soldiers (along with thousands of Iraqi noncombatants) have died because of Donald Rumsfeld's and Paul Wolfowitz's mendacity. Their neoconservative backers have flattered them into delusions of infallibility, encouraging them to ignore dissonant voices, however well informed, that come from outside their own closeted sect. Faced with criticism or dissent, they intimidate, smear, and snarl. They have therefore allowed the patriotic virtues of Plato's dogs to eclipse or infect the subtler virtues of the intellect, which is certainly not what Plato himself, the founder of Western higher education, had in mind.

To tease out the implications of this argument, I want to say a few words about injustice. All politically important attention to injustice is selective. Some injustices are taken seriously and remedied to the extent possible, while other injustices are flatly ignored. The distinction hinges not on the seriousness of the injury but solely on the power of the injured group. When Archbishop Desmond Tutu delivered to Nelson Mandela the scrupulously impartial findings of the South African Truth and Reconciliation Commission, detailing the injustices of every faction in the country's political spectrum, no one came to the ceremony. This is a depressing but not inaccurate commentary on human nature. People want to hear about the injustices that other groups have inflicted on their group. But they are not interested in being forced to contemplate the rank injustices that their group has inflicted on others. This generously forgiving attitude toward one's own group's misdeeds is an "original sin." It cannot be deleted from mankind's basic dispositions. It is not quite universal, admittedly, because there are always a handful of individuals who take a more or less impartial view, see all malicious and destructive behavior with a detached eye, and make no excuses for their own kinsmen, fellow sectarians, or countrymen. But individuals capable of looking, without averting their gaze, at all injustices impartially are very few. They are also politically weak, out of sync with most of their fellow citizens, and incapable of mobilizing intense political support. A perfectly impartial view of injustice may even be politically paralyzing. Genuine impartiality may somehow interfere with political acuity, with a nimble sense of timing and tactics. If true, this marginalizing effect of a commitment to impartial justice would explain why politics has always been shaped not by universally applied norms and Enlightenment values but by conflicts between groups, each of which has elevated into a sacred dogma a highly selective and self-exculpatory narrative of injustice. Only groups wearing blinders are strongly motivated politically. The impartial observer is an onlooker stuck impotently, without a fighting constituency, on the sidelines of history.

These reflections are not cheerful. But they are not necessarily defeatist. Benda thought that intellectuals who became spokesmen for nationalist, racist, or class hatred had betrayed their original calling. What calling did he have in mind? The activity of prenationalist "clerks" such as Leonardo, Malebranche, Goethe, Erasmus, Kant, and Renan was chiefly theoretical, and they were unable to prevent the laymen from filling all history with the noise of their hatreds and their slaughters; *but the clerks did prevent the laymen from setting up their actions as a religion, they did prevent them from thinking themselves great men as they carried out these activities.* It may be said that, thanks to the clerks, humanity did evil for two thousand years, but honored good.[10]

The political role of the politically detached intellect, according to Benda, is to keep alive public awareness of the limits of politics, to make sure that hopes for salvation and redemption do not spill over into politics, creating a public longing for a savior on horseback. This is a powerful thought and still relevant at a time when a tenaciously anti-intellectual American president, who sometimes suggests that he was selected by the divinity for a special role on earth, has yielded to a spectacular megalomania.

But skepticism about the ability of universities to play a positive role in our political life should not be overdone. The doubts aired above leave at least some room for creative action in the area of our immediate concern. Defending our institutions of higher learning from conservative demands for greater patriotism, for instance, can help us think through a positive political role for American universities today.

The first thing to say is that the United States is a more parochial country today than it was on 9/11. We have irresponsibly turned our backs on former allies and retreated into ourselves. More concretely, we are shuttering our embassies abroad and making it increasingly difficult for foreigners to study at American universities. Our unmatched military has invaded and occupied Iraq, to be sure. But the designers of this disastrous campaign turn out not to have known the first thing about the country they said they wanted to liberate. Their strategic failure resulted in no small part from their scandalous ignorance of the invaded country's culture, tribal structure, and language. We are truly a parochial superpower. Our monolingual generals and soldiers are just as clueless abroad as our monolingual senators and tourists.

Ignorance of the world is militarily disadvantageous. Something similar can be said about our lack of sympathy for non-American perspectives on America. Indeed, our inability to see ourselves through the eyes of others has become another grave threat to our national security. We do not have to accept the views of others, who may have their own psychotic reasons for hating us. But we have to know what they think and how they reason if we are to manage effectively our exposure to the world.

The unprecedented asymmetry of power in the world means that small actions by the United States, so minor that they hardly register domestically, can have devastating effects elsewhere. This is why Michael Walzer argues that America's continued military and economic presence abroad entails special responsibilities. We have a moral duty to know something about the lives we are shaping and in some cases destroying. We cannot honorably ignore the downstream consequences of actions taken in our name. As the only electorate in the world with a chance to hold the U.S. government accountable, we may conceivably have an extra moral duty to act as "virtual representatives" of the rest of mankind. But American citizens can hold their government responsible for its actions abroad only if they have an accurate and nuanced understanding of these actions, their consequences, and the feasible alternatives. Not extreme commercialization, therefore, but extreme public ignorance—which entails extreme vulnerability to being politically manipulated—is the most urgent problem to which universities can contribute an answer.

The political scandal of our time is that a secretive and intensely partisan administration has played cynically upon a traumatized citizenry, transforming public willingness to fight terrorism into support for an ill-conceived war in Iraq. But why did the country prove so easy to hoodwink? Why did so many Americans absurdly confuse Saddam Hussein with Osama bin Laden and Iraq with Al Qaeda? That abysmal ignorance and unfamiliarity with critical thinking offer partial answers cannot be denied. Our leading question can therefore be reformulated: What can universities do to remedy the scandalous parochialism and mental submissiveness of such easily manipulated citizens?

After 9/11, Americans circled the wagons. They sought to create as much psychological distance as possible between themselves and the frightening world "out there." They dreamed of prohibiting unshielded contacts with strangers. Even today, we can read articles by respected journalists that speak of the "three thousand Americans" killed on 9/11 even though everyone knows that hundreds of those killed on that day were foreigners. It is as if we could not tolerate the idea of mixing our dead promiscuously with the dead of other nations. The fear of being ambushed became the fear of the unknown, the foreign, the strange. It became fear of intermingling. It became dread of pollution. Such anxieties, in turn, bred delusions about the possibility of sealing our borders aseptically to wall out hostile forces. The damage caused by this unrealistic search for seclusion has been considerable.

The gravity of the problem was dramatically revealed in the television coverage of the Iraq war. American viewers saw a completely different war than viewers elsewhere in the world. There may have been just as much bias in French as in American TV reporting. I do not want to speak to that point here. What concerns me is the sudden disappearance of the kind of shared experience that provides the basis for mutually useful cooperation and informative disagreement. If a Democratic president eventually tries to revive the Atlantic alliance, he will have to confront the considerable gap in perceptions and interpretations that has opened up between Europeans and Americans.

American news organizations seem to have thought that their country at war needed to be spared, to use Cass Sunstein's phrase, "unanticipated encounters"—in this case, images that contradicted the fairy tale that America is a purely benevolent world power. The broadcast media spoon-fed the public encouraging images, airbrushing the invasion and occupation to stoke up patriotic emotions. They were willing accomplices in the Pentagon's made-for-TV Jessica Lynch "rescue." And they repressed an important part of that story, namely, the fact that our vaunted "volunteer" army is made up of young men and women from impoverished backgrounds who can find no appealing opportunities in a private economy under stress.

The whole country, in any case, was infantilized by disgracefully selective and even fictionalized reporting. Under the sway of intentionally patriotic broadcast journalism, the nation became an oversized "niche community" disconnected from reality by an echo chamber of self-reinforcing prejudices. The politically active citizenry fell victim to what Paul Krugman calls "incestuous amplifications." In other words, American TV watchers experienced the Iraq war in a kind of collective kindergarten, where unfiltered facts were not admitted. Nothing was allowed to disturb the legend of American invincibility, precisely at a time when it became obviously indefensible before a minimally informed audience. On Fox News, as someone said, America is always winning. Technologically induced collective autism—that is the rotten fruit of nationalistic news reporting. It may be comforting in the short term, but it encourages national delusions that are not compatible with an intelligent approach to foreign affairs. It also makes Americans psychologically unprepared to behave as reliable partners in an international security alliance.

Because they experience danger and adventure with the troops, embedded journalists tell a one-sided story, playing up heroism, playing down atrocity. This is why the Abu Ghraib scandal was broken by a soldier's family, not by any of the "investigative" reporters in Iraq. But the journalistic betrayal of American democracy goes deeper, since even the *New York Times* now admits to having made itself into a bulletin board for disinformation about WMDs in Iraq. By so doing, it contributed directly to the public sense of panic that allowed the Bush administration to stampede a grieving country into an unjustified war.

As if this were not bad enough, conservatives now want to make matters even worse. They apparently want American universities to reinforce American parochialism. They dream of embedded professors as well as embedded journalists. Campaigning to use the classroom to instill patriotic emotions, they seem to want to remake our students in the image of Plato's dogs.

That American universities do not presently please conservative ideologues is a constant refrain. According to David Brooks, for instance, American universities are citadels of liberal intolerance, where his conservative soulmates go sadly unappreciated and their students are blocked from pursuing dazzling careers on political grounds.[11] George Will once compared American universities to North Korea, hotbeds of far-left totalitarian extremists who harass and expel honorable conservatives. Patriotism is not even a required course. Such grumbling would be merely cranky if it did not contribute to the smearing (and in some cases to the defunding by state legislators) of institutions that have a vital contribution to make to American national security. Based on an out-of-date picture of our campuses today (where apolitical attitudes predominate and 1960s radicalism is a pale memory), neocon contempt for our centers of higher learning reflects the same parochial insularity and refusal to listen to voices outside the conservative bunker that have brought the country to its current plight.

Such flippant vilifications are annoying but basically harmless. If the United States is again subject to mass-casualty terrorism, however, conservative enmity toward the university may well take a sinister turn. The

assault will probably begin with the insinuation: are not the rootless cos-
mopolitans who populate universities actually a fifth column, preaching
tolerance and understanding and moral relativism, and therefore weakening our resolve in the terrible struggle that is upon us? Indeed, in one
sense, the conservative assault on the university has already begun. John
Ashcroft seemed bent on personally reversing the brain drain that
has drawn brilliant individuals from all corners of the world to seek
American citizenship and contribute to American power and prosperity.
His panic-induced xenophobia and hopeless attempt to keep out terrorists with a maze of "student visa" red tape by harassing foreign youths
who seek to study in American universities is another national scandal.
Something similar can be said about the inane roadblocks now being
thrown in front of visiting faculty from abroad. These foolish policies
will weaken our country, depriving it of an important asset. For one thing,
we could not maintain our graduate programs in the sciences without
foreign-born students. This is because students born in America are quite
attached to their historically rare freedom to be "late bloomers." They have
little desire to make definitive life plans before their mid-twenties. But
natural sciences demand that relatively young boys and girls make lifelong commitments. Foreign-born students, presumably under pressure
from their parents, are much more willing to make such a commitment
than native-born students.

But the real contribution of foreign students (and foreign faculty)
to our university life is another. They are one of the most important
resources available to fight the embarrassing ignorance of Americans of
the rest of the world. The danger of terrorists infiltrating the territorial
United States may be great. But an even greater threat comes from
American unawareness of political problems brewing in the rest of the
world and inexorably wending their way to our shores.

This ignorance of looming threats has concrete political consequences. Why did so many Americans believe that the invasion of Iraq
was an appropriate response to 9/11? The answer seems to be that most
Americans imagined that we were attacked *from nowhere.* As a result,
they granted our government the right to retaliate *anywhere.* "Nowhere"
does not really mean nowhere, of course. It refers to a country or countries about which we know nothing. U.S. citizens gave the administration carte blanche, in other words, because they were not conversant with
turmoil in Saudi Arabia and elsewhere in the Arab world. They justified

an unprovoked invasion because they couldn't distinguish one Muslim country from another. We also confined many innocent individuals in Guantanamo because our linguistically challenged troops were unable to distinguish, in Afghanistan, one bearded man in a long shirt from another. In Iraq, prisoner abuse resulted from the frustration of prison guards assigned to watch over prisoners with whom they could not freely communicate and whose private conversations they could not follow. And so forth.

A similar point can be made about the very idea of "preemption." The doctrine of preemption justifies anticipatory strikes against targets that might, sometime in the future, prove dangerous. The logic of preemption can best be understood by contemplating the local example of a checkpoint. If a pregnant Palestinian woman is rapidly approaching an Israeli border guard and refusing to stop as directed, the guard has a choice to shoot or not to shoot. A false negative will be fatal for him and a false positive will be fatal to her. This is a very stressful situation, ripe for miscommunications and unjustified interpretations of behavior. And Israeli border guards have occasionally shot innocent people. My point is not to criticize them, however, but rather to emphasize that *they* make "preemptive mistakes" even though Israelis can communicate much better with Palestinians than Americans can communicate with Iraqis. Americans kill more innocent suspects not because they are more sadistic but because they are more ignorant.

This is only one of the ways in which American ignorance of foreign languages and cultures "justifies" American violence abroad. America's universities, in my opinion, should be held coresponsible for the ignorance and parochialism of the American public as well as the ignorance and parochialism of the unimpressive politicians whom the public routinely elevates to high office. We are not as guilty as the broadcast media, perhaps, but we bear some share of the blame. The most urgent aim of university reform, therefore, should be to reduce the need for American violence abroad that stems, directly or indirectly, from the ignorance of Americans about the world.

The calamitous derailing of America's response to 9/11 was due not only to ignorance of the world but also to a basic failure of critical intellect. For example, the public, the press, the Democratic Party, and the television commentariat all went along with the administration's absurd assumption that the U.S. military could create a free polity in Iraq by destroying Saddam Hussein's autocracy. But democracy is not the same as the absence of dictatorship. That democracy is a rare system of governance with many positive preconditions is obvious to anyone who has studied modern history, even superficially. Only historically illiterate policymakers would act as if toppling a tyrant guaranteed the establishment of electorally accountable government. But it was not only our policymakers who acted this way. Our public is so grotesquely miseducated about basic facts and so unequipped to recognize elemental errors of reasoning as to allow the administration's gross malfeasance to unfold virtually without protest.

Another scandalous example of intellectual failure became visible in the immediate aftermath of 9/11. At that time, right-wing demagogues proved remarkably successful at convincing the country that we had been attacked by irrational fanatics. The 9/11 attackers were obviously cool and collected, able to mount a coordinated attack in a foreign country under difficult conditions. The obvious rationality of the means they employed suggested that there might at least be a residue of rationality in their goals. But the American right was intent on blinding the country to the obvious (if demented) *political* agenda of the hijackers and their puppet masters. They spread the slander that anyone who looked into the justifications of the attack ("Why do they hate us?") was unpatriotic, and was even dishonoring the fallen. They did this for political reasons of their own, namely, because they wanted to fend off, by stirring up public emotions, any attempt to question America's current foreign policy, especially regarding Israel. That the American public allowed itself to be psychologically bullied in this way is another damning commentary on our system of higher education.

The aftermath of the Iraq war provides a final example of the intellectual breakdown I have in mind. After the embarrassing failure to discover any WMDs in Iraq, the administration shifted its principal justification of the war to the liberation of Iraqis from Saddam's cruel dictatorship. This was a blatantly cynical move on the part of individuals such as Vice President Dick Cheney and Secretary of Defense Donald Rumsfeld, who had demonstrated, over long careers, their willingness to connive with dictators, including Saddam, and their indifference to the victims of oppressive regimes. But the extraordinary thing about this after-the-fact switch in justification was revealed in the frequently deployed expression "The world is better off without Saddam Hussein."

The explicit intent of this phrase was to discredit critics of the invasion and occupation by suggesting that they were appeasers who, at some level, were indifferent to the great human suffering caused by the Baathist regime. But the phrase revealed something else, namely, the administration's own shocking obliviousness to the very idea of opportunity costs.

A polity that placed a high value on critical intelligence would have offered greater resistance to such a transparently flimsy justification for war. Yes, the world is better off without Saddam Hussein. But that does not justify the war, not unless the administration can also show that the world would not be still better off had the $300 billion and other security assets of the United States been spent in other ways. (Securing more weapons-grade plutonium and uranium in Russia and dismantling more affiliates of Al Qaeda come to mind.) That the world has become extraordinarily dangerous, given the chance that WMDs will fall into the hands of terrorist groups that cannot be deterred, is undeniable. But this insight does not support the absurd doctrine of preemptive war. The threat in question is highly diffuse. Extreme danger can originate from any direction. If a catastrophic attack occurs in one place today, there is no reason to think another catastrophic attack will not occur somewhere else tomorrow. As a result, an intelligent response to the new national security threat facing the United States requires a prudent allocation of scarce national-security resources over space and time. When responding to one threat, no matter how serious, we must always keep some of our powder dry, anticipating that subsequent threats may suddenly emerge where least expected. But this is exactly the opposite of administration policy. Even if it had been justified in considering Saddam Hussein an imminent threat, the Bush administration would have been unjustified in its choice to leave the country deprived of resources to respond to other and subsequent threats. That the total recklessness of "preemption," even on Bush's own description of the threat we face, took so long to be raised as a public objection to Bush foreign policy is another damning commentary on the critical intelligence of our leading journalists and opinion makers. It also casts doubt on America's capacity to play the role of a responsible superpower in an increasingly dangerous world.

Actions are based on interpretations. Coarse and erroneous interpretations give birth to unintelligent and shameful actions. This is why universities, specializing in developing and criticizing interpretations of the world, have such a vital role to play in contemporary politics. They cannot free us from commercialization, but they can moderate the baleful influence of ignorance and stupidity. Institutional reform should aim primarily at improving the university's capacities in this regard. The disastrous decision to invade and occupy Iraq was based on a distorted interpretation of 9/11. A well-functioning system of higher education might have protected the polity to some extent against such mindless folly.

The rise of highly partisan think tanks—financially well endowed and focused full-time on cultivating access to policymakers—presents a new and still underappreciated challenge to American universities. Simplification factories, such as the American Enterprise Institute, have helped inject a "data mining" culture into the heart of government. They teach politicians that trawling for evidence and arguments to support preconceived policies is perfectly acceptable behavior in polite company. The consequences of this partisan and closed-minded approach to policymaking have not been favorable to American national security. Here again, universities should provide an aggressive response by showing, rather than simply saying, that "cooking the books" is dishonorable and self-defeating.

American conservatives frequently say that "moral relativism" is the gravest threat looming over our political culture. Universities should counter this banality by underlining the opposite truth, namely, that the greatest threat to human flourishing and survival in the current age is *false certainty*. Here I align myself fully, once again, with Cass Sunstein's argument above. A similar point was made earlier by Weber:

> The primary task of a useful teacher is to teach his students to recognize "inconvenient" facts—I mean facts that are inconvenient for their party opinions. And for every party opinion there are facts that are extremely inconvenient, for my own opinion no less than for others. I believe that the teacher accomplishes more than a mere intellectual task if he compels his audience to accustom itself to the existence of such facts. I would be so immodest as even to apply the expression "moral achievement," though perhaps this may sound too grandiose for something that should go without saying.[12]

This approach can help us lay down basic guidelines for university reform today. We need only ask: What are the "inconvenient facts" to which Americans must be exposed, for their own sakes and the world's?

Universities are not churches designed to satisfy spiritual longings. They are places of learning well positioned to remedy, to the extent possible, the cavalier attitude toward facts and logic characteristic of men of action. The world continues to change around us at an astonishing pace, and therefore we cannot safely fix our curriculum in stone. But we can certainly say the following. Only a massive and long-gestation investment in improving our students' knowledge of the world will permit Americans to assume their special responsibilities as citizens of an unrivaled superpower. Our best students today should all be taught how to communicate freely in at least one language other than English. They should all be encouraged to study abroad, at least for one year. They should be intimately familiar with comparative religion and political geography. They should study carefully the history of U.S. political, economic, and military behavior abroad, learning how foreigners understand the purposes of American power. And they should all have enough "literacy" in the natural sciences to enforce some sort of public accountability on our increasingly powerful scientific community. None of this will suffice, needless to say, unless they are also encouraged, by force of example above all, to develop critical minds.

These are just a few preliminary suggestions, obviously enough. I offer them only as tentative provocations to further thought. I have much more confidence about my general point. In the "war on terror," the fate of our country will depend on the quality of information we receive, our ability to interpret it in a reasonable way, and a tireless application of critical intelligence to government actions and explanations. It remains to be seen if our universities, and those who steer them, will prove adequate to this arduous but inescapable task.

NOTES

1. To employ the phrase of President Dwight Eisenhower.

2. This is a claim more or less prominent in the chapters by Benjamin Barber, Robert Calvert, Todd Gitlin, Michael Sandel, and Cass Sunstein.

3. Max Weber, "Science as a Vocation," in *From Max Weber: Essays in Sociology*, ed. H. H. Gerth and C. Wright Mills (New York: Oxford University Press, 1958), 149.

4. Derek Bok, *Universities in the Marketplace: The Commercialization of Higher Education* (Princeton, N.J.: Princeton University Press, 2003).

5. Stuart W. Leslie, *The Cold War and American Science: The Military-Industrial-Academic Complex at MIT and Stanford* (New York: Columbia University Press, 1993).

6. Plato, *The Republic*, 375e.

7. Plato, *The Republic*, 375e.

8. Plato, *The Republic*, 376a.

9. Julien Benda, *The Treason of the Intellectuals* (1928; repr., New York: Norton, 1969), 60.

10. Benda, *Treason of the Intellectuals*, 44.

11. David Brooks, "Lonely Campus Voices," *New York Times*, September 27, 2003.

12. Weber, "Science as a Vocation," 147.

CHAPTER TWELVE

The Civic Education of a Black American in a Great Big World

ROGER WILKINS

My country is at war with insurgents in Iraq, a continuation of the war against the Iraqi government of Saddam Hussein. Many young Americans have died, many have been wounded, and some have even been led to disgrace themselves. Many Iraqis have died or been wounded and many, many others have had their lives utterly shattered. If our government had exercised more patience, this war might someday have become justified in my mind and, more importantly, in the view of the international community as well. In that event, the occupation, carried out by a truly international force, might not have raised such opposition and the insurgency might not have occurred. But that is not what happened. And although I want a successful outcome with as little further damage as possible to our troops and to others, I think the way the war was developed by our nation was wrong, and that has led to a series of grave national errors that I deeply regret. I have dissented from these policies as vigorously as I know how, and some people in my government have suggested that dissenters like me are unpatriotic.

Yet I know myself to be a deeply patriotic American. The fact that I am free to say these words in public, even as our soldiers are in danger in a place far, far from home, deepens my patriotism and strengthens my conviction that the fundamentals of American government, American citizenship, and American history are essential elements of a good education, particularly if we expect to maintain our free institutions in roughly the same shape and strength that they now have. My deep belief in those institutions and the patriotism they engender in me is the reason I chose to open this discussion of participation and civic education with my profound dissent on the hottest public issue in America right now.

Despite the fact that I believe that hubris is our most dangerous affliction these days, I continue to believe that the institutions and the values and the practices of democracy in this country are the secular light of the world. I didn't always think like that. I've spent a great deal of my life deeply alienated from this country. I was born In Kansas City, Missouri, seventy-two years ago. Segregation, even before I was old enough to reason, began teaching me the brutal lessons that it was intended to teach. We lived in a little, isolated black neighborhood called Round Top. If you walked just a few blocks in any direction, to get to the streetcar line, for example, you left the black neighborhood. For some reason, I was called Little Roger when I was a child, so I thought my name was Little Roger. One day I asked my grandmother, "Why does everybody up to Twentieth Street smile and say hello to Little Roger and then everybody after Twentieth Street looks mean at Little Roger?" You can guess where the neighborhoods changed color.

My strongest childhood memory involves my father. He knew I loved what we called "streamlined trains" in those days and that my favorite came by on Sunday evenings. I recall that it was called the Santa Fe Chief and that I imagined it was on its way to that distant, mysterious place when it went zipping past us. My father would often take me down to the viaduct to see that train go flying by, and I remember telling him that I wanted to drive a train like that when I grew up. My father answered, "Well, Roger, I'm sorry. You won't be able to do that." And I asked why and he said, "Only white people are permitted to drive trains in this country." And again I asked why. He said, "Because they make the rules, and that's one of the rules they make." And I said, "But that's not fair." And he said, "You're right, that's not fair, and you must fight against that all your life."

Segregation and all of the things that were done to black people before that were designed to disable them. At the turn of the eighteenth century, Robert "King" Carter owned more slaves than anyone else in the

Virginia colony. When his plantation would receive a new shipload of labor prisoners, Carter would find the ones who seemed the least likely to be docile, and he would "season" them. He would have a finger, a toe, or an ear lopped off just to show the new slave how powerless he now was. Seasoning was designed to disable the new slave and all the witnesses in the sense of depriving them of any sense of their own humanity or belief in their capacity to master their own lives.[1]

Over the next three centuries, disabling of blacks took many new forms: denial of all freedoms, of course, and denial of education, denial of mobility, terror spread by the night riders and lawless lawmen, denial of the right to vote, lynching, denial of educational and economic opportunity, and, finally, segregation. The message that segregation—a full cultural shunning—was designed to deliver to us was that we were inferior and that we didn't really belong here and, finally, that the fruits of full citizenship were far beyond our limited capacities. Halfway through the third of those centuries a great freedom movement swelled within the United States, but died in the flames of black rage in northern cities where experimental poverty programs could not meet the enormous needs of the waves of blacks who, over several decades, had fled the parched and brutal poverty of the South. I was one of those young New Frontiersmen who stayed over to help Lyndon Johnson with the projects spawned by his domestic idealism.

By the time I left the government in 1969 at the age of thirty-seven, having spent the previous four and a half years working at the intersection of the U.S. Department of Justice and the angriest blacks in the smoldering cities, the bitterness that began in those childhood years of segregation had hardened into an awful knot. I, along with many other idealists in the Johnson administration, had worked my soul to the bone trying to persuade our government to respond to the misery and the profound needs of our poorest minority communities, but the enormous maw of the Vietnam War and the callousness of many powerful officials utterly defeated us, and then in 1968, the electorate turned its back on our hopes when it elected the candidate who had pursued a "Southern Strategy."

The wind of the civil rights movement had died just before it reached the poorest black people in our country. I was so exhausted, so devastated, and so angry that even though I had functioned near the highest levels of the U.S. government, I began to think of this country as "their" country—white people's country. And every time "they" would do something stupid, I was happy because "they" in their blindness and their arrogance were ruining "their" country. I even thought about going off to the south of France to write. After all of my early personal success I was on the verge of accepting the cruel conclusion dictated by the disabling strategy: America was "theirs," not mine.

It was the thought about France that turned me around because I knew I would lose traction as a person and as a writer because everything I wanted to write about was here. This was the place that provided the friction that formed me. This is the place that fed my furies and my rages, but also my loves and my hopes. It had given me the blues and baseball, Faulkner and Baldwin, the people I loved and the people I hated, and the First and the Fourteenth Amendments to the Constitution of the United States. So I climbed out of my funk and went back to work. By the time I was brought into teaching at the age of fifty-five, I had had thirty-five years of active citizenship—including an internship with Thurgood Marshall, my stint in the federal government, Watergate journalism, and participation in the leadership of the U.S. antiapartheid movement. Standing back a bit, I understood that notwithstanding the setbacks, the struggle for civil rights that had shaped my soul had also given me very powerful evidence of the virtues of our Founding values and the great satisfaction of deep involvement in important national and international issues.

Thus, neither I nor my conviction that the subject belonged in my courses had traveled to the classroom by a conventional academic route. I understand active citizenship and civic virtue through the prism of my own personal effort both to shrug off society's efforts to disable me and to reclaim for my ancestors some of the dignity they were not allowed to achieve in lives that were trampled by forces larger than any with which I have ever had to contend.

It also taught me the way to understand the incredible story of how the Constitution and American values have struggled with the issues of black people in America. It's a 385-year arc from the first black people who were brought to Jamestown in 1619 to now that reveals something profound about the power of America's Founding values. Blacks were the most despised people in this new land, and over the years many whites developed a deep psychic dependence on the prop that racism provided. But even though this racism was right there at the core of American culture, some citizens of the country returned time and again to our Founding idealism to mount semisuccessful attacks on our American caste system. In the late eighteenth century it was the abolition of slavery in northern states. In the nineteenth century it was abolitionism, the Civil War, and Reconstruction; and in the twentieth century it was the civil rights movement. Each time the struggle to match the behavior in the daily life of our nation with our Founding ideals fell short, but each of the struggles did manage to make the nation measurably more decent. And each effort gave the nation more pride in itself.

Nevertheless, the burst of idealism in the last century left us a great deal of work still to be done. Forty percent of black children are living in poverty. Poverty doesn't just mean ragged clothes. It often means inadequate prenatal nutrition, it means inadequate medical care after birth, it means few—if any—baby books in the home, it means meager language exposure for toddlers. It also means consignment to grossly inadequate schools that won't bring the child within a million miles of a place like DePauw. It might not bring the child within a million miles of a place in our economy. But the place to which it often brings that child is prison. It is estimated that 12 percent of all of America's black males are currently in prison or in jail. Now unless you believe in predestination or that there is some genetic moral inferiority in black people, these facts suggest that there is still something terribly wrong in our country.

But there is also something incredibly right here. This isn't the country that Washington and Adams and Jefferson and Madison and Hamilton and Franklin founded. It is not the country of Lincoln, of Teddy Roosevelt, or even of FDR. *It is so much better.* And it is largely because of the civic idealism and the structure of national ideals, some of which are embedded in our legal materials, which American blacks and their white allies have used to raise the level of civilization in this country so that it is able to produce a Condoleezza Rice, a Colin Powell, the billionaire Bob Johnson, or Michael Jordan and Barry Bonds, and, praise the Lord, Halle Berry.

At every step along the way there have been white allies. There was a rebel named Nathaniel Bacon who united poor whites and blacks in the seventeenth century, and in the eighteenth there was the Quaker Anthony Benezet, who was not only antislavery but also believed that blacks were equal in all their faculties to whites and started schools for blacks based on his beliefs. There were thousands of white abolitionists in the nineteenth century and the twentieth began with Mary White Ovington and William English Walling joining with W. E. B. DuBois to found the NAACP.

And there have been presidents who made massive contributions to the cause. Washington sent a powerful signal down through the halls of history by freeing his slaves in his will. Lincoln recast the founding at Gettysburg to extend the founding idea of equality to blacks. FDR created programs to improve the lives of poor people. Harry Truman embraced the cause of civil rights and desegregated the armed forces. John F. Kennedy ultimately came to a conclusion, which he shared with the country, that civil rights was a moral crusade for America. Then there is Lyndon Johnson, who dreamed of abolishing poverty and who carried the battle cry of the civil rights movement to the well of the House of Representatives. None of these leaders reached his policy decisions alone. Each was pressed to his conclusion by groups of highly motivated people who based their movements and their arguments on a vision, based on our Founding ideals, of what America could someday become.

President Bottoms asked me in our symposium—quite delicately, I must say—what, at my age (then seventy-one) I had to say to people who are eighteen to twenty years old. Most of the young people I see in my classes are Americans—a wide variety of Americans. Some have South Asian origins, some African, some Far Eastern, some Arabic, some Latin American, and some are African American, but the preponderance is still European American. The variety of these faces virtually demands that I teach about the America I know and something about the world that is yet to come. And yet I know that the specific racial experience I have had is foreign to them—even to the African Americans in the class. It was quite an education to have been a small child in the Depression, a preteen during World War II, draft age during Korea, and a young adult as the Cold War turned very warm. I also know that these young people have probably not been taught American history and civics as well as I was in public school in the 1940s.

When I was about to start teaching, I consulted my two older children, who had recently been college students, and asked them to tell me the things that had proved most valuable to them as students and what things stuck most in their heads. Then I reached back in my own memory to recall what in my college years had made the greatest impression on me and what things I wished I had been taught in college. Over the years I have listened with care to my students, just as I have listened carefully to my own daughter, soon to graduate from college.

So, putting my enthusiasm about the country and about the Founding together with those methods of devising a teaching strategy, I would answer President Bottoms's good question in the following way.

I love stories and I believe that stories, deftly used, have great pedagogical power. Over the years I have found that five of my favorite stories seem to leap over the fifty-year gulf in age and experience represented in that small distance between where I stand and the first row of student seats in the classroom. And so, here are the stories I generally manage to work into my courses or that shape the thrust of my teaching.

THE BEN FRANKLIN STORY

In the late spring and summer of 1787, fifty-five American politicians did something in Philadelphia that modern American politicians absolutely cannot do: they kept a secret. So when the Constitutional Convention was over, a Philadelphia woman is said to have asked Benjamin Franklin, "What kind of government have you given us, sir?" and Franklin replied, "A republic, madam, if you can keep it."

If you can keep it. Franklin understood that our form of government was not forever assured to the United States and that active citizenship was required to keep and enhance it. The contentious debates over the terms of the Constitution had confirmed what the Founders already knew, that democracy was hard work, and they left us a heroic example of how to do that work. The other stories I tell my students are part of this most basic of American stories.

THE "REAL" AMERICAN REVOLUTION STORY

In 1765 the English Parliament imposed a tax on a wide range of transactions that needed official papers of some kind or another to validate the business transacted. These papers required stamps, which could be obtained by the payment of a tax. Some colonists became enraged at the imposition of a tax on colonials to defray the costs of the English government, which were incurred without any consultations whatsoever with the colonials.

The colonials began to read all about this tax and how it was to be collected. They conversed with each other about it and began writing and circulating their opinions and learned position papers on all aspects of the dispute. And they even created new collaborative arrangements—committees of correspondence and a Stamp Act Congress. The government in England retreated temporarily. But soon other impositions by Parliament were adopted, and the colonists again began the round of communicating, protesting, getting to know people from other colonies better, organizing, and resisting.

Finally in 1774 they created a Continental Congress and then another one and then a skirmish at Lexington and Concord in April 1775. Then they created a revolution and an army. Reading, talking, writing, meeting, and organizing were the activities of that decade in which Colonial British subjects changed their minds and became Americans and citizens, a period and a process that John Adams—one of the most active and effective of those citizens—came to call "the Real American Revolution."

That was the kind of activity that Franklin clearly must have had in mind when he expressed the opinion that citizens had to act to "keep" the republic that had been made for them.

THE WEEPING PROFESSOR STORY

It is sad that the years wipe out the names of so many good people who have helped guide and shape us. Fifty years is a long time, and I remember the names of just a very few, but I had an activist professor whose name I will always remember. I took a politics course with him in the fall of 1952, and he was passionately involved in the presidential campaign of Adlai E. Stevenson. He made no bones about his partisanship, and he taught right down the middle. All opinions were welcomed in his class unless they were shoddily thought out, in which case your political affiliation didn't matter a whit. You got his withering dissection of your offering with the regular admonition that shoddy thinking wouldn't take you very far in the field of politics. Anyway, I think most people had concluded by late October that Eisenhower would win the election, but not our stouthearted professor. But the stout heart failed the day after the elections. Our professor came in, he tried to teach, his words caught in his throat, he tried again, and then he began to weep. Then he said, "I'm sorry. I'm very sorry. I can't teach today." That activist, weeping citizen-professor delivered that morning one of the most powerful lessons about caring about the country I have ever received.

When I teach, I never actually tell the story about the weeping professor. I do tell about Ben Franklin and John Adams, and I let them know about my passionate activism (which I try to do right down the middle, just as my weeping professor did so many years ago), and somewhere along the way I manage to tell them the fourth story:

THE DEMONSTRATION STORY

During the Washington-based antiapartheid movement twenty years ago, my colleagues and I would demonstrate late in every weekday afternoon in front of the South African embassy on Massachusetts Avenue, a major commuting artery to the affluent Maryland suburbs. We did it rain, shine, heat, sleet, or cold. We demonstrated on the day it was so cold that President Reagan's second inaugural parade was canceled.

Normally, an unending stream of homebound cars would pass us as we marched and chanted. A few drivers would honk in support. Most, though, would either gaze at us vacantly or in puzzlement. Some seemed never to notice as they drove on by.

On many days, groups of counterprotesters would show up. The police would restrict them to the other side of the avenue, where they would march, sing, chant, or yell out their support for the apartheid government of South Africa. Though I abhorred their views, I had far, far more respect for those counterprotesters—passionately involved in an important debate as they were—than I did for the bored or self-involved commuters who seemed intent only on getting home to their comfort. I think Ben Franklin would agree with me on this.

BLACKS AND THE VINDICATION OF THE FOUNDING IDEALS

But I've already told that story. I haven't really made the basic point, though. American ideals are very powerful as the rise of blacks from utter debasement to the far better position we now occupy demonstrates, and all of us—Americans of all backgrounds and religions—are the better for those changes. We are the better because generations of Americans used their heritage and fought for their national ideals within the contexts of their lives. America is not a flag to put in a lapel or to howled about in the local bar. The heart of America are the opportunities that we have for self-government not just in race, but in education, the environment, the political process itself, in health care—in just about any human activity imaginable—that are there to be picked up and used to change tomorrow for the better. Or not. To put Franklin's view of these opportunities into the modern idiom: Use them or lose them.

So, in answer to Dr. Bottoms's questions, that's about what I tell my students, and they seem to listen.

The final question is whether students should be required in the course of their studies to consider issues such as these or should they be permitted to sail through a four-year program without even skirmishing with this kind of history and these kinds of issues. Is there a question of choice here that trumps a teaching of some of the basic concepts of our democracy?

I would make two points. The first flows from the fact that we are faculty and they are students. Presumably there are reasons based on wisdom, training, learning, and experience that make us part of the professoriat. If that is the case, it would seem that we might have a bit of knowledge that would be important for young people to have whether they recognize it or not.

The second point is simply this: the twentieth century was a cakewalk for the United States compared to the challenges we are likely to face in the twenty-first. We can start with terrorism, since we did. It's not going away soon and it is likely to get worse. Deeply troubling nuclear proliferation is already taking place—do the words North Korea, Iran, and Pakistan make you lose some sleep? They ought to. And then there's China. Henry Luce dubbed the twentieth century the American Century. Luce loved China, but the China he loved is not the China that's coming. Our children may well live out their lives in the Chinese Century. Then there's our own transforming demography. Somewhere in the middle of this century whites won't be in the majority in this country. Some white Americans may find that deeply threatening, and white identity groups that have been on the periphery of our consciousness up to now may begin to play a more central role in our lives. Globalization and the rapidly changing shape of our work patterns are deeply upsetting in millions of American lives. The twenty-first century appears to promise us an almost unending series of crises—coupled with unprecedented opportunities if we are wise and lucky.

At times of crisis our leaders—this is a bipartisan observation—are not always strict in their observation of the limits the Constitution erects around their power. It is then when the nation needs citizens who are *alert to the need to keep their republic.* That is why I began this discussion with my dissent from our nation's current mode of war making. As I wrote earlier, some people argue that it is unpatriotic to dissent when we have troops in the field. People in power will always find a reason to try to quiet voices that they find inconvenient. But it is when the government finds discussion and protest and organizing most "inconvenient" that such discussion and action are most needed. That is when the requirement to "keep it" is most urgent.

Somebody has to teach young Americans those things and if it is not us, then, what's a faculty for?

NOTES

This essay is dedicated to my mother, Helen Jackson Wilkins Claytor (April 12, 1907–May 10, 2005), from whom I absorbed all the attitudes that informed this work.

1. Here and throughout I draw on my *Jefferson's Pillow: The Founding Fathers and the Dilemma of Black Patriotism* (Boston: Beacon Press, 2001).

CHAPTER
THIRTEEN

‑‑‑◉〰◉‑‑‑

Moral Education and Democratic Citizenship

MICHAEL WALZER

I have two purposes in this chapter: first, to argue that morality forms
a central part of a liberal education and to say something about how
it is properly taught; second, to argue more specifically that the moral
virtues required by democratic citizenship, and the rights and obligations that citizenship entails, should figure in the college curriculum (but
also in education more generally) and then to analyze some of the conflicts this "figuring" is sure to produce.

MORALITY AND LIBERAL EDUCATION

What do professors teach that is so vital that every student should be
required to study it?[1] Evidently, professors disagree about how to answer
this question, but one answer, suggested in the proposal for this symposium, seems to me worthy of an intellectual defense. That is the claim
that students should study moral and political philosophy and that their
attention should be focused on the problems of moral choice in political and professional life.

The claim is controversial. What morality should we teach, given that
morality itself is a "social construction" that has been differently constructed in different times and places and in different cultures within our

own multicultural society? How can the teaching of morality be made compatible with the value neutrality required by the "disinterested search for truth"? How can teachers avoid the reinforcement of hegemonic social and political ideologies? More simply, will moral education ever amount to anything more than the recitation of platitudes—like a class taught by Shakespeare's Polonius?

Anyway, can morality be taught at all? Can it be taught to young adults who are already living moral and political lives? It isn't a skill, like basic math. We don't say that someone is clever at morality. It isn't a body of factual knowledge, probably not a body of speculative knowledge either, such as might be presented in a first-year history or sociology course. Skepticism about the possibility or value of teaching morality is widespread; what underlies it, I think, is a deeply conservative understanding of human socialization. Moral life, on this view, is the virtually unconscious acting out of cultural norms inculcated in families and peer groups, in churches and synagogues, in everyday activities and relationships. And so morality should never be problematic. Whenever it poses problems, has to be studied, argued over, worried about, or "theorized," something is wrong. We have to consider likely causes: the decline of the family, the erosion of religious faith, cultural decadence, and media corruption.[2] All these are good subjects, no doubt, and some of them may well lie at the root of morality-as-a-problem. But I don't think that they justify skepticism about moral education.

In fact, the systematic study of morality by young adults (or, at least, by some of them, members of, or candidates for, the upper classes) is common throughout the history of civilization. Only in recent times did ethics become a minor specialization in academic departments where logic and epistemology were generally thought to be more important. But think of the Greek academies where representatives of radically opposed schools of thought explained their conceptions of the good life and the good society to aristocratic young men. Think of the Talmudic schools where important (and also commonplace) ethical matters were endlessly debated. Think of the great medieval universities where casuistry—the application of conscience to its cases—was a central part of the curriculum. Today even the words that describe these activities have become, for many, derogatory terms: academic, Talmudic, scholastic, casuistic. The words suggest an inordinate attention to irrelevant detail. Indeed, the work in those old schools was detailed, and it was academic, but it was also intimately responsive to social needs. One can read the history of every-day life out of the Talmudic and scholastic texts, and it is a special kind of history, thick with moral interest.

A similar interest was still visible in nineteenth- and early-twentieth-century American universities, though it gradually ceased to dominate the curriculum. Courses in moral philosophy, social ethics, and political theory were a standard requirement.[3] For a long time, it was central to our idea of a higher education that there was a common morality that each new generation of teachers and students needed to work on.

So what kind of society is it where morality has to be taught? It is the same kind of society it has always been. Why this fact had to be redis-covered, however, is a harder question. Somehow, over a period of many decades, we became increasingly hesitant and uncertain about moral education. Though I believe that things are changing today, the teaching of ethics still isn't easily or naturally associated with the other things we do. Our moral life was, one might say, repressed for such a long time (the way our immoral lives are supposed to be) that it is difficult now to regard it with equanimity. So a required course in ethics looks ideo-logical to many people—like a parochial imposition or an act of political domination.

The dissociation of ethics from the rest of academic work has been a complicated affair. Forty years ago, when I began writing about these questions, it derived in part from a one-sided conception of social science. In this view, statements of value, because they cannot be proven true or false, cannot be studied at all. Values can't be analyzed, we were told in those days, they can only be chosen, and the choice is irrational, ungovernable, without objective criteria.[4] Hence teaching is impossible, the presumptuous invasion of a mysterious (religious?) realm where professors, with their secular and scientific training, have nothing to say and should therefore say nothing. "Whereof one cannot speak, thereof one must be silent." The only legitimate course on ethics is a course on the history of ethical ideas.

Today, this conception of social science is widely criticized, chiefly through a "deconstruction" of the scientific ambitions of its protagonists. Conventional social science, we are now told, is rooted in cultural assumptions and historically conditioned ideas and interests—just as rooted as are the values it pretends to avoid. On this contemporary or "postmodern" view, you can indeed teach values as readily as you can teach anything else, but if you do that, you had better acknowledge that you are engaged in the reproduction of the prevailing cultural and ideological system. The only way to avoid the conventional wisdom is to teach a systematic skepticism or a radical relativism (I doubt that anyone is fully committed to the latter; it is too easily caricatured: "Some people think that murder is a bad idea; other people say . . ."). Now the only legitimate course on ethics is a course on the plurality of ethical ideologies.[5] What follows, it seems to me, is sheer loss: as in the earlier understanding of ethics as a historical subject, so in this understanding of ethics as ideology, the hard edge of analysis, argument, and application is blunted or given up altogether. What is the point of applying moral principles that have neither grounding nor stability?

But these professorial positions and the disputes they engender are probably less important in understanding American ambivalence about teaching morality than two deeply rooted cultural attitudes, which are, both of them, embodied by the major figures of our popular literature and cinema. Think of the hard, seasoned frontier loner and the tough, urban sophisticate—the cowboy, say, and the private eye. These are mythical representations of liberal individualism, and their influence is felt even in the academy. They are part of the common culture of teachers and students. How do these figures, as we know them in novels and movies, feel about morality?

First of all, they hold it to be deeply personal, almost secretive; in everyday conversation, morality is off limits. It isn't discussed among men or, better, among real men (maybe women talk about it among themselves . . .). The American hero is masculine and reticent, strong and silent—though in his urban embodiment, a stream of wisecracks conceals the deeper reticence. So there can't be any serious moral dialogue but only a kind of inarticulate contempt for unforgivable behavior. In public, we can only hold a man to his own standards: honor, sincerity, grace under pressure.[6] These can be talked about (though they hardly have to be), but moral argument focused on questions of virtue or goodness is called *moralizing,* and it is a sure sign of self-righteousness, priggishness, and hypocrisy. In contrast to all previous understandings, moral life in the United States has often been imagined as solitary, almost solipsistic. Maybe this conception fits somehow into liberal doctrine, but it is surely wrongheaded, for without other people, we would have no moral ideas (or even ideologies) at all.

The second attitude toward morality comes close to a nonphilosophical utilitarianism. Heroic reticence is the better part of wisdom, but when decisions are unavoidable, American heroes will make and defend them in hardheaded, tough-minded, utterly unsentimental ways. They must be worked out in terms of the actual or supposed desires of discrete individuals and the probable costs and benefits of proposed actions. The standards must be clear, so that the ultimate choice is as indisputable as addition or subtraction. There is, once again, no room for moralizing. At its practical worst, this is body-count morality; we saw it most clearly in Vietnam, where it was finally stripped of all heroic pretensions. In its current academic version (cowboys and private eyes, and tough-minded generals too, are left behind here), this moral reticence is expressed in equations; it involves the systematic application of economic models to moral and political life. The models are often useful, but they don't, it seems to me, enhance our moral understanding; they promote understanding of a different sort.

Intense subjectivity or radical objectivity: neither of these attitudes fits the life we actually live with other people. For the truth is that we are all familiar with the difficulties of personal relations and professional activity: we find ourselves in ambiguous situations, we worry about what to do, we make moral judgments, we criticize other people, we defend ourselves. We may sometimes be strong and silent, sometimes shrewd and calculating, but our moral lives are most of the time more discursive than these adjectives suggest. The language we actually speak is extensive in its structure and rich in its vocabulary; it includes personal honor and sincerity; it invites consequentialist calculation; but it also reaches beyond these two. It makes it possible for us to talk at length, to argue heatedly, about the most difficult issues in politics and personal life. And in this moral discourse, people are not only sincere and insincere, prudent and reckless, but also insightful and confused, courageous and cowardly, good and bad. The decisions they make don't only involve costs and benefits but also rights and wrongs, justice and injustice.

Our common understanding of moral life rests upon shared, though also often disputed, ideas—about the positive and negative rules of everyday life, about our obligations and rights, and about virtues like kindness and courage. No doubt, all these are "social constructions," and there are cultural differences in how they have been constructed. But though the differences are deep, I don't think that all of them go all the way down—otherwise we would not be able to talk about them the way we do; we would not be able to argue across cultural boundaries or to translate from one moral language into another. The negative rules, which are probably the most important, are also the most widely understood; a minimum set—don't murder, don't injure, don't deceive—comes pretty close to universal acceptance. That obviously doesn't mean that they are universally adhered to; it means that they have been "constructed" again and again, in different idioms, with different historical and textual references, but, still, in recognizably similar ways. Morality rests most profoundly on these prohibitions, expressed in our own culture by the three words, *Thou shalt not.*

The strong, silent hero presumably lives by those words, but he doesn't help to build a world in which the prohibitions they express can be maintained or, for that matter, criticized and reformulated. For the prohibitions are not best understood as a personal code. If they aren't publicly reiterated, debated, defended, revised, and passed on, they will be eaten away by private interest and partisan calculation.

Assume now that undergraduates are required to study the meanings and possible applications of (some set of) moral rules; assume that the teaching is argumentative and casuistic and that it aims to force students to analyze historical and hypothetical cases—as prospective lawyers are commonly taught to do. The teachers are certainly not neutral; nor is their teaching value free. How could it be? The only way to teach values is to defend or criticize them. A purely descriptive account won't give students any sense of what a value is or what it means to say that some principle or practice is valuable. Imagine a course that deals with (among other things) the ban on murder: teachers might probe the limits of the ban by considering, say, Albert Camus's play *The Just Assassins* or by providing examples of killing in war; they could talk about combatants and noncombatants, double effect and "collateral damage," the acceptance and imposition of risk. They might analyze different degrees of guilt in killings: premeditation, complicity, and negligence. They might discuss different theories of punishment. They would have views about all these things and express them, and, because they are (as I am imagining them) liberal teachers, committed to the value of disagreement, they would invite their students to express their own similar or differing views. It is not necessary that a course like this have a common curriculum; the teachers might choose different books, focus on different cases and issues. But they would be talking about murder, and they would not suggest, neutrally, that killing innocent people might or might not be a good thing to do.

I have already said that a course like this should be a required course; metaethics, by contrast, should be an elective. It is less important that students understand the "foundations" of ethics than that they have some grasp of the shape and structure of the moral world they already inhabit. But won't this educational program strengthen the existing shape and structure? Won't it reinforce established social hierarchies and cultural hegemonies? I am sure that the answer to these questions is yes, in some ways, which I will come to in a little while. But I want to stress now that the program also provides a language, perhaps the only possible language, for discussing what is right and wrong about the established moral world. A required course does not, as we all know, produce the same responses in all the students who take it. It certainly doesn't guarantee that students will subsequently make the choices that the powers that be want them to make. Some of them will do that, and some won't. Nor will it lead people inexorably to hold "politically correct" views and take a stand (as I would like them to do) against hierarchy and hegemony. Some of them will do that, and some won't. But if the educational program is effective, all the students will talk about morality and politics more knowledgeably, self-consciously, and critically than they did before; new groups of men and women will be brought into the discussion; and moral and political actors will be under greater pressure to defend what they do in public. To put the point clearly, students won't be more moral, whatever that means, after taking courses like the one I have described; they will be more intelligent about morality.

The strong, silent hero remains attractive. I would not want Humphrey Bogart to stop in the middle of *Casablanca* and deliver a lecture on just and unjust wars. But it is important to understand that his gut feelings and instinct for decency are dependent on long traditions of moral discourse. It is also important to understand that his reticence, while dramatically effective, is probably historically false. Throughout their moral lives, but especially in wartime, men and women face hard choices. And since the choices are not only personal but collective too, they need to think out loud about what to do; they need to argue with one another. Watching from a distance, what they say is less important than their ability to say something coherent and intelligent. On these occasions, it is not all that helpful to be heroic but inarticulate.

We have to learn to talk about the choices we make. I want to turn now to the specific kind of learning required by democratic citizenship.

POLITICAL EDUCATION, CULTURAL DIVERSITY, AND DEMOCRATIC CITIZENSHIP

Imagine a country much like our own, which is divided culturally, religiously, ideologically, and economically. I am going to focus on the religious divisions, because these generate the most interesting curricular debates, but it is important to stress that in this imagined country no aspect of public life is free from controversy. Let's imagine further that insofar as these controversies require political decisions, the decisions are made more or less democratically. Whether more or less depends on the number of citizens who are, to some significant degree, engaged and knowledgeable, ready to take responsibility for the character and direction of their country. But some of the country's religions, chiefly the fundamentalist or orthodox religions, have little interest in democratic decision making, and so their believers are not taught by their parents or pastors the virtues necessary to citizenship. Now, what kind of civic education should this country's public schools and its colleges and universities provide? And what demands should this country make upon private schools and universities run by churches or religious sects?[7]

I assume that students should be taught something about each other, about the different cultures and religions to which they are committed. But I want to address questions only about their political education. What do they need to know if they are to vote in "our" elections, where the reference of the possessive pronoun is simply the body of adult citizens? There are, I believe, three critically important curricular requirements, which apply equally to secular (public) and religious (private) high schools and to all colleges and universities.

The first requirement is probably best met at the high school level, since it involves something like what used to be called "civics." Students need to learn a practical political science of democracy; they need a how-to-do-it course, where the everyday working of government ministries, representative assemblies, courts, parties, social movements, and so on is studied. This is the least controversial part of democratic education, certainly the easiest for religious schools to accept (though they should be bound to attend to all three requirements). But there is nonetheless important educational work to be done here: to teach students to think of themselves as future participants in political activity, not merely as knowledgeable spectators. And since the spectacle is often unedifying and uninviting, teachers must stress that the democratic system is never closed, its character never finally decided. There are always opportunities for people with new or different ideas (here I sound like a democratic Polonius, but a little of that is all right). Students should be encouraged to experiment with political ideas and taught how to argue about them in front of their peers and within specific institutional settings.

Second, students need to study the history of democratic institutions and practices from ancient Greece onward—and alongside this they need to learn about and engage with the preference of various religious groups for nondemocratic forms of government. Maybe teachers in Catholic, Jewish, or Muslim schools will look for ways to naturalize democracy within a tradition that has actually been hostile to it, but I am inclined to favor an honest confrontation with the preferred forms of rule—of kings or priests or religious sages. After all, democracy is a culture of criticism and disagreement. There are different ways to help students feel at home in a democratic society, and the claim that all of us have always lived there is not necessarily the best way. It is certainly not the most honest way, and young people generally recognize and recoil from dishonesty. That said, I don't think it is wrong to tell the Catholic, Jewish, or Muslim story in a version that stresses possible points of access for a democratic understanding.[8] But one must also tell the Greek story and dwell on the genuinely formative moments in the history of democracy.

The third requirement is, to my mind, the most important: a course on the philosophy or political theory of democratic government, with all the standard arguments critically reviewed. This should obviously include the arguments about constitutional arrangements, but it should be focused on the practices and attitudes that constitute a democratic political culture: the equality of citizens (men and women alike), their freedom to speak and associate, the right of opposition, tolerance for disagreement, the need (sometimes) for compromise, skepticism about authority, and so on. These are, of course, the practices and attitudes of *liberal* democracy, but in this case the adjective doesn't qualify but merely reinforces the noun; I doubt that an illiberal democracy could maintain for long the equality, inclusiveness, and right of opposition that are necessary features of democratic politics. The best way to teach these practices and attitudes is to exemplify them in the classroom: so the theoretical texts in which democracy has been explained and defended (or criticized) should be studied *democratically*, with freewheeling discussion, open-ended inquiry, a sense for the unfinished character of the democratic project. The arguments should never be reduced to a catechism, especially not for the purposes of the final exam.

Every faculty will have to argue, obviously, about the right texts to assign to its students. I don't think that agreement is impossible, though it will always be temporary. The arguments have to be renewed, and should be renewed, every decade or so, since faculties define themselves by arguments of this sort, and the creative destruction of curricula is an important feature of democratic education. The exact balance of required courses and electives is also something that has to be argued over—and will perhaps change (and change back) over time. But I don't think that there are any good reasons for abandoning the balance altogether—no good reasons for a set curriculum without electives, or for a supermarket of optional courses without any requirements. After all, the society that the students have already entered is a mixed world of freedom and constraint, and the moral life they have already begun is a mix of choice and obligation. Schools should mirror this reality, and professors cannot escape the task of establishing the proper educational mix.

To committed democrats, and especially to secular democrats (however they feel about requirements and electives), the courses I have proposed will seem innocuous enough. But to some religious groups, they will look like a program for cultural subordination. Free inquiry, gender equality, the rejection of hierarchical arrangements, the liberal practice of "making up one's own mind"—all this can be said to undermine religious authority. Orthodox Catholics, Jews, and Muslims may feel that their children are being "Protestantized," since Protestant congregationalism is much closer to democracy than their own organizational practices are. At the same time, fundamentalist Protestants may feel that their children are being secularized or, as some of them have complained, initiated into the fake religion of "secular humanism."[9] Clearly, a democratic education will impact differently on different religious communities. Insofar as it is successful, it will bring significant changes to some of them, while confirming or even reinforcing the practices of others. Should this matter?

One response is to insist that modern societies are sufficiently compartmentalized so that their members can act differently in different spheres, without compromising their religious beliefs. Catholics can elect representatives to Congress while accepting an ecclesiastical hierarchy over which they have no similar control. Orthodox Jews can criticize political leaders while never daring to criticize their nonelected sages. Certainly, traditional authority structures have considerable staying power: priests, rabbis, mullahs, old families, local notables all continue to shape communal opinion long after modernity has called into being a host of eager successors. So why can't democratic politics coexist with religious cultures even if it isn't equally in tune, as it were, with all of them?

We know that it can and does. But the coexistence is harder for some religions than for others, since for some of them religion isn't a "compartment" of social life but the whole of it. Religious precepts are all-encompassing, controlling all the believer's activities in all spheres of society. And so the political education that I have described is hegemonic in this crucial sense: that it presses students to accept the prevailing independence of politics from religious control, the famous separation of church and state. Of course, religious beliefs legitimately influence political opinions and choices. But students will be taught that these beliefs, insofar as they have practical consequences for other people, need to be discussed and defended in the public forum, where they will be criticized by nonbelievers. And however firm their own beliefs are, religious men and women who argue in public are committed in principle to listen to the inevitable counterarguments. Dogma is still a feature of some religions, but it is not a feature of democratic culture. In practice, of course, political sects are as dogmatic as religious sects, but while religious education legitimately reinforces dogmatic belief, political education (in a democracy) ought to undermine it.

Still, we need to acknowledge that orthodox religion isn't alone in aiming at a radically unified and coherent social life. National-republican political theory, in its hard Rousseauian version, has a remarkably similar aim: to create a political community whose members "fly to the assemblies," where they are wholly focused on the public good. Here in the United States, Rousseau's educational impact, mediated by John Dewey, has been wholly different from the impact he sought to have on Polish schools in his *Government of Poland*.[10] But the argument about how to produce and reproduce committed Polish citizens fits, I think, the theory of the *Social Contract*, and it makes for a useful contrast with the requirements of a liberal democracy. Patriotism and commitment are the crucial goals, virtually the only goals, of the educational system, the civil religion, and the public culture that Rousseau prescribes for Poland. The citizens of his republic have as little room in their lives for other-worldly religion as devout believers have for secular politics. When a Polish citizen reaches the age of twenty, Rousseau says,

> he must be a Pole, not some other kind of man. I should wish him to learn to read by reading literature written in his own country. I should wish him, at ten, to be familiar with everything Poland has produced; at twelve, to know all its provinces, all its roads, all its towns; at fifteen, to have mastered his country's entire history; and at sixteen, all its laws; let his mind and heart be full of every noble deed, every illustrious man, that ever was in Poland. . . . I do not, as this should make clear, favor putting the youngsters through the usual round of studies, directed by foreigners and priests.

Rousseau believed that republicanism and nationalism went together, but it is easy to imagine a purely nationalist version of this curriculum—and also right and left sectarian versions. There may well be many parents with strong political commitments, as there certainly are many parents with strong religious commitments, who would like to rescue their children from the "usual round of studies" directed by unbelievers and liberal teachers.

Rousseau's curriculum would definitely not be right for a liberal and multicultural democracy. At the same time, much of his list could, and does, figure in a democratic education: at roughly the age of twelve, I was able to write the names of the sixty-some counties and county seats of the state of Pennsylvania on a blank map. And I knew quite a bit about the noble deeds of American patriots. The problem with Rousseau is that he believes that nothing else, nothing "foreign," should be taught to young people—and that makes his republic into a monolith and turns citizenship into a totalizing experience. But even a more modest democratic education, like my own in Pennsylvania in the 1940s and 1950s—indeed, any education that avoids ideological certainty and acknowledges cultural pluralism—would be very threatening to parents with nationalist or sectarian commitments, just as it would be threatening to parents struggling to reproduce an all-encompassing religion. Freewheeling study and debate about issues in political theory, history, and sociology would challenge students who had been taught at home that the deeds of Americans are always "noble," or that proletarian dictatorship is historically inevitable, or that patriarchal rule is divinely ordained and eternal. Education is not a neutral activity. Teaching the most conventional version of liberal democratic theory and practice, in a liberal democratic state, will certainly have "normalizing" effects on the children of illiberal or antidemocratic communities. I should add, however, that teaching a critical or "postmodern" theory would have very similar effects. The communities will be marginalized or subordinated in either case, and the faith of their children will be put at risk. So, again, and finally, does this matter?

The U.S. Constitution forbids the establishment of religion, but (this point is so obvious that it is rarely stated) the Constitution provides for an establishment of politics. We don't have an established church, but we do have an established state. And this is a state of a particular sort, just as any religious establishment would be: it is a liberal democratic state. It follows that while our public schools and colleges cannot teach Christian theology (except in a course, say, on the philosophy of religion), they can teach liberal democratic theory. Constitutionally, that is a permitted activity. But it also seems to me a politically and morally necessary activity, because the students in our universities are just becoming active citizens, and they will soon be making critically important decisions that will determine the quality, perhaps also the physical safety, of our common life. The education of every child affects every other child. Given democratic decision making, the children of religious parents, the children of political sectarians, will help to decide the fate of my children. There are no possible exemptions here, unless a religious community decides to opt out of citizenship altogether and adopt the status of resident aliens. Perhaps we should allow that, but I see no reason to allow future citizens to avoid or escape an education for citizenship. The stakes are too high.

Think of citizenship as a political office: surely future officeholders should learn something about the responsibilities the office entails. Or better, the current officeholders should teach the next generation what they think they have learned about those responsibilities. For the reproduction of democratic politics is never a sure thing. We have to prove to our children that we really believe in the values that make democracy possible. That means, first of all, that we have to live by those values; it also means that we should not be afraid to insist on their study. For very good reasons, citizenship, unlike medicine or law, doesn't require a license; students don't need a passing grade in democratic politics. But they should definitely take the course.

Notes

1. I draw here on an article that I wrote long ago for the *New Republic*, "Teaching Morality," June 10, 1978, 12–14.

2. See any of the standard neoconservative lamentations: the work of William Bennett, for example: *The Index of Leading Cultural Indicators Updated and Expanded* (New York: Broadway Books, 1999); and *The Book of Virtues* (New York: Simon & Schuster, 1993).

3. See the Harvard University catalogue for 1915–1916 (Cambridge, Mass., 1915), which includes a set of courses on Social Ethics, listed separately from Philosophy and Government. Forty years later, courses like that would be unimaginable.

4. This is the popularized conclusion of a much more subtle philosophical argument; see, for example, J. O. Urmson, *The Emotive Theory of Ethics* (London: Hutchinson University Library, 1968).

5. My reference here is mostly to everyday conversation in the contemporary academy, but Stanley Fish's book *The Trouble with Principle* (Cambridge, Mass.: Harvard University Press, 1999) provides an intelligent and sophisticated version of this argument.

6. My own years of reading and moviegoing provide the basis for this account of American culture; I suppose that Hemingway's heroes might serve as the best public representation of the figure I am talking about (though a novel like *For Whom the Bell Tolls* raises doubts about the rejection of sentimentality).

7. I have been helped in answering these questions by Yael Tamir, ed., "Democratic Education in a Multicultural State," special issue, *Journal of Philosophy of Education* 29, no. 2 (July 1995).

8. For a Jewish version of this sort of thing, see Irving Agus, *Urban Civilization in Pre-Crusade Europe* (New York: Yeshiva University Press, 1965).

9. See the arguments in and about the important court case *Mozart v. Hawkins County Board of Education*: Amy Gutmann, *Democratic Education,* rev. ed. (Princeton, N.J.: Princeton University Press, 1999), 298–99; Jeff Spinner-Halev, *Surviving Diversity: Religion and Democratic Citizenship* (Baltimore, Md.: Johns Hopkins University Press, 2000), 136–37, 140.

10. Jean-Jacques Rousseau, *The Government of Poland,* trans. Willmoore Kendall (Indianapolis: Library of Liberal Arts, 1972); the quote can be found on p. 20.

Utopias Gone Wrong
The Antipolitical Culture of the Modern University and How to Change It

ROBERT E. CALVERT

I shall take the *political* to be an expression of the idea that a free society composed of diversities can nonetheless enjoy moments of commonality when, through public deliberations, collective power is used to promote or protect the well being of the collectivity. *Politics* refers to the legitimized public contestation, primarily by organized and unequal social powers, over access to the resources available to the public authorities of the collectivity. Politics is continuous, ceaseless, and endless. In contrast, the political is episodic, rare.

SHELDON WOLIN[1]

Politics I take to be the activity of attending to the general arrangements of a set of people whom chance or choice have brought together. . . . [A]s we have come to understand it, the activity is one in which every member of the group who is neither a child nor a lunatic has some part and some responsibility. . . . Now, attending to the arrangements of a society is an activity which, like every other, has to be learned. Politics make a call upon knowledge.

MICHAEL OAKESHOTT[2]

But diverse groups hold together, firstly, because they have a common interest in sheer survival and, secondly, because they practise politics—not because they agree about "fundamentals," or some such concept too vague, too personal, or too divine ever to do the job of politics for it. The moral consensus of a free state is not something mysteriously prior to or above politics: it is the activity (the civilising activity) of politics itself.

BERNARD CRICK[3]

My first aim in this chapter is to claim that active political participation is necessary to the legitimacy of a polity, our own, that is at once liberal, democratic, and a republic. Second, I will argue that over the last century the public schooling Americans have conceived as appropriate for the American citizen has harbored two competing conceptions of purpose and authority that have been implicitly utopian and thus deeply antipolitical, and in effect hostile to active political participation. Third, I will try to show that these tacitly utopian visions have become the conceptions of educational purpose and authority that now dominate the modern American university and thus help to explain why an education for citizenship, understood specifically as participation in what can be called the politics of the nation, is so little honored in the higher education of today. One of these utopian visions, the warped version of the American dream called *meritocracy,* though thoroughly modern in its assumptions, is reputed vaguely to be "conservative" in its implications; the other, a version of multiculturalism issuing in *identity politics,* is championed by the postmodern "left" and offers a "radical" critique of existing American culture and society.[4] Finally, I will suggest a kind of undergraduate instruction for citizens that is political in the dual sense that it embraces both conflict and commonality (of all sorts) and sees them as interdependent. This is a pedagogy, moreover, that is altogether consistent with the legitimate aspirations of those two utopian visions, brought down to earth, and consistent as well with the principles of liberal education properly understood.

ACTIVE CITIZENSHIP AND WHY IT IS IMPORTANT

In the beginning were thirteen small republics, but also, in the language of the Declaration of Independence, "one people," united, at least during the Revolution, by the desire to govern themselves without a king. Thus was the problem of *E pluribus unum* originally stated. James Madison's Constitution, aiming at a "more perfect union" grounded in the authority of "the people," created a single "elevated" and "extended" Republic, and by its institutional structure guaranteed both that it would be a *liberal* republic in which individual rights would be secure and that the "one people" Jefferson spoke of would rarely if ever speak with one voice. For their part, the Anti-Federalists (later reinforced by the Jacksonians), distrusting the new government and in this and other respects representing a majority of the people, saw to it that it would also be a *democratic* republic, but one in which the actual political life and affections of the people would be focused for the most part locally and sometimes in opposition to the central governing institutions of the Republic itself. From the beginning, then, the Madisonian Constitution has posited a "unity," a commonality, a sense of the *political*, whose very existence and meaning to the members of the polity thus created is "constructed" in part by the *politics* in which its members engage.

To draw on an old metaphor, we can think of such a polity, or regime, or "constitution" in the broadest sense, as resting on a three-legged stool. The political participation of active citizens assures that each of the three legs supports the polity itself; and if any one of those legs fails, the polity will collapse, or fundamentally change its character, and hence become illegitimate. *Democracy* clearly requires that a majority of citizens help prescribe the rules by which they are governed. *Liberalism* just as clearly requires not only that the rights of individuals be protected by that same government against infringement by other citizens but also that the government itself, however democratic, be restrained. If eternal vigilance is the price of liberty, citizens worried about their liberties must see to it that the institutions that both enable and restrain government are kept in good working order. For a liberal democracy also to be a *republic*, some unspecified number of citizens must be moved to participate in public affairs by their sense of ownership of the "public thing." Through their sacrifices large and small, they will have "invested" something of themselves in the whole of which they are a part. They will have come to identify with it, indeed to love it. They will be patriotic.[5]

Each of these three supports of the liberal democratic republic has its pathologies, ever a threat to the integrity of the whole. Democratic participation, unrestrained, can threaten individual freedom at any of the levels. Liberalism can promote an individualism so self-centered, so complacent, so atomistic, so egoistic, as Tocqueville put it, as to shun all political participation and thus invite despotism.[6] Republicanism, when joined with democracy, can produce a regime so all-embracing as to entail a totalistic nationalism—a liberal nightmare. But the only enduring remedy for any of these excesses is counteractivity on the part of the others. Put another way, participation helps to stave off political entropy, the natural tendency of an essentially "headless" polity to dissolve if not actively maintained by its members.[7] Political action is necessarily action through institutions, and thus if each tendency in the political culture pursues its own interests, the integrity of the whole will be maintained, as Adam Smith perhaps would have argued had he been more politically oriented. We in any case can argue that political participation is necessary not only for bringing about change but also for preserving the institutions that define the political order itself and make orderly change possible. Thus, we can say, to return to an earlier claim, that political participation, politics, or what Michael Oakeshott called "attending to the arrangements" of society, both presupposes and is itself central to a political education. As if this were not complicated and tenuous enough, democratic, liberal, and republican modes of political participation are inspired by and tend to foster different and conflicting conceptions of characteristically American political and social goods—freedom and equality, for example, or local community, or national solidarity in times of crisis. The radical democrat, or at any rate the social democrat, may work for equality of condition, the liberal, here speaking for the vast majority of Americans, for equality of opportunity, and the republican for a kind of functional equality, or equality of contribution, according to talents, to the common good. These are vastly different and incommensurable conceptions of equality.

With respect to freedom, the real tension is between liberalism and republicanism. The former cherishes what for the last half century and more we have called "negative" liberty, the freedom of individuals to pursue unhindered, or with as little restraint as possible, their own conception of their private, subjectively defined happiness. This is a citizenship defined by rights, chiefly property rights broadly understood, with the citizen connected to other citizens essentially through contractual obligations enforced by law. The liberal citizen's main concern in becoming active in politics is to see to it that such private rights are secure; and (for one kind of liberal) to seek through government action their extension to those not already enjoying them, seeing the public good as essentially a regime in which such private rights for all are equally protected. In good times, in a prosperous society and an economy of abundance, however, such a citizen is apt to be passive and to regard public life, including government itself, to be a distraction. By contrast, the republican citizen acts politically not for the sake of individual rights or private happiness, or not only for those ends, but with a view to the public or common good, and even for the sake of the action itself. The republican citizen may find the affluent society the liberal citizen passively enjoys to be a threat to the liberty and public-spiritedness he prizes. This is to speak of what Charles Taylor variously calls an "exercise-concept" or a "self-realisation-concept" of freedom. John Pocock links this positive conception of freedom directly with an "Aristotelian" citizenship and political participation, in contrast to the passive or "Gaian" conception of negative freedom:

> To Aristotle and many others, politics (alias the activity of ruling and being ruled) is a good in itself, not the prerequisite of the public good but the public good or *res publica* correctly defined. What matters is the freedom to take part in public decisions, not the content of the decisions taken. This nonoperational or noninstrumental definition of politics has remained part of our definition of freedom ever since and explains the role of citizenship in it. Citizenship is not just a means to being free; it is the way of being free itself.[8]

So at best American citizens participate in politics, when they do, out of mixed motives, but participate they must, or some of them must, if the government itself is to be legitimate. Only through citizen participation in some form do citizens and their government come to a common understanding about the purposes the polity is to serve, and it is also through such participation that citizens and government are reassured in their respective roles as leaders and followers. Democracy understood as popular rule, or rule with the consent of the governed, offers only thin and formal conceptions of political purpose and authority. With the voice of the "sovereign" people muted, filtered through a complex and conflicting maze of rights-protecting institutions, it isn't easy to discern the "will" of the people, though some will claim with unwarranted confidence to know what it is. So what will be done in the name of the people and by their authority is a matter of "politics," with the winners, for the moment, claiming legitimacy, but always open to challenge—if challengers there are. Politics is *about* sorting through and deciding which, or whose, purposes are to be served, and whether those purposes are or are not consistent with the good of the whole.

The typical American citizen is of course not wholly or solely any one of the three types described above, though no doubt pure types of each can be found. On the contrary, we are composites, and each element in some measure is necessary. Unless a person has some democratic sentiments, believes in individual rights, and grants that there is at least on occasion something that could be called either good or bad for "the country" as a whole, it would seem doubtful that such a person is an American citizen at all. Yet it will readily be seen in the above that it is the *republican* impulses that now are most lacking in that composite creature we call the American citizen. Indeed, when observers speak about the decline of political participation among Americans generally over the last several decades, and especially among young people, they mostly have in mind that set of impulses and convictions in the American citizen I have identified as republican. Indeed, it may be said, it is really only the republican part of American political culture that identifies lack of participation as prima facie a problem. Our republican selves have worried about this from the beginning, seeing an inert citizenry, or a people devoted overmuch to private purposes, especially to the accumulation of wealth, to getting and spending, which early Americans castigated as "luxury," as a sure sign of corruption, of citizens and of the republic itself.

Finally, not the least of the benefits of political participation is that it is itself an indispensable kind of political education. It teaches all of us about limits. If liberals do their job properly, they will teach democrats who are too enthusiastically republican that individual rights and private lives must be respected. If republicans are alert to their responsibilities, they will teach democrats who are only privatistic liberals that "particular estates," as John Winthrop put it, "cannot subsist in the ruin of the public."[9] But if political participation sets limits to public and private excesses of citizens, it also teaches politicians the sources as well as the limits of their own authority, while also making manifest the collective purposes they are empowered to pursue.

Although political participation itself is an indispensable form of political education, Americans from the beginning have believed that citizens must be prepared for actual political participation by a prior education. Public schooling, as we will see, was thought to be indispensable to the health and well-being of this new democratic society, but prior even to schooling, or together with it, the character of the liberal democratic republican would be shaped by what today we would call the institutions of civil society, by families and religious institutions, of course, but also by a variety of forms of economic activity. Only after boys and girls are properly brought up to be men and women can they be expected to have developed the foundations of social and moral capital upon which citizenship itself can be built. *Can be built*, and without a formal higher education, as was shown by everyone's favorite example, Abraham Lincoln, and more recently by James Stewart's Rick Rescorla. And there are in communities across the land today any number of latter-day civic heroes, mostly unsung, quite ordinary republican citizens, who never attain those storied heights but who regularly transcend their immediate private interests and leave their communities better than they found them—and all this without the benefit of higher education. The point is, as the best social science is telling us, there are declining numbers of such persons, especially among those young people whose college educations would seem only to enhance their capacities as citizens.

Next I consider what I take to be two of the more formidable obstacles to teaching young men and women of college age about the means and ends of good citizenship in our time. These obstacles are formidable because together they presently constitute the operative and rarely challenged purposes of American higher education. One of these tendencies originated in primary and secondary schools in the first half of the twentieth century, and then, filtered through the counterculture of the 1960s, migrated into higher education. The second tendency has been a central feature of American universities at least since the late nineteenth century, and perhaps for much longer, but took on a new life with the adoption of the Scholastic Aptitude Test in college and university admissions policies. I refer to the university as a training ground for a professional elite. Superficially in tension, the first of these tendencies radical, the second conservative, they have in practice converged, I will argue, to create a pervasive antipolitical culture in the modern university with pronounced utopian features. Understanding in some detail what these tendencies are, and how they have fortuitously come together to make those of us in higher education comfortable in the belief that the political education of citizens is not our responsibility, may also suggest, or so I hope, that it is not inevitable that the modern university must remain civically dysfunctional—part of the problem instead of part of the solution.

Utopia in American Education and Its Antipolitical Deformations

If a child of their [the Rulers'] own is born with an alloy of iron or brass, they must, without the smallest pity, assign him the station proper to his nature and thrust him out among the craftsmen or the farmers. If, on the contrary, these classes produce a child with gold or silver in his composition, they will promote him, according to his value, to be a Guardian or an Auxiliary.

PLATO[10]

By that part of our plan which prescribes the selection of youths of genius from among the classes of the poor, we hope to avail the state of those talents when nature has sown as liberally among the poor as the rich, but which perish without use, if not sought for and cultivated.

THOMAS JEFFERSON[11]

They must send out into the country all citizens who are above ten years old, take over the children, away from the present habits and manners of their parents, and bring them up in their own ways under the institutions we have described. Would not that be the quickest way our polity could be established?

PLATO[12]

Public agitation, propaganda, legislative and administrative action are effective in producing the change in disposition which a philosophy indicates is desirable, but only in the degree in which they are educative— that is to say, in the degree in which they modify mental and moral attitudes. And at the best, such methods are compromised by the fact that they are used with those whose habits are already largely set, while education of youth has a fairer and freer field of operation.

JOHN DEWEY[13]

By "utopian" I mean the portrayal of a *good* place which is also *no place*, a society or polity located only in a writer's imagination and also outside conventional understandings of time. The ancient model, of course, is Plato's "city in speech," whose continued existence, once created, presupposed the stopping at its apex of the ancient Greek conception of cyclical time. In the modern age, after the emergence of the idea of progress in its several expressions, the utopia "exists" at the end of a historical process, which "solves" the problem Plato could not of how it comes into being—modern utopian writers never have to venture to Syracuse. Utopias of whatever historical period are also, as was Plato's *Republic*, a depiction of the perfect time and place and hence a fundamental criticism of the society in which it is created. Finally, and this is the most important feature of utopias for our purpose, *they have banished politics*. Governed as they are by a kind of knowledge that exceeds the capacities of ordinary people and leaves no room for disagreement, there can be no *legitimate* conflict, no politics, either within the governed, between the governed and their governors, or within the governing class itself. The unity and the commonality they invariably depict is neither politically generated nor politically maintained.

Progressivism Writ Small

To understand the antipolitical culture of the contemporary university requires a brief return first to the Progressive Era generally (the thirty years or so ending about 1920) and then specifically (our main concern) to the educational phase of the Progressive movement.

The incipient utopianism of the Progressive Era was based on those two distinct but complementary components of cultural modernity, *voluntarism* and *scientific rationalism*, contained in the idea of progress itself, that "master idea of modernity" as it has been called.[14] Voluntarism (not to be confused with volunteerism), rejecting both divine command and teleology, makes unfettered human will the only source of ends or purpose in human life and is reflected in such modern ideas as sovereignty (both Hobbesian and popular), the market conception of freedom (the "sovereign" consumer) described by Michael Sandel in his chapter, and radical individualism in its several expressions. Scientific rationalism refers to the means modern societies have developed for achieving the ends set by voluntarism. It·is expressed both as a distinctly modern form of epistemic authority, specifically in technology and bureaucracy. Both of these twin and complementary components of cultural modernity are profoundly antipolitical, and both were deeply a part of the out- look of Progressivism, including, as we will see, its educational phase.

The Progressive utopian impulse grew out of the reformers' outrage at the rampant political corruption of the times, the unholy alliance between politicians on the make and the plutocratic "special interests" brought powerfully to light by the muckraking journalists of the day. This was the crisis of democracy, to which the reformers responded basically in two ways. On the one hand, when they invoked the undifferentiated will of "the people,"[15] they embraced the voluntaristic principle. On the other, in the second expression of the culture of modernity, the Progressive reformers placed their faith in scientifically trained experts to implement the will of the people, which of course is the principle of administrative rationality. Hence the campaign on the part of the reformers to get this or that bit of public business "out of politics" and into the hands of the experts. In the first instance these would-be career civil servants (experts for hire would soon follow), denied by the Pendleton Act of 1883 any ties to the corrupt political parties, were expected to use their science-based expertise only in the public interest. So instead of the unholy alliance between the "interests" and the politicians, there would be a holy one, between the experts and the virtuous people.[16] Thus abolished—theoretically—were political parties, to say nothing of the myriad ways in which the interests exerted their influence, which is to say that in principle all institutions mediating between the people and their government, all *political* institutions, were implicitly deprived of legitimacy. The will of the people, the only source of purpose, as well as of (ultimate) authority, would be implemented by the scientifically trained experts, acting in the interest of the people but by a new kind of nonpolitical authority based on that infallible kind of knowledge known as science. It would be a government of the people and for the people, but by the smartest of the people.[17]

It is important to mention one additional article of the Progressive faith, indeed an expectation central especially to the American incarnation of the idea of progress, which is the belief in a continuous expansion of material well-being. The Progressives hardly invented this American faith, as it had been a characteristic feature virtually from the beginning of what Herbert Croly called the Promise of American life.

Moreover, that this "promise" pointed to a kind of utopia has long been recognized.[18] A society of free, rational, industrious individuals, acting in their own self-interest, would naturally and automatically produce such a wealth of the nation that the scourge of poverty would be forever lifted. And on such a foundation of material plenty would rise a society whose further improvement would know no limits. Croly himself, describing the beliefs of his countrymen, spoke of "a sort of Utopia up to date, situated in the land of Good-Enough, and flying the Stars and Stripes."[19] This popularized Enlightenment vision, consisting of a lot of Adam Smith with a nod to Condorcet, was of a society whose government, while providing an economically necessary infrastructure, existed primarily only to guarantee an order in which equality of opportunity prevailed, and in which all important social as well as economic decisions were made by individuals in and through the market. To this essentially laissez-faire vision add only, as the Progressives did, that modern science had provided the means to the realization of these ends, first economic and then social, and we have the base levels upon which would be built the ideal polity, of that pyramid of ideas called the idea of progress. Condorcet's optimism, of course, was unlimited; Smith's was such, notwithstanding his "realist" talk about self-interest, that Reinhold Niebuhr could find in him one of the Children of Light. Progressive Americans were nothing if not optimistic, their idealism tempered only by the fact that a good many of them regarded themselves as only *living toward* their ideal.[20]

When the Progressive enthusiasms waned and the country under Harding returned to "normalcy," these Progressive intimations of utopia—the professionalization *and* the democratization (as well as the prospering) of America—persisted, but after a point they parted company and pursued what seemed different goals, only to be reunited much later in the century in the modern university. The fixation on professional expertise remained a permanent feature of American life, linked as it was with the aspiration to socioeconomic status of the American middle class, and came eventually to dominate and transform American higher education. The Progressive passion for democracy, however, found its way into the university not, as one might expect, through the now self-consciously professional discipline of political science, which, committed to a "value-free" science of politics, could study American democracy but *not* espouse it.[21] Rather, the Progressive passion for democracy "bubbled up" into the university from the public school, reconstructed and made a force for the democratization of all of American life. Let us deal with these in order.

Expertise in the University

As it happened, even before the Progressive movement hit its stride, the universities were already devoted to training a professional elite. Responding specifically after Pendleton to the requirements of civil service reform calling for experts rather than "spoilsmen" in the growing bureaucracy, but more generally to what Burton Bledstein calls the emerging "culture of professionalism" in the late nineteenth century,[22] American universities in the twentieth were increasingly understood as gateways to the status so eagerly being sought by middle-class Americans as larger and larger aspects of American life were coming to be regarded as the objects of scientific knowledge and hence of professional expertise. The older professions, law, medicine, the ministry, were now joined by a host of new ones, engineering, journalism, teaching, business, the reformed civil service—virtually any activity Americans found useful involving more "brain" than "hand" work—and all of these, and many, many others, were now regarded as "careers" for ambitious young men and, later, women.

The emergence of this culture of professionalism, it should be noted, coincided broadly with the supplanting of religion by science as the dominant worldview of the American middle class. This entailed also an important if sometimes subtle shift in the way in which aspirants to professional respectability thought about and justified to themselves and others how they would spend their lives. In the religious terminology applied to the older professions, one followed a "calling" or "vocation," a concept of Protestant Christian origins designating one's life's work as commanded by God. The new science-oriented professionals, on the other hand, would pursue a "career," which initially seemed consistent with a conception of a profession as old as Plato. Instead of serving the greater glory of God through serving others in their community, the new professionals devoted their energies and knowledge to serving "society" or the "public interest." In either case, service to others (one's clients) rather than self-interest was to be one's dominant motive. There would come a time, however, in the twentieth century, when it would be commonplace for a career, however professional, to be understood almost exclusively in individualistic terms, as an indication of socioeconomic "success." This would be service not to God or society but to oneself. But this is to get ahead of our story.

Let us now move to the middle of the twentieth century. The near utopian vision of the new professionalism was accompanied by an American version of the Napoleonic era's "careers open to talents," which eventually made manifest its self-regarding implications. The vehicle by means of which this evolved form of professionalism was imported into twentieth-century higher education, with far-reaching effects on the whole society, was the Scholastic Aptitude Test, the rationale for which was set forth by its most prominent advocate, James Bryant Conant, in a revealing essay published in the *Atlantic Monthly* in 1940.[23] Later espoused by Clark Kerr of the University of California, making the movement national, Conant's aim was nothing less than to create, through higher education, a Jeffersonian "classless" society. As president of Harvard, Conant had developed a strong dislike for the sort of privileged upper-class students who treated a Harvard education as a rite of passage to a guaranteed place in the nation's upper crust.[24] Conant proposed that through rigorous scientific testing, young men (women would soon be included) from all walks of life would have the opportunity to indicate their talents and abilities and thus their promise for a professional life, the training for which would be the first office of the nation's universities. And a society thus enshrining equality of opportunity in such a systematic fashion would render impossible, Conant thought, the hierarchy toward which mid-twentieth-century America constantly tended. Jefferson's own vision would finally be realized. That was the promise. The reality has turned out to be very different.[25]

At its core, meritocracy, and its key principle, equality of opportunity, begins and ends with the assumption of *inequality*, in intelligence, in effort—that is to say, in merit. $IQ + E = M$, where intelligence plus effort equals merit, is the formula in the classic dystopian novel *The Rise of the Meritocracy* by Michael Young. The meritocratic assumption is that however equal "all men" may in principle be at birth, when put to the real-world test some are measurably brighter and harder working than others, and thus more valuable to "society," and therefore also more entitled to the rewards society has to offer.[26] Indeed, to follow rigorously the logic of meritocracy is to arrive exactly at a kind of inverted Platonic justice based on the lower parts of the human soul. Those baser talents and abilities are nurtured by the right sort of education, which is to the best appetitive advantage of each individual as well as to the society itself. Indeed, to follow this logic to its conclusion produces exactly not an egalitarian or classless society but its opposite, a graded hierarchy defined by wealth and social status, with the intelligent and industrious at the top and the stupid and lazy at the bottom. Besides Young's dystopia, the ultimate deformation of the utopia implicit in "equality of opportunity" may be said to be a society in which James Stewart's Wall Street crooks are somehow the norm. Conant himself evidently anticipated, as did Jefferson, that the few "geniusses . . . raked from the rubbish . . . to be instructed at the public expence, as far as the grammer schools go"[27] would be a public-spirited elite. No doubt assuming the older meaning of "profession," Conant in any case emphasized heavily the recruiting of superior students who would become leaders in the various professions. But the SAT does not measure public-spiritedness or sound the depths of the civic self. It takes social and moral capital for granted, and the elites thus produced exploit but do not replenish that kind of capital.

Democracy in the Progressive School

Certain tendencies in early-twentieth-century Progressivism, as I have suggested, were implicitly utopian—their heady faith in the promise of science as a solution for all imaginable social ills, their confidence that a restored democracy, purged of corruption, would yet realize Lincoln's vision of a government of, by, and for "the people." When the Progressive movement collapsed after the Great War, these hopes and expectations didn't evaporate. They went underground—became embedded in the very definition and self-understanding of the emergent education profession in the public schools, led by its major source of theory and inspiration, the Progressive Education Association, founded in 1919. Those enthusiastic men and women of the PEA were in turn inspired chiefly by the writings of America's philosopher, John Dewey. Even before Dewey's enormously influential *Democracy and Education* was published in 1916, those in charge of the new "progressive" schools across the country were passionately committed to "democracy." At the same time, as aspirants to the status of professionals, armed with their own science of education and hence possessors of expert knowledge, they saw themselves, and themselves alone, as qualified to lead the nation into the future promised by Progress.

Did this produce in the Progressive educational mind a fusion of utopia and democracy? It did indeed. But we must be careful of the terms. Critics of what came to be called progressive education who have used the term "utopian" have usually meant to express only their sense that the democratic vision embodied by the theories and practices of the progressive schools, like some of the reforms of the parent Progressive movement, was simply naive or unrealistic. But I wish now to argue that Progressive educational theory was "naive" and "unrealistic" in a way that makes of it a quite explicit if largely unrecognized form of American (educational) utopianism. To bring out its utopian features, as outlined above, will help put us in a position to identify and assess its influence on higher education today.

The utopia envisioned by the progressive educationists was a "place," a "democratic" *society* that had never existed anywhere but was destined in the fullness of time to come into being in America. I emphasize "society" because the democracy embedded in progressive educational theory was not a *polity* so much as a kind of social democracy, reminiscent, but only vaguely, of the democratic alternative to the revolutionary socialism of that era. It was not a polity because it had nothing to do with either government or politics, as those activities are understood in democracies spatially and temporally located. Dewey had told his legion of committed followers that "democracy is more than a form of government; it is primarily a form of associated living, of conjoint communicated experience."[28] His followers quickly concluded that democracy, properly understood and provided for, was not a form of government *at all*, and as a form of associated living had nothing to do with, no need for, politics. This was a kind of conflict-free democracy certain progressives had glimpsed over the rainbow and hoped would be ushered in by the appropriately reconstructed school. And its very "existence" in the educationists' vision constituted a critique, more or less radical, of what American democracy had become. Put another way, we can see the educationists as the professional experts devoted selflessly to implementing the will of the people. But "the people" turn out to be schoolchildren who themselves need to be democratized, their wills properly formed.

The generic obstacle to progress according to the eighteenth-century philosophes was precisely ignorance, the antithesis of Enlightenment, and so education was always the necessary condition of progress. But it fell to American progressive education theorists to see in the democratized school virtually the *sufficient* condition. "If we seek the kingdom of heaven, educationally, all other things shall be added unto us," Dewey assured his followers, "which, being interpreted, is that if we identify ourselves with the real instincts and needs of childhood, and ask only after its fullest assertion and growth, the discipline and information and culture of adult life shall all come in their due season."[29] Well, the real needs and interests of childhood were certainly not being met by the traditional school, with its rigid discipline, its imposition on children of "subject matter" remote from actual life, the insistence on strict obedience from naturally active children—indeed the school's essential separation from society itself. But a school brought into contact *in the right way* with society, with actual life, would meet the real needs and interests of children and also serve as an instrument of a progressive transformation of the larger society itself. Here Dewey indicates what flows from this "right way":

> To do this means to make each one of our schools an embryonic community life, active with types of occupations that reflect the life of the larger society and permeated throughout with the spirit of art, history, and science. When the school introduces and trains each child of society into membership within such a little community, saturating him with the spirit of service,[30] and providing him with the instruments of effective self-direction, we shall have the deepest and best guaranty of a larger society which is worthy, lovely, and harmonious.[31]

The idea of progress, recall, was often expressed in metaphors of "growth" and "development" toward the highest stage of human flourishing, the latter presumably a kind of Aristotelian telos, or final cause, the realization of which was the ultimate end or "purpose" of the thing changing, in this case society itself. Dewey is here saying that the school needs to be linked intimately, even "organically," with the emerging industrial society of his day, indeed, as we'll see, to incorporate that society somehow within itself as expressed in "art, history, and science." The really key term here, however, is that the school is seen in essence as an *embryonic community*, expressing itself in and through the activities characteristic of the society "outside." Well, embryos grow and develop, don't they? Properly constructed and conducted in the right way and spirit, the school eventually will create a society after its own image. So the school and society must be joined: "Can we connect this 'New Education' with the general march of events?" Dewey asked. "If we can, it will lose its isolated character; it will cease to be an affair which proceeds from the over-ingenious minds of pedagogues dealing with individual pupils. It will appear as part and parcel of the whole social evolution, and, in its general features at least, as inevitable."[32]

Children in the reconstructed school will be shaped by the "outside" environment, but it will be both a simplified and a purified version of it, the simplification required to keep children from being overwhelmed, and the purification to guarantee that children would not be exposed to miseducative influences. It is here that we can see the invitation to utopian theorizing:

> It is the business of the school environment to eliminate, so far as possible, the unworthy features of the existing environment from influence upon mental habitudes. It establishes a purified medium of action. Selection aims not only at simplification but at weeding out what is undesirable. Every society gets encumbered with what is trivial, with dead wood from the past, and with what is positively perverse. The school has the duty of omitting such things from the environment it supplies, and thereby doing what it can to counter-act their influence on the ordinary social environment. By select-ing the best for its exclusive use, it strives to re-enforce the power of this best. As a society becomes more enlightened, it realizes that it is responsible *not* to transmit and conserve the whole of its exist-ing achievements, but only such as make for a better future society. The school is its chief agency for the accomplishment of this end.[33]

The conception of a reconstructed school incorporating into itself the "progressive" features of the society outside bespoke a vision of a stately but gradual march, an evolution really, of a school-led society toward the inevitable self-realization of American democracy, albeit a democracy oddly bereft of any government other than the unobtrusive authority of the progressive teacher in the background, and certainly bereft also of politics in the much-decried adult sense of the word. Much of this would change as progressive education matured.

At a 1932 meeting of the Progressive Education Association, George S. Counts, a professor of education at Teachers College, Columbia, gave a speech provocatively titled "Dare Progressive Education Be Progressive?". In a trenchant critique of the prevailing theories and practices in the movement since the foundation of the Progressive Education Association in 1919, Counts called on the members of the association, wedded as they were to a child-centered, thoroughly nondirective education, to overcome their deep suspicion of "indoctrination" and "imposition" and rise to the challenge presented by a nation in a deep depression and with its democratic principles in jeopardy. Progressive education, Counts charged, had come to represent the educational outlook of a liberal-minded but well-to-do and comfortable class of Americans whose educational principles tended in the direction of "anarchy or extreme individualism,"[34] even as their class interests inclined them otherwise toward conservatism. Instead of striving to direct the "growth" of each individual child to the ultimate flowering of his or her fullest potential, what was needed was precisely the "imposition" on children of genuinely progressive ideas, ideas that would chart a course and move the nation forward, toward the realization of the democratic ideal latent in the nation's history. Discounting the skepticism of the "learned and wise" and endorsing the opinion of ordinary people about the power of education, Counts's real challenge to the progressive schools was captured in the title of the book incorporating his address: *Dare the School Build a New Social Order?*

Had Counts wanted to specify a target in his critique of progressive educational theory and practice during the two previous decades, he could have pointed to Harold Rugg and Ann Schumaker's *The Child-Centered School*, a progressive education statement of the 1920s that captured most of what the movement was about,[35] as Counts's own work did for the 1930s. The "anarchy or extreme individualism" he noted in the movement as a whole was contained succinctly in what Rugg and Schumaker called progressive education's "new articles of faith"—freedom of the children to express themselves actively and creatively versus the rigid control imposed by the authority of the traditional teacher; the freedom of the children to study what interested *them*, not what the teacher thought they ought to know—pupils themselves would set the educational agenda; pupils would *actively* pursue their interests rather than listen passively to the teacher; each child would be regarded as a budding artist, whose creativity and self-expression would be given free rein; and through a host of group activities pupils would both learn that they were unique as individuals *and* be initiated into "successful social cooperation."[36] Though not overtly a call for social reconstruction—Rugg himself would come out strongly in favor of using education as a means of social reform later in his career—the child-centered school was in its way as much a plan for a "new social order" as was Counts's explicit program for social reconstruction. The "new school," they said, "is evolving its informal real-life organization, encouraging common aims and purposes, the interpenetration of minds, producing in the school a life of happy intimacy—creating a 'wholesome medium for the most complete living.'"[37]

In sum, the portrait of "the individual" was extreme indeed, and it did border on anarchy. In the school the child was free of parental control, of course, but also, except for the shadowy presence of the teacher in the background, free of *all* adult authority. More than this, the portrait was pure in the sense that "the child" as such was the central figure in this picture, without accompanying characteristics of gender, race, or other defining features—indeed a diminutive version of "the individual" that was also at the center of the modern political theory from Hobbes through Rousseau, here with an emphasis on the latter. But as those theorists had not, Dewey and his followers abolished all economic constraints as well, anticipating by nearly half a century Galbraith's proclamation of the "Affluent Society." With the "school" as the "natural" home of this child cum modern individual, the progressive educational theorists had created a ready-made, an existential state of nature, which summoned their deepest theoretical speculations.[38]

If progressive education was a microcosmic extension of Progressivism writ large—Progressivism gone underground, so to speak—the generation of the 1960s in its several expressions represented its resurfacing. Indeed, progressive education—child-centeredness, hostility to the formal discipline represented by "subject matter," indeed the anti-intellectualism of the education profession itself,[39] the child as creative artist, the celebration of spontaneity, the idealization of youthful purity, the quest for the intimate community, the radical egalitarianism, the passionate search for democracy, the presumption of material plenty, the belief in the transformative powers of the school, in short, utopianism redux—was on a collision course with Conant's blueprint for the professionalized yet "classless" meritocracy in the making, not to mention Kerr's multiversity as "social service station." These two powerful forces in American education and life met head-on in American universities beginning in 1964. There is scarcely anything of any significance in either progressive education or the meritocratic vision that did not serve as either a critique or a defense of that incarnation of the modern university and of the political, social, and economic order it willy-nilly represented. Add as catalysts the baby boom, the Vietnam War, and television, and the battle unfolded along predictable lines.

What Culture Wars?

That battle is not *now* being fought in universities, at least not very vigorously; on the contrary, the combatants have in effect declared a permanent truce—have come to recognize that their most fundamental interests are not in conflict after all—and have thus created a political desert, a rapprochement that quietly ends the conflict over "difference" without achieving any sense of a shared life or common good. The most important characteristic of *today's* "modern university" for our purposes is that it has synthesized the radical "progressivism" of the "sixties" generation and the liberal (if relationally conservative) meritocratic orientation of the universities of that day into an ideologically eclectic university in our own, whose purposes and authority have little to do with either liberal or political education.

It is by now an old story about how the New Left, its own utopian project failing in the larger society, returned as professors and administrators to take control of the universities they had once seemed determined to destroy. But if the now aging radicals are "in," it doesn't mean that the "establishment," the "power structure," the society created and largely dominated by modern corporate capitalism, is "out," and this for two very practical reasons. First, when the baby boom ended, universities had to scramble in the new buyer's market for students, most of whom, intent on scaling the heights of the corporate and professional worlds, cared little about those old battles. This demographic imperative meant marketing themselves in terms calculated to appeal precisely to the upwardly mobile young Americans, now sorted out, raked from the rubbish in Jefferson's phrase, by the SAT. So a university education is still, indeed more than ever, the pathway to success in American life as measured by wealth and social status. University admissions officers know this and depend on it. As ever, that is, as Michael Sandel describes in telling detail, American universities are in the business (yes, business) of producing an educated elite for the professional and corporate worlds.

In the meantime, as the "modern" university itself had become modern indeed, that is more corporatized, the modernizers came to regard the traditional department heads (now known as "chairs"), for example, in the same way Louis XIV did the territorial nobility. And deans and provosts (officers unknown to the corporate world) evolved into centralizing vice presidents, who spoke of themselves as "senior management" as they set about neutralizing such traditional centers of academic power and authority in the name of institutional efficiency.[40] This in turn meant both guaranteeing a highly professionalized faculty, whose research interests were ever more specialized, not to say esoteric, and a campus climate ever more hospitable to the causes championed during the 1960s and their aftermath—recognizing and dignifying the identities of those hitherto oppressed segments of the population, especially racial minorities and women, and urging peace and justice generally—indeed attacking the myriad wrongs perpetrated by a racist, sexist, homophobic nation, at home and abroad.

Moreover—and this cannot be overemphasized—the new-modeled university would create an elite that looks like America. Once the erstwhile members of "the movement" became ensconced in academe, they transformed the university even as they were transformed by it. Subsequent generations of "radical" professors, no less than the students recruited by appeals to careerist self-interest, were upwardly mobile, and in time the university became *their* establishment, *their* power structure, by means of which they could continue, in David Bromwich's phase, "politics by other means."[41] And while devoting themselves internally to this embedded blend of radical and status quo utopian politics, American universities abandoned "real" politics to the growing "conservative" movement in the outside world.[42]

AGAINST UTOPIA: A POLITICAL EDUCATION IN THE MODERN UNIVERSITY FOR HERE AND NOW

To begin, it is altogether appropriate that universities help to equip our young men and women in all their diversity for well-paying and socially prestigious ways of earning a living. Universities, even those devoted to liberal education, have been doing that for centuries. It is also a good thing that we guarantee on the nation's campuses an academic and social atmosphere friendly to persons who in any way are outside the white, male, Protestant, heterosexual mainstream, a climate in which they are free to explore their cultural identities, indeed to assert, to stand up for, who and what they are. Again, any education worth the name during the critical years between late adolescence and early adulthood is inevitably and quite properly a time for "finding oneself," indeed, as Socrates had it, for coming to "know thyself."

But if we stop there, something important is missing in both cases. It should be part of our students' *political* education that universities require students to "contextualize," as we say, their deepest and most personal interests—in the one case to recognize that the "ladder to success" they seek to climb does not stand alone but is framed and supported by a set of political and governmental institutions and *their* moral underpinnings, without which that ladder could not exist. They should be required to consider too, that, as presently formulated, the American meritocracy virtually *guarantees* an unequal and unjust society, and that their "individual" life's plan is fraught with moral consequences.[43] In the second case, students should be required to understand that particular "cultural" identities are also in part formed, and sheltered, by those same institutions, defined by those same three principles, democracy, liberalism, and republicanism; and that pursued single-mindedly a politics of identity turns out to be no real politics at all but an expression of group narcissism. That is, students must be made aware of the shared institutional and ideational context that is the necessary condition for both the pursuit of socioeconomic aspirations and the flourishing of particular cultural identities. I mean, of course, the three legitimating principles of the American political creed outlined in the first part of this chapter—democracy, liberalism, and republicanism—that require an active citizenry.

This in turn will require a set of courses, if not a whole curriculum, devoted to challenging the "self-evident" belief encouraged by the modern university as presently market oriented and culturally fragmented—the belief that the so-called politics of identity (cultural, gender, sexual orientation, etc.) within a "commonality" defined by upward social mobility, "making it," is really all there is to being a citizen in a liberal democratic republic. That is, the university must stop being a "place," isolated from the outside world, in which for four years young people are rarely asked to transcend their "own" (as they see it) self-defined purposes in life. The university should become instead a base camp for explorations into the conditions that make possible the politically guaranteed "way of life" our students take for granted but mostly don't understand. That is, the unmediated, abstractly formulated aspirations of would-be meritocrats and of would-be cultural separatists point to no kind of viable society, let alone a "good" one, but rather to one or another sort of deformed utopia.

Such courses would be defined by what they ask students to know and how they are to go about knowing it. In the first place, their content would be the interplay between democracy, liberalism, and republicanism examined historically—not, or not simply, as exercises in the history of political ideas, or only as "abridgements" (Oakeshott's term) of our own ways of doing politics and offered as a kind of enculturation; rather, the three indispensable ways of understanding human beings as political animals should be examined *concretely,* that is, as they have grown out of past political experience, have in turn helped shape subsequent institutional practices, and now offer possibilities for action in the never-ending quest for justice broadly understood as the defining characteristic of the good American society. I can think of no better beginning for this sort of instruction than the chapter by Roger Wilkins in this volume.

But just as would-be meritocrats or identity politicians must see their particular quests in a context larger than the antipolitical culture of today's university, so must they be led to understand the American nation-state itself, and hence their membership in it, in the broadest possible context. On the one hand, they must be put in touch with the historical succession of "terminal" political communities, of which the present nation-state is only the most recent. This means a vertical exploration of what "politics" and "the political" have meant from their beginnings to the present, for the roots of our own political self-understandings are deep. The "Greek story," as Michael Walzer says, must be told, but so also the Roman story; and, as the bearer and transformer of those ancient political traditions into the modern age, the Judeo-Christian story.[44] Critical reflection on the continuities and innovations in the tradition to which those stories have differently contributed are an invaluable source of our own self-knowledge. And guiding as they have the forming of institutions of all sorts, "the arrangements" to which citizens must attend, understanding those stories is indispensable to our political education, providing as it does the "tacit" political knowledge of which Wolin speaks.[45]

Moreover, along the way—as helping to meet the need for knowledge about the world beyond our borders identified by Stephen Holmes, perhaps as part of the second semester of William Galston's proposed course—the story should be told of those who have imagined one form or other of a "world state" or a "global citizenship," and why, given *that* arguably utopian set of assumptions, the realization of such a vision might mean, for good or ill, the end of the political life as we have known it. On the other hand, also to broaden our students' knowledge of the world, if we compare ourselves with polities past, we must also compare our own politics today with the ways in which other peoples do politics, concentrating on how they have both enjoyed and used their own inherited political traditions and institutions—I mean instruments of governance as well as specifically political institutions such as parties—as those have projected a set of ideas about politics similar to and different from our own. No antiquarian preoccupation with the past, in the first case, or romantic idealization of systems other than our own in the second, the point in both kinds of "comparative" study ultimately is to understand ourselves.

We can easily imagine a suitably focused two-course survey in which the key participants, professors and students, would each undertake to treat these broad subjects not as material merely to be "learned" but as controversies, on the level of ideas and over the structuring of institutions, to be discussed and debated with all the intensity the actual historical record reflects.

But it is in courses with a more restricted and topical focus that the most fundamental features of a political education can be seen to reject the antipolitical educational utopianism outlined above. This would also be a liberal education that, far from worrying about a "politicized" university, would embrace a pedagogy that legitimates courses exemplifying—not merely analyzing detachedly in the spirit of value neutrality—a liberal, a democratic, and a republican politics at their best. The problem with higher education today is not that it is politicized but that it isn't, strictly, *political* at all. Such courses would presuppose an educational epistemology that rejects both the postmodern denial of truth and the *scientistic* positivism that equates truth to the certainty achieved by the following of a rigidly prescribed method thought to guarantee "objectivity." Actually, though in principle very "democratic," neither of these conceptions of truth (or its impossibility), the one underpinning meritocracy, the other identity politics, in fact supports a political way of knowing. The pedagogical approach in such a course, while satisfying the intellectual perquisites of citizenship urged by Todd Gitlin, would also be based on a conception of liberal education that draws as much on the "oratorical" as on the "philosophical" tendencies in the Western tradition.[46]

Any really fundamental issue facing the American people that occasions vigorous debate in the outside political world—any of the issues in the so-called culture wars, for example, but a lot of others besides—would be suitable for such a course. I have in mind such deeply divisive issues as abortion, the status of the family, same-sex marriage, race relations, affirmative action, immigration policy, the gap between rich and poor, corporate scandals, a professional versus a conscripted military, the meaning of "profession" in American life, whether the mass media foster or discourage democracy, the neo-imperial presidency, the place of religion in our politics, indeed, whether our government can remain legitimate in the face of declining political participation, among many others.[47] Each of these large and complex issues can be broken down analytically into its component parts (or in some cases combined into more comprehensive issues), with students assigned to defend and oppose different sides of each controversial component of the larger problem. The classes should be small enough for every student actively to participate (about twenty students would be optimum), structured so as to *require* such active participation by every student, and large enough to provide the atmosphere of an "audience" for those debating the several issues. Ideally, such a course would be team taught, with two or more instructors advocating—openly, in their own voices—this or that position in opposition to their colleagues. (A bit of "role-playing" would no doubt be required of all concerned.)

Such courses (if properly structured and focused) would not only be lessons in the meaning of democracy, liberalism, and republicanism—concretely, historically, and philosophically considered—but they would also teach lessons in civility, the excitement of participation—intimations of what Adams and Jefferson meant by "public happiness"—and the importance of debate and deliberation as integral to political action. To enhance even further this dimension of such a course, some of the sessions could usefully be open to the public. In view of *what* was being investigated and *how* that investigation was conducted, they would in fact represent the fusion of the student and the citizen—a very political education indeed.[48]

As for the university itself within which such an education is to take place, it is not at all to give in to the utopian impulses I have criticized in this essay to suggest that it may be understood as a kind of miniature liberal democratic republic. Indeed, as something akin to a realistic version of John Dewey's "embryonic" democratic community, it would be infused not only with the "spirit of service" to be absorbed by the elites we inevitably educate but also with the drive to achieve its common "political" educational aim through a robust educational "politics" represented by the internal debate about the world outside.

Yet I concede that this conception of a politically responsible university will be rescued from utopianism in the conventional meaning (as "naive" and "unrealistic") only by an administration able to see beyond its market considerations and willing to work to foster among at least some of the faculty such an educational version of a liberal democratic republican polity in which being a "good university citizen" would take on a new meaning. This would mean encouraging faculty to engage in what Ernest L. Boyer called the "scholarship of teaching,"[49] which affirms a commitment to teaching and to a kind of scholarship less and less to be found on the nation's campuses, even of small liberal arts colleges, once thought to be "teaching" institutions. This is to be distinguished from the model of "the modern university" generated in the late nineteenth century and now reiterated throughout virtually the entire system of higher education.[50] I would suggest that part of William Galston's second prong in his own "investigative" model of a political education could entail faculty engaging, with each other, with students, and with gusto, in the "politics" of curriculum planning and course construction necessary to the courses proposed in several of these chapters. Were the courses described above in fact team taught, with students drawn from a variety of fields of study, career interests, and cultural identities, and (in part) publicly presented, the discussion thus generated, intense controversy and all, might well have the effect of drawing professors as well as students out of their current disciplinary and professional isolation, and thus go some way toward unifying a fragmented and privatized university.

Finally, the problem, for which a genuine political education is at least a partial solution, is that in this arguably most modern of all societies in the world today, the central elements of our political culture, our commitments to democracy, to liberalism, and to republicanism, threaten constantly to degenerate into a radical egalitarianism, a radical individualism, and a totalistic nationalism. These then become, in a culture becoming increasingly more modern, so many centrifugal forces, harbingers of a radical fragmentation, the political entropy to which I have referred. As it happens, those same elements of our political creed, understood as three complementary motives for political participation *and* for a liberal education worthy of the name, are the only adhesive, the only *centripetal* force, the only *defensible* source, finally, of the American patriotism that might hold this diverse society and problematic polity together.[51] By committing itself to a politically informed liberal education, the contemporary university could promote even more effectively and responsibly its present vocational and cultural missions, could emancipate itself from its self-imposed utopian isolation from the polity that shelters it, and, through making its students simultaneously practically and theoretically aware of the obligations of citizenship, also make itself a force for discouraging the worst and promoting the best in our political traditions.

NOTES

1. Sheldon Wolin, "Fugitive Democracy," *Democracy and Difference: Contesting the Boundaries of the Political*, ed. Seyla Benhabib (Princeton, N.J.: Princeton University Press, 1996), 31.

2. Michael Oakeshott, "Political Education," in *The Voice of Liberal Learning*, ed. Timothy Fuller (Indianapolis: Liberty Fund, 2001), 159–60.

3. Bernard Crick, *In Defence of Politics* (Chicago: University of Chicago Press, 1962), 19.

4. The quotation marks around these conventional ideological labels are meant to indicate some doubt about their adequacy in this context. What

Americans tend to conserve, as Gunnar Myrdahl pointed out long ago, is liberalism and even a species of radicalism; and the postmodern or cultural left has a hard time making its case without tacitly relying on certain very "traditional" American norms and values. See the instructive chapters by David Paris, "Multiculturalism / Political Correctness ('MC/PC'): Old Wine in No Bottles;" and John Searle, "The Storm over the University," in *Neutrality and the Academic Ethic,* ed. Robert L. Simon (Lanham, Md.: Rowman & Littlefield, 1994).

5. We might think of this as a crude application of Locke's labor theory of value in explaining the patriotism generated by political participation. When you mix your labor with that (the polity) which is held in common, when, that is, you invest *yourself* in the republic, you become part owner of it. And what you come in that way to own, you cherish.

6. Alexis de Tocqueville, *Democracy in America*, ed. Harvey C. Mansfield, trans. Delba Winthrop (Chicago: University of Chicago Press, 2000), esp. vol. 2, pt. 2, chaps. 2–4.

7. "Entropy" is Sheldon Wolin's term characterizing Hobbes's state of nature, *Politics and Vision: Continuity and Innovation in Western Political Thought* (Boston: Little, Brown, 1960), 262. It also suggests more broadly, I think, the condition of radical or pure modernity as such, the triumph of pure voluntarism coupled with pure scientific rationalism, though Hobbes's own conception of "science" is not entirely congruent with the latter term. As for America's headless polity, the republicanism of the Revolution, rejecting the hierarchy of the medieval order, followed by the liberal (and republican) distrust of concentrated power reflected in the Constitution, guaranteed respectively that the American polity would have neither a traditional "head" nor a modern "sovereign."

8. J. G. A. Pocock, "The Ideal of Citizenship since Classical Times," in *Theorizing Citizenship,* ed. Ronald Beiner (Albany: State University of New York Press, 1995), 32.

9. John Winthrop, "A Model of Christian Charity," ed. Alam Heimert and Andrew Delbanco, *The Puritans in America: A Narrative Anthology* (Cambridge, MA: Harvard University Press, 1985), 89. This is of course not to say that Winthrop would have endorsed the modern American liberal conception of individual freedom, certainly not its negative version. It is rather to say that modern liberal rights, notably property rights as those are variously defined, depend on a viable "public estate" for their protection.

10. Plato, *The Republic*, trans. F. M. Cornford (New York: Oxford University Press, 1945), 107.

11. Thomas Jefferson, *Notes on the State of Virginia*, query 14 in *Thomas Jefferson: Writings*, ed. Merrill D. Peterson (New York: Library of America, 1984), 274.

12. Plato, *The Republic*, 262–63.

13. John Dewey, *Democracy and Education: An Introduction to the Philosophy of Education* (New York: Macmillan, 1916), 328–29.

14. The terms are from Samuel H. Beer, *Modern Political Development* (New York: Random House, 1973), chap. 5.

15. With a number of reforms aiming at something approaching direct democracy—the initiative, referendum, recall—they sought to get government out of the hands of the corrupt politicians and urban bosses and to put it back into the hands of the people, where democratically it belonged. The perception of "the people" as a unified and virtuous body capable of direct rule in opposition to a corrupt governing elite points to the strongly *republican* character of Progressive democracy, even if its notorious fragmentation as a movement also bespoke its liberal character. It's not too much to say that Progressives at the time—Herbert Croly being a clear exception—were unable to recognize just how far "the people" had already been corrupted (as the republican would say) by the anticipation of material plenty, that indeed the "promise" of American life was already being understood as merely equality of opportunity. Then, too, the manifest diversity of the American society, owing to wave upon wave of immigration, not to mention the end of slavery, didn't deter them from positing a unified people. Ironically, the scientifically self-conscious political scientists of the day, most notably A. F. Bentley, were at the same time constructing a group or pluralist model of the political system that virtually denied any reality to the people as a collective entity, to say nothing of a common good.

16. This is the thesis of chap. 3 of James A. Morone, *The Democratic Wish: Popular Participation and the Limits of American Government* (New Haven, Conn.: Yale University Press, 1998).

17. The more expansive and self-confident expressions of such professionalism came to be known as technocracy, and indeed harbored a contempt for what ordinary citizens, as well as politicians, think they know.

18. See Adam Ulam, "Socialism and Utopia," in *Utopias and Utopian Thought*, ed. Frank E. Manuel (Boston: Beacon Press, 1966), 116–34. Cf. Christopher Lasch, *The True and Only Heaven: Progress and Its Critics* (New York: W. W. Norton, 1991), esp. "What Progress Really Means," 47–49.

19. Herbert Croly, *The Promise of American Life* (1909; repr., Boston: Northeastern University Press, 1989), 5.

20. While practical-minded Americans may have found extreme the philosophes' lyricism about the indefinite perfectibility of mankind, it was nevertheless generally believed that we Americans were the foreordained representatives of the human race. And such change for the better, or progress, was automatic, the motive force for which was contained in the thing itself, an industrializing society

free from traditional restraints. This is to say, then, that this version of American utopianism was deeply embedded in the most fundamental assumptions of nineteenth-century American liberal culture and was only made manifest by the new professionalism that reached a kind of apogee in the Progressive response to industrialization. It isn't too much to say that a similar utopian tendency can be detected in the headier projections today about globalization.

21. On the impact of professionalism and the quest for scientific respectability on American political science, see David M. Ricci, *The Tragedy of Political Science: Politics, Scholarship, and Democracy* (New Haven, Conn.: Yale University Press, 1984). See also notes 3, 7–10, and 12 in the prologue to this volume.

22. Burton J. Bledstein, *The Culture of Professionalism: The Middle Class and the Development of Higher Education in America* (New York: W. W. Norton, 1978).

23. James Bryant Conant, "Education for a Classless Society: The Jeffersonian Tradition," *Atlantic Monthly*, May 1940. The article grew out of the Charter Day address delivered at the University of California on March 28, 1940.

24. It was this period that gave rise to the notion of the "gentleman's C," a term still used at Harvard, if with some irony, during my time there as a graduate student in the early to mid-1960s. It was the grade assigned as a sort of entitlement to a well-to-do but otherwise undeserving student.

25. For a detailed account of the rise of the SAT and its long-range effects through higher education on American society, see Nicholas Lemann, *The Big Test: The Secret History of the American Meritocracy* (New York: Farrar, Straus & Giroux, 1999).

26. Michael Young, *The Rise of the Meritocracy* (1958; repr., New Brunswick, N.J.: Transaction Publishers, 1994).

27. Jefferson, *Writings*, 272. The spelling is Jefferson's.

28. Dewey, *Democracy and Education*, 87.

29. John Dewey, *The Child and the Curriculum and The School and Society* (1900; repr., Chicago: University of Chicago Press, 1956), 60.

30. We might wonder about how much of today's emphasis on "community service" as a surrogate for a rigorous political education in today's universities might be traced to this vision of the Progressive school.

31. Dewey, *Child and Curriculum, School and Society*, 29.

32. Dewey, *Child and the Curriculum, School and Society*, 8.

33. Dewey, *Democracy and Education*, 20. Emphasis in the original.

34. George S. Counts, *Dare the School Build a New Social Order?* (1932; repr. Carbondale: Southern Illinois University Press, 1978), 5.

35. Lawrence Cremin, *The Transformation of the School: Progressivism in Education, 1876–1957* (New York: Vintage Books, 1961), 183.

36. Harold Rugg and Ann Schumaker, *The Child-Centered School: An Appraisal of the New Education* (Yonkers-on-Hudson, N.Y.: World Book, 1928), 54–67.

37. Rugg and Schumaker, 67, in part quoting James S. Tippett et al., *Curriculum Making in an Elementary School* (Boston: Ginn & Co., 1927).

38. For passages in Dewey's seminal writings that gave his followers license to speculate about this miniature and purified community that was the school as though the economic problem had been solved, see *Child and Curriculum, School and Society,* 32 and *Democracy and Education,* 317. As much as any other feature of educationist thought, this projected triumph over scarcity, which was quite consistent as well with as the idea of progress itself, signifies the utopianism of this period in American educational writing.

39. Richard Hofstadter, *Anti-Intellectualism in American Life* (New York: Alfred A. Knopf, 1963), especially pt. 5, "Education in a Democracy," 299–390. This is also a central theme in Diane Ravitch's recent *Left Back: A Century of Failed School Reforms* (New York: Simon & Schuster, 2000).

40. Efficient modernist centralizers in academia could argue with some cogency against the old departmental structure on the grounds that such pluralism represented mere departmental or disciplinary self-interest, which militated against the unity necessary in a modern university intent on providing a coherent liberal education. But the real problem with the "traditional" decentralization was that it validated a plurality of centers of power and of *academic* authority, which no modernizing administration can tolerate. Neither was a coherent liberal education the issue. The contemporary university with the proliferation of studies programs is much more fragmented, more "diverse," by far than the traditional one, which makes quite impossible, it would seem, even the *idea* of a coherent liberal education. Such fragmentation has produced a "multiversity" of a kind that Clark Kerr could scarcely have imagined.

41. David Bromwich, *Politics by Other Means: Higher Education and Group Thinking* (New Haven, Conn.: Yale University Press, 1992).

42. It is only in the conventional (and parochial) American sense that the Republican party of the second half of the twentieth century is the party of conservatism. At best, that party seeks to "conserve"—no, radically to extend—a kind of political economy (and individualist culture to match) identified above as a species of American utopianism, which, in its effects on civil society, is nothing if not corrosive, even, in the long term, revolutionary.

43. There are two powerful critiques of "equality of opportunity" that any defender of meritocracy ought to have to confront: John H. Schaar, "Equality of Opportunity and Beyond," in *Legitimacy in the Modern State* (New Brunswick, N.J.: Transaction Publishers, 1981), chap. 9; and Christopher Lasch, "Opportunity

in the Promised Land: Social Mobility or the Democratization of Competence," in *Revolt of the Elites and the Betrayal of Democracy* (New York: W. W. Norton, 1995), chap 3.

44. Indeed, the intertwining of political and religious thought has been such as in some respects to make them inseparable. More than this, American political culture in particular is so permeated by the Judeo-Christian tradition, particularly as represented by Protestantism, that any analysis pretending to be complete must see democracy, liberalism, and republicanism as ultimately unintelligible if religion in America is omitted from it.

45. Sheldon S. Wolin, "Political Theory as a Vocation," *American Political Science Review* 63, no. 4 (December 1969): 1070.

46. See Bruce A. Kimball, *Orators and Philosophers: A History of the Idea of Liberal Education* (New York: Teachers College Press, 1986).

47. Such a debate-structured course could well draw on a number of the other chapters in this volume that speak directly to these issues.

48. The intimation of such a course is implied in Christopher Lasch's chapter, "The Lost Art of Argument," in *Revolt of the Elites*, chap. 9. Yet, in Oakeshott's terms, though "arguments" would undoubtedly be deployed, such political discourse is less an "argument" than a "conversation."

49. Ernest L. Boyer, *Scholarship Reconsidered: Priorities of the Professoriate* (Princeton, N.J.: Carnegie Foundation for the Advancement of Teaching, 1990), 23–25. In Boyer's analysis the scholarship of "discovery," of "service," and of "application" precedes and in some ways culminates in the "scholarship of teaching." Quoting Oscar Handlin, Boyer concludes his section on the "scholarship of service" by saying that "scholarship has to prove itself not on its own terms but by service to the nation and the world." This is one of the benefits of a political education in the modern university.

50. According to Charles W. Anderson, "The philosophy and structures, the procedures and rituals, of the research university have largely become standard for the system. They are the universal model for all institutions of higher education. The liberal arts colleges no longer in general have a special role, for all their protestation to the contrary. They have simply become more intimate versions of the same thing. The tone is set by the graduate schools, themselves little differentiated, which provide a standard model of the professional research scholar and distribute it throughout the system. . . . The very universality of the model set by the research university tends to confirm its 'naturalness' and its legitimacy." *Prescribing the Life of the Mind: An Essay on the Purpose of the University, the Aims of Liberal Education, the Competence of Citizens, and the Cultivation of Practical Reason* (Madison: University of Wisconsin Press, 1993).

51. I have said very little about patriotism in this chapter, in part because there is little I could add to the eloquent statement by Roger Wilkins. Yet the very concept is so controversial, especially in the academy, as virtually to have been banished as a topic of analysis or discussion—all the more so today, when, as in the Vietnam era, "patriotism" is being appropriated in support of the heatedly disputed war in Iraq. But not entirely, as the 2004 Democratic Convention suggested. See also the rich discussion in Martha Nussbaum's *For Love of Country* (Boston: Beacon Press, 2002), many of whose contributors offer what strike me as compelling arguments for a properly grounded patriotism, which they distinguish from the sort of jingoistic nationalism that has given patriotism itself such a bad name among those unwilling to make the distinction. For an earlier argument based on this same distinction, see Schaar, "The Case for Patriotism" (1973), *Legitimacy in the Modern State*, chap. 14. Schaar's defense of patriotism was against the Berkeley radicals (who denounced it), with whom in other respects he was sympathetic. More recently, see Wilfred M. McClay, "The Mixed Nature of American Patriotism," *Society*, November/December 2003.

Index

think tanks, 202
Thomas, Diane, 49
Thrasymachus, 16, 25n1
Tocqueville, Alexis de: on American
  traits, 10, 26n8; on education, 35, 40;
  on individualism, 234; on liberty, 60;
  on religion, 172; on slavery, 102–3;
  on society, 3
tolerance, 176–77, 197–98
Truman, David, 28n12
Truman, Harry, 210
trust, 2, 6–7, 10, 12, 26n4, 29, 42n2,
  180
truth, 120–21, 254–55
Tutu, Desmond, 193
tyranny, 10

universities: admission to, 113; anachronism and, 187–88; authority of, 4,
  9–10, 13–14, 24; character and, viii–ix,
  163–68; citizenship and, viii–ix; civic
  education and, 40–41; civic involvement and, 41, 88–89, 186–87; commercialization of, 61–64, 185–86;
  corporatization of, 49–50, 251; culture
  and, 35–36; democracy and, 241–42,
  244–50; diversity and, 33, 188–89,
  251–52, 261n40; economy and, 6–7,
  49–54, 250–51; financial aid and,
  51–52; foreign students in, 198; freedom and, 186; funding for, 34–35,
  52–53, 62–63; globalization and,
  188–89; ignorance and, 194–95,
  197–99, 201–3; liberal education and,
  261n40; market model of, 49–54;
  morality and, 166, 197–98; parochialism and, 187, 188–89; patriotism and,
  190–94, 197–98; pluralism in, 261n40;
  politics in, 4–5, 40–41; privatization
  of, 63–66, 69; professions and, 237–38,
  241–44, 249–51; public forum doctrine and, 100; purpose of, 187–89;
  rationality in, 166–67; recruitment by,
  viii–ix, 6–7, 33–34, 51–53, 250–51;
  religion and, 167–68; research model

of, 17, 33–34, 36–37, 57–58, 188,
  262n50; tolerance and, 197–98
University of Alabama, 53
University of New Hampshire, 53
University of Richmond, 53
University of Southern California, 51
University of Virginia, 53, 56
Unno, Tai, 161–62
utilitarianism, 157–58, 221
utopia, 239–50, 256–57, 259n20

values, 14–16, 24, 26n7, 79–92, 92n1,
  219–23. *See also* character; morality
Veblen, Thorstein, 34
violence, 85
vocational education, 36–38, 47, 49–50,
  57–58. *See also* professions
Voice of the Faithful, 149–50
voluntarism, 239–40
voting, 2–3, 25n2, 30–31

Waldo, Dwight, 26n7
Walling, William English, 209
war: character and, 138; civic involve-
  ment and, 190; ignorance and,
  194–202; interdependence and, 70–73;
  parochialism and, 194–203; patrio-
  tism and, 191–93, 196–98, 205–6, 215;
  terrorism and, 131. *See also* jingoism
Washington, George, 12, 156, 210
Weber, Max, 26n7, 186, 202
Weiss, Paul, 163
Welch, Joseph, 162
"The White Man's Burden," 128
Whittle Corporation, 66
Wilkes, Robert, 144
Wilkis, Robert, 121, 123–25
Will, George, 197
Windelband, 167
Winthrop, John, 236
Wolfowitz, Paul, 192
Wolin, Sheldon, 28n12, 231, 254, 258n7

Yankelovich, Daniel, 30
Young, Michael, 243

About the Editor
and Contributors

Benjamin R. Barber is the Gershon and Carol Kekst Professor of Civil Society and Distinguished University Professor at the University of Maryland, and a principal of the Democracy Collaborative, with offices in New York and Maryland.

Robert E. Calvert is professor of political science at DePauw University.

Jean Bethke Elshtain is the Laura Spelman Rockefeller Professor of Social and Political Ethics at the University of Chicago.

William A. Galston is the interim dean, School of Public Policy; Saul I. Stern Professor of Civic Engagement; and director, Institute for Philosophy and Public Policy, at the University of Maryland.

Todd Gitlin is professor of journalism and sociology in the Graduate School of Journalism at Columbia University.

Stephen Holmes is the Walter E. Meyer Professor of Law at the New York University School of Law.

Leroy S. Rouner is professor of philosophy, religion, and philosophical theology emeritus at Boston University.

Michael J. Sandel is the Anne T. and Robert M. Bass Professor of Government at Harvard University.

James B. Stewart is the Bloomberg Professor of Business and Economic Journalism at Columbia University, and chairman of the Board of Trustees of DePauw University.

Cass R. Sunstein is the Karl N. Llewellyn Distinguished Service Professor of Jurisprudence at the law school and a member of the political science department at the University of Chicago.

Michael Walzer is professor of social science at the Institute for Advanced Study at Princeton.

Roger Wilkins is the Clarence J. Robinson Professor of History and American Culture at George Mason University.

Alan Wolfe is professor of political science and director of the Boisi Center for Religion and American Public Life at Boston College.